A. J. Gollov
The Destiny Code
matrix

The way to the true Self

Book content:
text, illustrations, cover design, lyrics by Anastasia J. Gollov

Interior book design and illustrations by:
Asia Yara

Cover book design by:
Maria Meshko, Konstantin Puppo

Translated into English and edited by:
Simon Geoghegan (simon.geoghegan@gmail.com)

No part of this publication may be republish, reproduced, stored in a retrieval system, or transmitted in any form or by any means, electronic, mechanical, photocopying, recording, or otherwise, without written permission from Anastasia J. Gollov.
Author contacts: ajgollov@gmail.com

"The Destiny Code" guides its readers on a fascinating journey to discover the true self. The book you are holding in your hands provides you with a highly effective tool to learn all about yourself - a special methodology that allows you to calculate and interpret your Destiny Code using your date of birth. It not only allows you to work out what your own special number code is, but using the prism of esotericism leads its readers to a revolutionary understanding of themselves and the wider universe. This book provides a fascinating way to discover the true self and is imbued with a caring and responsible attitude to its readers. It contains the author's own deeply considered verses in the Native American lyrical epic style, which have been designed to help the reader contemplate the energies present within them through the historical experience of the intersection of sacred knowledge and the human perception of existence.

ISBN: 979-8-218-95871-8   © by Anastasia J. Gollov

CONTENTS

INTRODUCTION 6
   AUTHOR'S FOREWORD 9
CHAPTER I. CHAKRAS 13
   GENERAL CONCEPT 13
   THE FIRST CHAKRA — THE MULADHARA 16
   THE SECOND CHAKRA — THE SVADHISTHANA 18
   THE THIRD CHAKRA - THE MANIPURA 19
   THE FOURTH CHAKRA — THE ANAHATA 21
   THE FIFTH CHAKRA — THE VISHUDDHA 22
   THE SIXTH CHAKRA — THE AJNA 24
   THE SEVENTH CHAKRA — THE SAHASRARA 26
   CHAKRA PATHOLOGIES 27
   OPPRESSION 28
   RIGIDITY 31
   BREACH 34
   HYPERACTIVITY 36
   BLOCKAGES 39
   LIGHT AND DARK CHAKRAS 43
   LIGHT AND DARK PEOPLE 47
   WHEN LIGHT PEOPLE WANT TO BE DARK AND VICE VERSA 50
   A SHORT LEGEND ABOUT YIN AND YANG 54
   CHAKRAS IN CHILDREN 58
   THE MULADHARA IN CHILDREN 59
   THE SVADHISTANA IN CHILDREN 60
   THE MANIPURA IN CHILDREN 62
   THE ANAHATA IN CHILDREN 64
   THE VISHUDDHA IN CHILDREN 66

- THE AJNA IN CHILDREN 68
- THE SAHASRARA IN CHILDREN 70

CHAPTER II. CASTES 73
- GENERAL CONCEPT 73
- THE ASSEMBLAGE POINT 75
- CHAKRAS AND CASTES 78
- THE FIRST CASTE 81
- THE THIRD CASTE 102
- THE FOURTH CASTE 110
- THE CASTE PYRAMID 120
- TRANSITIONAL CASTES 121
- FROM A ONE TO A TWO 122
- FROM A TWO TO A THREE 124
- FROM A TRHEE TO A FOUR 124

CHAPTER III. THE DESTINY CODE MATRIX 127
- A UNIQUE TOOL 127
- WHAT THE DESTINY CODE LOOKS LIKE 128
- CALCULATION 129
- THE SIGNIFICANCE OF THE ZONES AND 136
- CHARACTER (COMFORT ZONE) 138
- PORTRAIT 139
- THE HIGHER ESSENCE 140
- CHILD-PARENT KARMA 142
- MATERIAL KARMA 144
- THE PROSPERITY LINE 146
- THE SKY LINE AND THE EARTH LINE 149
- THE ANCESTRAL SQUARE 150
- THE LINE OF MEN AND THE LINE OF WOMEN 152
- THE KARMIC TAIL 155

- DESTINATIONS 159
- THE HEALTH CHART 164
- THE COMPATIBILITY FORMULA 165
- CHAPTER IV. ENERGIES 167
  - THE 22 ARCANA OF DESTINY 167
  - ARCANUM 1. THE PIONEER 169
  - ARCANUM 2. THE SECRET 175
  - ARCANUM 3. FEMININITY 183
  - ARCANUM 4. MASCULINITY 189
  - ARCANUM 5. KNOWLEDGE 197
  - ARCANUM 6. LOVE 209
  - ARCANUM 7. MOVEMENT 219
  - ARCANUM 8. JUSTICE 229
  - ARCANUM 9. THE HERMIT 237
  - ARCANUM 10. THE WHEEL OF DESTINY 245
  - ARCANUM 11. STRENGTH 253
  - ARCANUM 12. SACRIFICE 263
  - ARCANUM 13. DEATH 271
  - ARCANUM 14. MODERATION 279
  - ARCANUM 15. THE DEVIL 287
  - ARCANUM 16. THE TOWER 293
  - ARCANUM 17. THE STAR 301
  - ARCANUM 18. THE MOON 309
  - ARCANUM 19. THE SUN 317
  - ARCANUM 20. JUDGEMENT 325
  - ARCANUM 21. THE WORLD 333
  - ARCANUM 22. THE FOOL 343
  - 26 PROGRAMS OF THE PAST 351
- CONCLUSION 364

INTRODUCTION

At the source of the Pomunkey River,
Where the willows of the ancient forests respectfully bow their branches
To the surface of the still waters
Where the echoes of the ancestors still linger,
The song of those human souls who have already travelled the human way,
By the will of the gods tarry to this day

Calling out to all their descendants
Until the time comes when the 'People of the Light' will arrive.
For ten moons, the spirits of the forest determined
Who would take this burden upon themselves,
Who would show the way and the nature of the burden,
That each is destined to carry.

The young hearts of the Pohwatan people
Bowed their knees before the Great Spirit.
Securing their compact with warm blood,
They vowed to observe their covenant.

Like the Waters, the Earth or the Sky,
Like the Fire or Wind through the leaves,
Not all living people are equal
And neither can they be equal.

And now the Young Hearts of the Pohwatan people
With beating hearts, strong feelings and faith,
Ignoring their common nature and kinship,
Immersed themselves in rivers of blood
With the words and cries of warring clans.
And through the trials of war and conflict.
They will tenderly honor and bravely protect
the memory of the departed ancestors with their songs.

Native Americans have been living along the Rappahannock River on the territory of what is now Virginia in North America for hundreds of years, constantly feuding among themselves for the resources available there. One day, one of their young chiefs Wahunsenacawh decided to unite the warring tribes in order to create a large alliance — the union of Algonquian-speaking Tribes. The great sun god sent protectors to his children to defend the human race and keep peace among those living in these lands. Thus, the Northern peoples were given a common guardian — the wise and majestic American Bald Eagle. And the tribes of the Southern lands began to live under the wing of the mighty Golden Eagle.

Wahunsenacawh argued that all the Native Americans were one people, and the path of each tribe was one. Moreover, it was his opinion that the destiny of all his people is indivisibly intertwined with the cycle of life, which has been predetermined for the whole world.

The indigenous peoples believed that with the change of the ages, the people of the Light would come and destroy those of the Dark who are the enemy and superfluous and alien to this Earth. They saw in the ancient legends, the light of hope and the harbinger of happiness, so they waited with enthusiasm for the coming of the liberators. At the beginning of the 17th century, "fair people" really did come to these lands.

However, contrary to the indigenous peoples' expectations, the white people began to decimate the indigenous peoples of the northern coast, conquering more and more tribes and 'liberating' the land for themselves. The pale-skins had come to destroy the "dark people" — who, it turned out were the native Americans themselves. Wahunsenacawh tried to establish relations with the incomers, but it soon became clear that their forces were far from equal, and the new guests wanted to make themselves overlords. Thus, the end of one nation gave rise to a new one. And the ancient legend came to pass.

Legends preserve bright truths that are passed down from generation to generation. The simplest songs contain thousands of useful stories and facts — this is precious knowledge that should help keep the descendants on the true path. This treasure trove of information not only preserves the past as a chronicle of life, it carries warnings and hints about the future. The knowledge of the past reveals the secrets of what is yet to come.

From time immemorial, the shamans knew that the time of awakening would come, and then true knowledge would be revealed to every person on Earth. The path towards understanding the truth will lead people to the universal path of Light — to a single goal — and will open the 'forgotten' connection between everyone and everything in the Universe.

"Our songs contain secrets from the beginning of the beginnings, from the time of the emergence of the first tribes," the shamans said, "but the hour will come when the Circle of Life closes and the cycle begins again – then the time will come to reveal meanings, passing on knowledge to new peoples."

According to legend, there will be a change in the cycle and the Wheel of Life will again begin its journey from its starting point. And the Bald Eagle and the Golden Eagle, circling together in the sky, will symbolize the New Circle of Life. Mighty beasts will gather from all over the world to see them dance. Each animal will bring something special only to them and share it with the others. This occasion will open up the Energies of Rebirth and Awakening.

The indigenous peoples of China, the East, Siberia, the countries of Oceania, Australia and many less populous nations from the most distant lands also have their own totemic animals. According to legend, their meeting will symbolize the New Age, in which great knowledge will be revealed that will awaken every person on the Earth.

In 2014, New York hosted the first World Indigenous Conference, organized by the UN, at which representatives of ethnic groups from all over the world gathered together for the first time. On the very lands of the wise Bald* Eagle and the mighty Golden Eagle.

It is remarkable because the period we are now living in is witnessing an unprecedented surge of interest in secret sacred meanings — people have begun to discover more and more new tools to help them gain self-knowledge, centuries-old spiritual practices have acquired thousands of new followers and proponents.

The techniques and methods expounded in this book 'The Destiny Code' is no exception. It has become available to potential followers during this very period of the increase and development of human knowledge of ancient sacred truths.

Anticipating salvation from the white invaders and the advent of a New World, the Native Americans people made a fatal mistake — their interpretation of their ancestors' legends was too positive. Those parts of these legends that contained an element of warning were perceived to be a cause for tremulous expectation.

Indeed, what we desire does not always coincide with what actually happens and we have to be prepared for this. The more you come to know yourself, discovering the most subtle things inherent within you, the better you will be able to get the best out of yourself from a material and spiritual point of view.

Humans are a balance of the negative and positive. You need to be able to take on board not only the positive aspects of what is happening around you but to see the reverse side of the coin. And it is only when we are able to perceive both sides that we can see a complete picture of ourselves and, accordingly, the world around us.

AUTHOR'S FOREWORD

When a person develops their spirituality, they do not become smarter — they just learn to understand themselves better.

MY WAY

Why do people strive to know themselves? To find happiness? To achieve self-affirmation in life and attain the status of an all-knowing sage? To discover the way the World works? What is the end goal of all this striving?

Since ancient times, mankind has sought to discover the secrets of existence and comprehend the truths of life. Year on year and century after century, people have accumulated priceless knowledge by striving for a single goal — to find themselves and embark on the true path.

In its attempts to find answers, humanity has made discoveries that allow one to look beyond the bounds of reality, the bounds of the visible, the conscious and the accessible. Mankind has learned the secrets of the sacred, perceived the presence of higher Energies and been given the opportunity to control its Destiny. Moreover, it has opened up for itself the opportunity to help others in their quest for these things.

I set out on my path in search of the esoteric in my youth when my innate curiosity to learn something secret and take a glimpse into the future led me to my first acquaintance with Tarot cards. By practising interpreting and plunging ever deeper into the meanings of the cards, like Alice, I found I was able to pass through the Looking Glass of reality into a land of wonder. In this fantastic world, answers to every question could be found in the most amazing way, and, it turned out, every action bore a deep meaning.

Over the years, I have learned to read many things that are inaccessible to others and this has completely absorbed me. The skills that I acquired, which had initially seemed impossible and beyond the realms of reality, eventually became simple truths of life. Reading Tarot cards was not just an unusual activity that could surprise and amaze the people I knew. The cards became a tool that could literally influence life situations that could not be resolved on their own by themselves.

Nevertheless, the nature of the information I received from the cards remained figurative and did not contain clear recommendations and concepts. The metaphorical images of the Tarot and other fortune telling cards did not satisfy my innate desire to receive clear guidance and instructions to take this or that course of action.

Widening my circle of knowledge, I strove to study other systems that reveal a person's functions and abilities. Thus, I discovered the incredibly simple, but at the same time highly complex system of chakras and castes and dabble in the theory of Kabbalah Sefirot Magic. I came to perceive and understand the nature of Energies.

As I studied new ways to develop myself spiritually, I strove to immediately apply the knowledge I acquired in practice in order to master additional tools that I could work with to improve reality for myself and for those people who came to me for help.

One way or another, curiosity often leads the seeker in the most roundabout ways to the most unexpected corners of the unknown. One day, while, once again, exploring the latest trends in modern applied Magic, I happened across an interesting methodology with the intriguing name — The Destiny Code. The fact that it was so different from anything I had previously studied instantly enchanted me. In addition to its captivating philosophy (the thinking and meanings underlying it), it provided me with clear instructions on how and what to do — right here and right now. This advice could immediately be applied to real life, coordinating and guiding its course. It provided specific instructions in a given situation, explanations and reasons why everything in life happens this way and not otherwise. To my amazement, this unique technique met all the criteria that I had set myself on my quest for a New Knowledge system fit for our New Age, but had not been able to find it within the framework of a single methodology and practice until this moment.

When a person develops their spirituality, they do not become smarter — they just learn to understand themselves better. Herein lies the answer to the question why a person needs to develop spiritually. Primarily, it is to understand yourself.

I have always been of the opinion that the point of any quest for self-development lies in the fact that, having embarked on this path, and having gained knowledge, applied it in practice and discovered new facets of perception, a person can immediately and confidently take the next step forward. And that the value of this or that spiritual practice is to sense these changes in the here and now.

I was struck by the fact that this newly acquired practice could provide me with exactly the form of interpretation I needed, I began to understand more deeply the techniques and methods required to read and interpret the Destiny Code. Since then, my life has been divided into "before" and "after".

Several sources and theories exist regarding the origin of the Destiny Code technique. According to some, this practice was conceived by the spiritual master Natalia Ladini. She saw the 'Mandala of Destiny' in a dream and after this spent many years devising the form and structure of a complex system of meanings and characteristics. Subsequently, in the early 2000s, Ladini opened her own school, where she taught this new knowledge to others and spread her technique and methodology to the public.

According to other sources, the Destiny Code method is based on a very old way of dealing Tarot cards using only the Major Arcana of the classic Tarot deck — a kind of modified form of the Celtic Cross layout, which is based on the correspondence of the numbering of the Arcana to the numbers in a person's date of birth. There are many schools now that have completely different legends regarding the origin of this method, but they are united by their clear correspondence to the same general structure — the same common values and characteristics of the points of the matrix.

By reading the Destiny Code and creating a matrix, one can not only see an individual's personal traits, their special features and the specifics of their character but also understand how they look at the world. You can clearly interpret the specific algorithms of actions and calculate the probability of certain events occurring in their lives, thus predetermining and controlling them. You can clearly see the individual programs, functions and tasks set for them by the Universe that they need to pass through in this life.

Now anyone can find the answer to any question that might occur to them regarding their knowledge of themselves and other people. Every event in life has a specific purpose. Everything that a person does — how he or she thinks, what he or she strives or does not strive for — all this has its rationale. Everyone has their own role to play in the Circle of Life, the Universe has its individually tailored plan for everyone, and everyone is capable of finding the most productive way to develop themselves in order to ultimately improve the world for those who follow them. All you need to do is remember your date of birth and insert it in the matrix.

Remember this moment. The knowledge you are about to discover in this book will change you for good. And Life will never be the same.

A.J.G.

CHAPTER I. CHAKRAS

GENERAL CONCEPT

C alculating your Code of Destiny is easy. The book that you are holding in your hands provides a step-by-step description of the matrix's characteristics and the precise formulas you need in order to work yours out. On the journey to find your personal 'Self' set out on these pages, you will immerse yourself in the study of the chakras, get to know the meaning of the key areas and points of the Destiny Code and learn how to decipher the features of the Tarot Arcana depending on their location in the matrix. Therefore, by the time you have finished reading this book, you will have a unique tool at your disposal to discover the many facets of your own personality and those of your loved ones, or any other person you might have taken an interest in.

However, in order to better understand the unique nature of this wonderful tool, you must first address the main concepts that underlie the way it works. And the first of these concepts is Energy.

As we know from school, each of us consists of atoms, and an atom, in turn, consists of protons, neutrons and electrons. The movement of particles creates energy that fills and envelops our physical bodies. As a result, we are simultaneously a source of energy and its recipient.

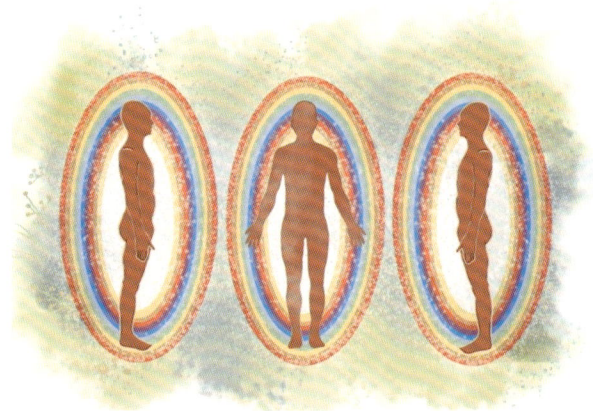

The energy emitted and absorbed by every human being is known as their biofield. Modern technologies allow us now to even produce photographic images of it, which not only proves the existence of the biofield as a scientific fact but also allows us to develop algorithms to help us diagnose its condition. And, of course, technological progress has opened up the opportunity to correct a person's energy flows, adjust their spiritual and physical state and thus improve the quality of their life. Energy circulates in the body, and its currents move along routes that pass through the chakras.

Chakras are energy vortexes on the body's biofield that radiate and absorb energy. They are the points at which vital life resources are lost and acquired. In Sanskrit, the word 'chakra' means 'disk' or 'wheel'. And indeed, in most illustrations and body maps chakras are depicted as flat disks. However, this two-dimensional depiction is slightly misleading. In reality, the chakra is a funnel that is shaped like a cone.

If you were to depict the human body in profile and place the chakras on this image, then the principles governing how they work would be a lot clearer. Energy centers are a funnel of energy flowing like a vortex from the outside world into the human body and back out again from it. If we were to show the same illustration face on, then we would see the usual image of the chakras in the form and shape of spinning disks.

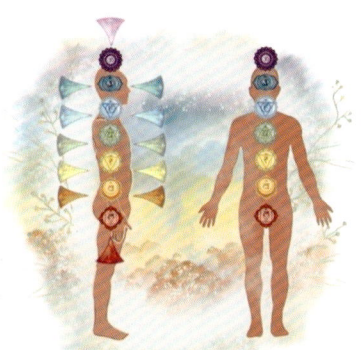

Naturally, the obvious question arises: if this energy is spinning in a vortex, then in which direction does it move when it passes through the chakra? It is important to remember that when energy is moving in a clockwise direction, it is being emitted into the outside world. In this instance, it has been produced by the person in question and is being shared with the outside world. When energy moves in a counter-clockwise direction, it is being absorbed from the outside — in other words, it is being absorbed and received by the person. The direction that the energy is rotating in the chakra is the most important factor that determines its type — whether it is a Light or Dark chakra.

On the classic chakra map of the human body, there are seven main chakras. Chakras are counted from bottom to top from the first to the seventh. And each of them bears a specific set of characteristics: its name, position relative to the physical body, color and function. The first chakra (the Muladhara) points downwards. The seventh (the Sahasrara) points up. The second to the sixth chakras are located in a straight line along the spine, expanding from the center of the physical body to the sides, front and back.

It's worth mentioning here that the chakras are not tangibly present in the physical body, they cannot be felt. They are manifested in the form of a frequency range of energies, which are projected onto the body's biofield. Each internal organ in the human body functions at a certain speed, thereby creating its own frequency of energy — or vibration.

The physical body's various internal organs and systems form general centers towards which the energy created (or absorbed) by them flows.

The positions of the chakras are those points in the body at which this energy is localized.

Each chakra can indicate how the body is functioning, how productive and stable it is. You can determine not only a person's physical but also mental well-being depending on the condition of their chakras. In addition, an analysis of the chakras can help one determine the degree and development of a person's spiritual power.

Each energy center has specific tasks and functions, and a detailed study of this system allows us to understand which areas of our lives require adjustments. Having read this book and undertaken a deep analysis of their chakras a person can determine those areas of his or her body that are experiencing problems and identify the reference points of his or her personality. In the Destiny Code matrix, the chakras act as special markers that describe the exact nature of what is happening in life and indicate the reasons for a particular choice.

I would like to briefly consider the classic characteristics of the seven chakras that I have presented here. It is vital that you know them in order to further successfully study the methodology and technique behind reading and interpreting the Destiny Code.

THE FIRST CHAKRA — THE MULADHARA

In Sanskrit, the first chakra is called the Muladhara, the root chakra. The color of this first chakra is red. The Muladhara's symbol is a red or pink lotus flower with four petals. The Muladhara is located at the bottom of the spine, in the pelvic area. Energy is localized from the coccyx down the legs.

Of all the chakras, the first chakra has the lowest frequency, is the slowest, and forms matter with its vibrations. Everyone's physical bodies are actually a byproduct of the Muladhara. It is here that the supply of vital energy for the human body is localized, which determines the health and quality of the life of the organism (its cells). Everything starts with the first chakra — it is here that life is formed.

The Muladhara is responsible for basic human needs such as sleep, food, security, procreation, stability and physical health. In simple terms, the first chakra is responsible for the primary needs that keep you standing firmly on your feet.

The first chakra is aligned to the following aspects of life:

- the health of the physical body;
- your relationship with the material;
- your basic needs (sleep, food, reproduction);
- your social role (where you belong socially);
- your groundedness and balance;
- your stability and resilience;
- your security (your ability to adapt and survive).

The main task of the first chakra is to give a person the necessary energy to carry out and fulfil the above aspects of life.

If everything is fine with a person's Muladhara, then they will want to live life to the full, have a family, children and a stable position in society, they will be physically resilient and healthy and have faith in the world, knowing that the Universe will always take care of them. This person will want to live in the here and now, he or she will have no fear of death, realizing that everything is just a part of the cycle of life. This sort of person wants to thrive and knows how to go about it. When the First Chakra is functioning normally, people understand that they are a part of life itself and accept the fact that nothing in this world belongs to them, except they themselves to themselves. The Muladhara functions as it should when a person is happy that they can simply 'be'.

THE SECOND CHAKRA — THE SVADHISTHANA

The second chakra is the Svadhisthana, the sex chakra. The color of the second chakra is orange. In women, it is located from the pubis to the navel, in men — from the perineum (prostate) to the navel.

The Svadhisthana is the chakra of pleasure. It is responsible for sex purely for the sake of pleasure, the ability to get joy from life, to earn money quickly and communication in any of its manifestations, as well as for relations in general: social position, public behavior, parties, friendship groups and interpersonal relationships.

The second chakra governs the following areas in human life:

- pleasure;
- emotions;
- sexuality;
- cash (material goods) flow;
- flexibility of body and mind;
- relationships and connections;
- bodily sensations.

The Svadhisthana generates sexual energy and forms the Etheric body with its vibrations. This body can be characterized as a haze or figurative trail. The etheric body is four-dimensional and exists simultaneously in different temporal realities. To get a rough understanding of what the etheric body is, imagine the effect that spirits have on the human body. Just like the scent of a perfume, the ethereal body leaves a trail behind itself (in the past) and, ahead of a person, creates a foretaste of his or her appearance (in the future). In a certain way, it's a kind of energy trail.

When a person knows how to enjoy life, he or she can provide him or herself with everything they desire. When a person has many connections and satisfies their need to communicate with other people, when a person is capable of giving him or herself the things that will give them joy, then the Svadhisthana is functioning normally.

THE THIRD CHAKRA – THE MANIPURA

The third chakra — the Manipura, is the solar plexus chakra. Its color is yellow. The Manipura's energy is centered from the navel to the ribs. It is responsible for the working of the abdominal organs, the digestive system and the nervous system.

The energy of the Manipura forms the Astral body. This body is able to separate from the physical body and travel not only in space but also in time.

The Manipura is the most important chakra for the purposes of the Destiny Code. It is the true essence that a person is really all about. All meanings, causes and effects are embedded in the energy of the Manipura.

The energy of the third chakra characterizes how a person's personality manifests itself in this world. If the third chakra is not functioning normally, then very often this person becomes invisible on the 'radar' of life, they simply drag out their physical existence without taking into account their connection with the world and without working out their personal destiny.

The Manipura is responsible for leadership qualities, the ability to achieve goals, social status, success and the ability to get things done. The Manipura's spheres of influence are as follows:

- the ego;
- inner core;
- self-realization;
- strength of will
- personal potential;
- social image;
- actions;
- striving to obtain 'experience'

A correctly functioning Manipura is very important for the system of a person's overall energy flow. The state of the third chakra determines the quality of a person's connection with the world. The value of a person to the Universe is directly dependent on the quality of the energy in this chakra.

When a person is self-realized, when they live in harmony with their principles, when their inner 'Self' has been formed and they are free in their desires, when they see their place in life and have determined their path in life, the Manipura is working well. This means that a person is visible to the Universe, they are on the path set out for them and performing their function in the overall universal flow of energy.

THE FOURTH CHAKRA — THE ANAHATA

The fourth chakra is called the Anahata — the Heart Chakra, the chakra of love and spiritual values. Its color is green. This is the only chakra whose position is slightly to the left of the spine closer to the physical location of the heart.

The vibrations of the Fourth Chakra create the matter of the Mental body. This is a special form of energy that can release certain additional flows to influence external factors in a person's environment. The mental body has its own temperature depending on the intensity of the energy flow in the Anahata.

The Anahata is responsible for feelings. Primarily, for love, sincerity, compassion, altruism, patriotism and duty. An important function of the Heart Chakra is the ability to feel, recognize and build the mutual relationship between everyone and everything in the Universe and to understand the causes and analyze the consequences of actions and events.

The Anahata is responsible for the following areas and aspects of human life:

- the senses;
- emotions.
- awareness;
- acceptance;

The Anahata is a very vulnerable chakra. The wider the spectrum of energy it distributes, the thinner the shell of the Energy body. The Anahata is working normally when a person is able to accept feelings and emotions and when he or she can share them and control the interconnection between these processes. An important aspect when analyzing how well the fourth chakra is working is the presence or absence in a person of 'acceptance' as a factor in their life. The ability to accept what is happening with dignity is key to the healthy functioning of the Anahata. The qualities of sensitivity and the ability to control oneself are the most important functions of the fourth chakra.

THE FIFTH CHAKRA — THE VISHUDDHA

The Vishuddha is the fifth chakra and is also known as the throat chakra. It is the chakra of voice and sound. It is blue in color and has a high sound range. It is located in the throat area.

The vibrations of the Vishuddha form yet another type of energy body. It is customary to call it a Causal body, which means that it is the 'Body of Cause' or 'Body of Karma'. It is believed that it is precisely this body that records a person's karma and forms an overall image as a fact in and of itself. The Body of Karma bears the Image of a person's self-realization and broadcasts it to the world. A person can be whatever they like on the inside (in the Manipura), but their environment and the world will perceive him or her in accordance with their Vishuddha as the person that they are at the present moment.

The main functions of the Vishuddha are: talents and their manifestations, self-expression, creativity, speech, skills and expertise. But it is also this chakra that is responsible for lies and deceit, often to oneself.

The Vishuddha is responsible for the following areas of human life:

- self-expression;
- speech and voice;
- openness and communication skills;
- ideas and meanings;
- clarity;
- creativity (in the global sense of Creation);
- Karma.

The Vishuddha is functioning normally when a person has their own voice, when their word is heard and listened to, when they are able to express themselves and their thoughts, when they are comprehensible to the world around them, and the world is comprehensible to them in return. The fifth chakra is functioning correctly when the realization of a person's abilities moves in the overall global direction of creativity, when a person is a creator, and not a 'doer'.

THE SIXTH CHAKRA — THE AJNA

The sixth chakra is the Ajna. It is the chakra of intuition and intelligence. Also known as the 'third eye'. The color of the Ajna is dark blue. This chakra is located in the region of the pituitary gland which projects between the eyebrows on the front of the forehead.

The sixth chakra symbolizes alternative vision and the ability to perceive the vibrations of energy flows and read information from without.

The symbol of the Ajna is a lotus with two petals, one of which is directed to the right and the other to the left. The lotus petals are channels to connect the chakra to the energy sources and internal organs in a person's physical body. In the case of the Ajna, the chakra is connected to the left and right hemispheres of the human brain. Receiving information from without, processing it and accepting it, the Ajna stimulates energy flow not only through itself, but also in the brain, providing energy via electrical impulses within itself.

The energy of the sixth chakra forms a high-frequency and an almost imperceptible Spiritual body. According to other sources, this body is called the Buddha body, which means the body that connects with God. The reason that it is referred to as the Spiritual body is justified by the fact that a person's subconscious is formed at the level of the Ajna, in other words, the totality of the spirit's memory of its soul's past incarnations. In my view, it is the seventh chakra that is responsible for our communication with God.

The most important function of the sixth chakra is perception in any of the manifestations that it may take. It is through the Ajna that any kind of information is received, accepted and processed. A person's ability to receive this or that flow of information is determined by the size of the sixth energy funnel. The development of the Sixth Chakra brings a person to the highest spiritual level. The Ajna is the pathway of spiritual energy.

The Ajna is responsible for the following areas and aspects of human life:

- reason;
- vision (the ability to see);
- perception.
- memory;
- subconscious;
- logic and intuition;
- intellect

The Ajna provides a person with the ability to receive information, consider what is going on around, analyze and draw conclusions. It allows a person to 'see' people and things in their true light, to perceive their true essence. The sixth chakra forms a person's worldview, and the brightness of colors and the range of shades that make up this person's picture of the world depend on the quality of the energy in the Ajna.

When a person is able to use all of the above skills, it is a sign that their Ajna is working as it should be. But, unfortunately, in practice, for the majority of people, their Sixth chakra contains pathologies and is in need of 'repair'.

THE SEVENTH CHAKRA — THE SAHASRARA

The Sahasrara is the Crown Chakra. It is usually represented by the color purple. It has a thousand petals, which symbolizes the countless neural connections inside the human brain. The energy of the Sahasrara is located just above the head and is projected onto the crown of the head.

The vibrations of energy in the Sahasrara create the finest high-frequency energy body, which is a kind of conductor for contact with the Universe (Higher Matters).

The Sahasrara affects all spheres and is reflected in all aspects of human life. This is the most changeable, fragile and resonant energy flow. However, it should be highlighted that the most important aspects of the flow of energy in the Sahasrara influence are primarily:

- the awareness of the Higher 'Self';
- the connection with the Egregore and the universe;
- the vision of the Path;
- extrasensory perception.

From an esoterical point of view, the seventh chakra is considered the most important one to develop and work on. In the context of the Destiny Code system, the Sahasrara indicates those energies that are responsible for inspiration and depression: the talents and skills that the Universe has endowed a person in their current life, the connection with the Higher powers, the Universe, God. The Crown Chakra is responsible for self-awareness, understanding of the meaning of life, orientation towards the true path and the acceptance of one's destiny. The energy in the Sahasrara opens up the flow of the Higher 'Self'.

CHAKRA PATHOLOGIES

Just like any person's internal organs, when the chakras are in a healthy state, they will work and perform their functions properly. When the energy flow is as it should be, a person's life is fruitful and happy, nothing bothers him or her and everything goes well. But, unfortunately, this is not always the case. Our chakras are as important to us as the heart, lungs or circulatory system. Like our internal organs, they can also be exposed to negative and destructive external influences. Our chakras also require healing and protection. Unfortunately, few people pay due attention to their energy organs and subsequently let them get into a bad state.

When a chakra is in a bad state this is known as a pathology. Just as in medicine, where our internal organs' pathologies need to be examined and treated, so the condition of our chakras need to be corrected in a timely manner if necessary.

There are several conditions (pathologies) that affect the chakras: oppression, rigidity and breach. When a chakra experiences excessive activity this also becomes a pathology and is known as hyperactivity. In addition to these pathologies, sometimes blockages occur that inhibit energy flows, clogging the chakra.

Balance is an important factor when receiving and giving energy. The same is true in nature: in order for a flower to grow, you need a balanced and proportional correlation between the earth, the rain and the sun. If a flower does not get enough water, then it will lack the necessary strength to grow. If it gets too much water, it will become waterlogged. Without the light of the sun, life and growth are not possible at all. And the same is true with our chakras.

If the flow of energy in one of our chakras exceeds that flowing through others, this chakra will begin to swell, grow and take on an unhealthily dominant role. In this way, our other chakras become oppressed, which results in the destruction of our 'energy bodies'. Or vice versa: a chakra might not get the energy it needs and becomes shrunken. Incidentally, these pathologies can even be seen at the physical level. For example, imagine a man with a broad chest, correct posture and straight shoulders — this is a clear indication of a person with a pronounced Manipura. And now, on the contrary, imagine a timid man suffering with a pathology of his third Chakra whose outward appearance looks stooped, crooked and as if his entire chest area had caved in.

Have you ever noticed that people whose professional activities are related to speech almost always have a wide and large mouth? Whereas people who are not talkative and reticent very often have thin lips and a small mouth. These are clear manifestations reflecting the state of their Vishuddha — the chakra responsible for speech, for the ability to have your own voice and to express your own opinion.

In order to use the Destiny Code technique productively, it is important to learn how to diagnose the state of the chakras. When you begin to understand where and how much energy is or is not being spent, whether your chakras have pathologies or are working normally, you can begin to build a strategy to balance your energy flows, analyze any weaknesses and redirect energy to the right places and in the right direction, thereby bringing yourself back to your normal, i.e. fully-resourced state.

In the next section, I propose taking a look at the pathology of the chakras. We will analyze the techniques available for diagnosing the condition of a person's chakras using illustrative examples.

OPPRESSION

Oppression is perhaps the least threatening type of pathology that can affect the chakras. In a situation where a chakra has been healthy, but as the result of certain life circumstances and minor everyday external influences — for example, the influence other people might have on a person — it can become oppressed and crushed. If you can figure out the source of this oppression and remove it, the chakra will quickly return to normal without any additional serious corrective treatment being necessary.

An example of a person with an oppressed Muladhara might be a man living in a family where everything is decided by the woman — she is the one who works and controls the life of the family. A man in this scenario forfeits his right to be the master of the house and make decisions, he finds himself reliant on the woman and is thus deprived of some of his primary root needs (to be strong and responsible). Another clear example of oppressed root chakras can be found among people who are in prison or deprived of their freedom for other reasons. A person has a natural need to be physically present in 'their own place', to possess their own things and to have the right to decide what they will be and how and where they might be kept. Prisoners, homeless people or those who are struggling to provide themselves with the necessities of life such as sleep, food and basic security — are deprived of these natural needs. Another example are people who have been driven into a situation where they are financially dependent (people with debts and loans), their Muladharas can also be oppressed.

There are many case studies of people with an oppressed sacral chakra that apply to a lot of people. I can say with absolute certainty that every person who reads this book will have experienced oppression of their Svadhisthana at some stage or another. And what's more, we all have to fight for the needs of the second chakra day in and day out and, apparently, we will have to continue doing so until we draw our final breath. Let me remind you that we are talking about the chakra responsible for comfort, socialising and pleasure. The most striking and simple example of an oppressed sacral chakra is when a person has to do a job they hate or is in a relationship with a partner they don't love, or experiences no joy in their sex lives, or is constantly on a diet. In general, any prohibition or restriction imposed by someone else or oneself that influences those aspects for which the Svadhisthana is responsible will end up suppressing the pleasure chakra. But I must also disappoint those of you who plan to fix their Svadhisthana by now joyfully running out and stuffing their faces with chocolate bars — the golden rule regarding balance still very much applies here! It is very important to sense the impulses and needs of the Svadhisthana and not overload it with excessive

energy. Because this is how energy is drained from other spheres of life so that other chakras are left without the necessary resources they need.

When talking about the Manipura, it is important to remember that in the context of the Destiny Code, this chakra is of paramount importance, and diagnosing the state of the energy flows in the Manipura is of vital importance when trying to realize your destiny.

When people find themselves in a situation where they are not allowed to defend their opinions or when their circle and environment do not take them into account. The following are examples of an oppressed Manipura: the inability to express your own character, a lack of self-confidence and always having to comply with the will of others. However, the third chakra needs to be approached with great care because the boundaries dividing its pathologies and those of the other chakras are very thin here.

Perhaps the most obvious example of an oppressed Anahata would be when people find themselves in an environment where they are not allowed to show their true feelings and are forced to conceal them. For example, a secret unrequited love or charitable feelings that may not be considered acceptable in the circles one finds oneself in. For example, a person might sincerely want to help a homeless person with money or accommodation for the night but because of the potential criticism this might provoke in their social circles, they are forced to do nothing.

A typical example of an oppressed Vishuddha is a situation when a person is forced to remain silent and hide the truth, or when a person is denied the right to express themselves. In addition, being forced into deception is also a sign of the oppression of this energy center. People are often forced to deceive others and themselves when they are under pressure as a result of external factors such as their parents, peers or teachers.

The Ajna and Sahasrara chakras are blocked in as many as 80% of people. It is important to be able to sense the fine lines separating the pathologies affecting the condition of these respective chakras. Often they are suffering from several pathologies at once. To ensure the highest and subtlest energy flows and the balance of the energies circulating at the level of these chakras requires a high level of spiritual development.

An oppressed Ajna often occurs when a person chooses to live in a society where they do not need to think for themselves. Everything has already been decided for this person. They are given precise and clear instructions at their work, they buy everything that advertising execs or salesmen tell them to, and throughout their lives, they act largely on the advice of others.

The Sahasrara becomes oppressed when a person does not see the path they need to take and does not feel the need to find it in order to return to their rightful place in the Universe's overall energy flow again. In other words, the moments in life when people lose sight of themselves.

RIGIDITY

All people are more or less born in exactly the same way... But later on in life, each of us follows a unique, inimitable path. The conditions of life, the trials of fate, the people that a person encounters along their path are the strongest factors influencing the course of the development of a human life. Everything is connected, everything flows between one thing and another. Everything that happens, bears its own meaning and purpose.

Rigidity occurs when a chakra is too set in its ways and immune to outside influencing factors. In the context of the Destiny Code, a pathology of rigidity in a chakra indicates that the energy center has not initially been developed sufficiently. From early childhood, a rigid chakra has been deprived of the flow of energy it needs. If a pathology of this nature is detected, then this means that this person's chakra has been in this state from the very beginning of their life.

It is difficult to bring a rigid chakra back to its normal state. Such a pathology requires a very long process of treatment in order to restore the energy flows, and the longer a person remains in this state, the more time and effort it will take to normalize their energy balance.

 A rigid Muladhara often occurs in people who have not been taught to create order in their lives from their childhood. When parents put away their children's toys for them or when they make simple decisions for them (for example, what to wear, what to play with, who to be friends with), they fail to teach them the most basic everyday life skills. They thus influence the child's root chakra, interfering with its development. The longer a person is subjected to such an influence, the faster their energy funnel atrophies.

Rigidity can influence the development of events in a very interesting way. The restriction of energy flows in the chakras can provoke extremely bipolar reactions. In other words, this sort of person can manifest themself in a totally negative or a totally positive manner. And in both of these cases, these conditions are considered to be pathological, because they disrupt the overall balance of energy flows and destroy a person's spiritual aspect. Thus, a person with a rigid Muladhara can either be an extremely slovenly person, or a manic pedant for cleanliness and order. In both cases, these are an indicator that this person's chakra is suffering from a pathology of rigidity.

 Birthday cake, candies as an incentive, limiting one's desires and deliberately not satisfying them, treating sex as if it were a chore and a duty — all of the above are indicators of a rigid Svadhisthana.

As with medicine, when analyzing the state of a person's chakras, it is vital that the correct pathology is diagnosed: the more accurate the diagnosis, the more productive the resulting treatment will be. And in much the same way as in psychoanalysis where it is believed that the causes of most mental illnesses are rooted in childhood so when working with pathologies in a person's chakra system, one should look for factors that have been influencing the chakras from an early age. Therefore, when a pathology of rigidity is diagnosed, one of the first things we look at is the subject's childhood.

The majority of cases involving rigidity in the Manipura are likewise the consequence of some circumstance or other that has occurred in childhood. The key word here is the verb 'to do'. When a child is not allowed to be independent, his or her personality is oppressed, his or her individuality and personal characteristics are not taken into account and all these actions lead to the violation and rigidity of the Manipura.

A typical case example of a rigid Anahata is the oppression of energy in the earliest years of a person's life. The heart chakra will become rigid in people who have not experienced feelings of love, support and acceptance in childhood. And if a family doesn't talk about feelings with their children and fails to show sympathy and empathy towards them in general, then they will grow up deprived of the ability and skills to love, sympathize and worry about others.

A rigid Vishuddha is a little more difficult to diagnose. Here, it is important to be able to tell the subtle difference between this pathology and a rigidity of the Manipura. A person with a rigid Vishuddha Chakra does not know how to express or defend their opinions and rights. Whereas someone suffering from a rigid Manipura is incapable of forming their own opinion at all. A person with a rigid Vishuddha (throat) chakra has their own point of view but cannot express it, let alone defend it. They remain silent and conceal their true 'Self' under the pressure of external factors such as parents, peers and teachers.

An example of a rigid Ajna is the lack of desire to think for yourself. The brain has not undergone the requisite development in childhood, its neural connections have not been established and as a result, these people do not know how to think for themselves and do not strive to make their own decisions. On the whole, they are not taught to analyze information and, accordingly, are not able to draw their own conclusions about many questions in life. In their family lives, their elders and betters are always deciding things for them and advising them what to do and how to do it. A lack of imagination is also a feature of a rigidity in the Ajna chakra. In this way, the level of a person's intellect and intuition is directly related to the state of the energy flow in their sixth chakra.

When a person grows up in an atmosphere of disbelief, with a complete or partial denial of spiritual values, their Sahasrara will be rigid. Examples of this are when a child does not believe in miracles, magic, goodness or God. Faith is simply not instilled in them from their earliest childhood.

BREACH

When a chakra has been subjected to a sharp impact from external forces, then a breach can be said to have taken place. The extent of the breach can be so destructive that the chakra may not be able to recover at all.

An example of a breach inflicted on the first chakra might be a person who has lost their home in a fire or other difficult circumstances that have radically changed their usual way of life — for example, if they have been left without any source of income and livelihood. The most severe instance of this pathology is when a person is deprived of one of their body parts (limbs) or internal organs. In this case, a compensation mechanism kicks in, which involves the partial redirection of energies from other chakras to strengthen the Muladhara. However, after such an impact a person's energy center can never fully recover and restore itself.

The Svadhisthana might become breached when a person is deprived of a source of pleasure or when a source of pleasure causes it to be breached. For example, when a person has been betrayed by a loved one or fallen out with a friend. The most difficult cases occur when people who have been addicted to smoking, alcohol, drugs, overeating, or abusive partnerships are undergoing rehabilitation or are in compulsory treatment.

However, the most striking example of a breached second chakra occurs in instances of sexual violence. In the majority of these cases, the chakra is not restored to its normal state at all after such a blow. However, a transformational program to normalize the overall energy balance and compensate for the lack of energy in this zone can be applied.

Examples of a breach inflicted on the Manipura can be found in every person's life story. The extent of the breach may vary but the result is the same — the Manipura is badly hit. Some typical situations are when people are subject to extreme shame, humiliation and persecution.

For example, a lawyer might decide to become a farmer but the environment and circles he finds himself in do not support his aspirations and his dreams are rudely and thoughtlessly trampled underfoot. He expresses his cherished idea but instead of support he receives nothing but criticism and ridicule, which ends up traumatizing him.

Many instances of this sort occur when a person's personality, character, enthusiasm or any other feature of their individuality are not accepted by the society around them, which furthermore often subjects them to cruel condemnation and ridicule. But the most complex situations are probably those when a person disappears altogether such as an accident, criminal act or an act of war. The severity of the breach caused as a result of this can not only hit the Manipura but also spread to other chakras, reducing the entire biofield to a state where it is extremely vulnerable.

Rejection in love is the most common example of a breach being inflicted on the Anahata. A difficult relationship breakdown, the loss of a spouse, infidelity and serious betrayal at the hands of others — all of the above can cause a serious breach to the fourth chakra. After an incident of this sort, a person slows down the flow of energy to the heart chakra and often closes it up altogether with such expressions as: "I will never love again", "I don't believe in anything anymore", "all feelings are a lie".

When a breach has been inflicted on the Vishuddha, it is often visible to the naked eye. Direct signs of this sort of breach can be impaired speech, stuttering, bad teeth, incoherent speech and frequent sore throats and colds. When a person finds themself in a situation where they are being "shut up", this can be a blow to their fifth chakra and may end up disrupting the flow of energy through it.

A breach to the Ajna occurs when a person's natural thought processes are placed under pressure. For example, when someone joins the military or starts a new job where they are literally ordered to switch off their independent thinking processes: "You aren't here to think, you're here to do a job!" This process can cause deep trauma to the Ajna Chakra. Typical indicators of a breach to the Ajna are when people are broken by a situation they find themselves in and then force themselves "not to think" independently in their own lives or when people shift the responsibility for making any decision onto others.

"There's no such thing as Santa Claus! Unicorns are the stuff of fairy tales!" — these are the sort of statements that are often uttered by children and adults alike and can cause a breach to the Sahasrara. Although, on a more serious level, what we are talking about here is the nature of faith and those situations that can cause it to be undermined (this can be faith in God, faith in justice, faith in yourself and, indeed, unicorns and Santa). In a single moment, someone else can destroy another's faith in something, depriving them of support and possibly an important source of strength. One careless word and something can happen, something might crack and smash into smithereens — and a person can lose all meaning in their life, rejecting the true intended path that they were meant to follow.

HYPERACTIVITY

Chakra Hyperactivity is an excessive flow of energy into a chakra, this happens when, at a certain given moment, the incoming energy becomes more than is required. If the flow of energy is only slightly higher than the desired level, then a person may well be able to correct it on their own. But if the discrepancy is very large, then the resulting activity ends up drawing energy from other chakras solely into itself and thereby depriving them of the necessary vital energy that they need.

In a normal (natural) state, chakras radiate and absorb energy, but there are also situations when a chakra absorbs much more energy than it requires. This is a good place to introduce the idea of Light and Dark chakras. If a chakra is Dark, a person absorbs energy from other sources, which easily circulates in the body, finding an outlet in their most active chakra. This might be a completely harmless incident at some insignificant stage of life, but in the future, it might cause a breach to certain energy flows. Chakras can become so seriously breached that they lose their energy altogether. For example, people with light energy are often unable to 'digest' the excess amounts of energy they produce. As a result, the energy ends up settling in the body on the physical level and the person ends up putting on weight.

People with a hyperactive Muladhara are often obsessed with getting their everyday chores or problems sorted. This sort of person ends up directing all their energy into maintaining order and cleanliness or observing their own strict and limited rules towards life. These are the sort of people who enjoy physical labor. As a rule, in terms of their external appearance, they are stocky, with their large feet planted firmly on the ground. If you look at a photograph of a farmer, for example, you will notice that he is standing foursquare on the ground his body weight evenly distributed between both legs, as if he were organically at one with the earth. It is particularly difficult to work on the Muladhara with people who suffer with an obsessive-compulsive disorder (OCD). If a person suffers from an obsessive-compulsive disorder, the energy from the first chakra needs to be directed to the Anahata and its movement in the direction of the Muladhara needs to be partially blocked, which over time restores balance to the overall energy flow.

A hyperactive Svadhisthana leads to hypersexuality. However, here, in most cases, this hyperactivity acts in concert with any number of other pathologies. Therefore, should hyperactivity be discovered in the Svadhisthana chakra, pathologies in other chakras can often be found at the same time.

A hyperactive second chakra can be best visualized as a man with his pelvis jutting forward, his hands gesticulating toward his body, with a wide, sweeping gait and an extremely brazen and forward manner.

A hyperactive Manipura often manifests itself physically in the form of a large extended belly or a deliberate expansion of this part of the body using clothes or other accessories. Those people who are lucky enough to be afflicted with this condition tend to be very influential in life. They often speak loudly, know how to resolve issues using threats and actively manipulate situations using their considerable 'weight in society'. It's very easy to identify a hyperactive Manipura and they are common among politicians, businessmen, celebrities and other influential people.

A typical example of someone suffering hyperactivity of the heart chakra would be a person who constantly strives to love everyone, to sympathize and empathize and even weep for them beyond all the bounds of reason. They have an excessive desire to protect and care for others, and this uncontrollable sense of 'love' and 'care' leads to many situations in their lives when their 'big heartedness' ends up turning against itself. Outbursts of sentimentality and emotions create barriers in communicating with other people and, therefore, create difficulties for these people throughout life.

As a rule, people with an excessively active Vishuddha chakra are artistic, political, and public figures. These are the sort of people who promote their ideas and objectives using sound, writing and speech. Or, more often than not, the type who talks non-stop, spreading gossip and constantly lying. In the case of pathological liars, it is worth noting that these people are also suffering from another pathology. This is evidenced by the nature of lies themselves because they are not only a sign of excess energy but also a deformation of the way it flows.

Typical examples of people with a hyperactive Ajna can be found among philosophers, scientists, writers, artists and all those who need to process huge flows of information. Outwardly, these people often have low-set eyebrows, and a deep and heavy gaze, their heads are slightly bowed, as if their necks cannot cope with the weight of their heads due to the energy that has accumulated there.

It's fairly difficult to provide examples of hyperactivity in the Sahasrara chakra in everyday life. In theory, these people are often psychics, people with supernatural powers, religious fanatics or people who are fanatically obsessed with a big idea that will change the world. All these people use the seventh chakra as their main channel of energy. As a general rule, their lives are ruled by the promptings of the Spirit rather than the Body. Of course, one could easily be tempted here to cite various master thinkers, the most advanced representatives of religious movements and practising mages and sorcerers. But no, this is not the case! It's very important to take on board a very subtle but vital difference. The aforementioned people are usually balanced individuals with their energy evenly distributed between all seven chakras according to their needs. These people are on a completely different, higher level of spiritual development. Although this is a subject we will touch upon later in this book, it is worth noting that these people are all members of the highest caste.

BLOCKAGES

Every event that happens to a person in their life leaves a mark upon it. Some give a person strength, others deplete their resources or destroy, break and deform their spirit — their energy flow. After all, every action has its consequences.

However, the ways that blockages in the chakras occur are very different. In most cases, a blockage is formed after an impact. It can emerge in a breached chakra where the blow has been so strong that a hole has subsequently formed. In these cases, it is very difficult or even impossible to restore the chakra back to its natural state.

Energetic influences can also create a blockage in the chakras. This is because people receive energy in different ways. Any person, provided that he or she is more energetically powerful, is capable of causing great harm to an opponent, even with a seemingly simple and innocent word. This is how applied magic works, when a psychic or, in other words, a person with a strong energy field, is able to attack an object, directing a deliberately negative energy blow at it (the evil eye, contamination, conspiracies, possession). This kind of magical influence can be applied to any of the seven chakras individually or simultaneously to all of them.

And there are also instances when a person can end up creating a blockage within him or herself. As a rule, a complex series of disturbances in the workings of an individual's energy flows needs to be identified here. These are cases when a pathological chakra creates a negative energy background that spreads to the neighboring chakras and settles in them. This can be compared to a side effect in the physical body. For example, when you "stub your toe and hear a ringing in your ears".

A good sign of a blockage that a person has created for him or herself is the regular use of the phrase: "That's the last time, I'll ever..." Having got through a difficult experience, a person can get hit. And to drown out and remove the pain, he or she plugs the hole with a cork. But because the energy cannot pass through the blockage, it has to seek different ways out in order evenly distribute itself to the other chakras. In this instance, the chakra that has been blocked ceases to perform the functions that it is meant to, and the 'blocked' individual no longer lives a full life.

The following are a few examples indicating the presence of a blockage in a person's chakras. For example, after a difficult breakup, a person might say to him or herself: "I will never fall in love again!" Someone who has lost their home in a fire or under other circumstances might vow to themselves: "I will never have my own home again." A teenager who has been kicked out of the house and torn away from their family after a big quarrel with their parents might leave with the words: "I don't have a family anymore". Statements such as: "I will never believe again", "I will never do that again", "I will never…" are all clear markers indicating the presence of a blockage.

For the sake of clarity, let's take a look at some more examples that might indicate the presence of a blockage in each of the seven chakras. This will be a useful exercise not only in terms of strengthening our general understanding of this particular pathology in the chakra system but also in the context of the methodology to which this book is devoted.

When a person says or thinks the following sorts of phrases: "I will never have any stability in my life", "I will never have my own home (car, wife, husband, child, job)", "I will never have peace", "I will never be happy" — it is a sure sign of a blockage in their Muladhara.

Statements indicating the presence of blockages in the Svadhisthana are often formulated as follows: "I can't afford to…", "I'm never going to touch another candy again", "I'm never going out ever again", "That's the last time I ever have anything to do with men/women any more". Another very interesting fact here is that asexual behavior, asceticism and entering into a monastery can also be signs of a blockage in the Second Chakra. But in this instance, one needs to very carefully and attentively analyze the behavior of the energy in the subject to say for sure.

The Manipura is both straightforward and complex at the same time. The psychological prescriptions people impose on themselves in their life are very similar to the creation of a blockage in the chakra. You will recall that everyone and everything in the universe is connected. A good example could be those situations when a person lacks the energy to manifest his or her true impulses and desires, thereby blocking the flow of energy in the third chakra with such groundless assertions and statements as: "I will never make the first move again", "I will never stick my neck out again", "I will never act on my own initiative again".

Things are slightly easier when there is a blockage in the fourth chakra. In this instance, a person tends to assert their limited position in the manifestation of any feelings. The demonstration of such dogmatic attitudes as "I will never love again", "I won't help others", "I will not open up my heart to anyone" and similar phrases using the word "Never..." is a clear sign indicating a blockage of the Anahata.

Expressions such as "I'm never going to tell the truth ever again", "I'm not going to say anything", "my opinion is of no interest to anyone anyway" are tell-tale signs that there is a blockage in the Vishuddha Perhaps on one occasion, a person speaks out, expressing their opinion and receives a sharp 'slap down' for their pains – the energy from this event hits their fifth chakra hard and their energy flow is breached so badly that they can't bounce back from this traumatic event. A situation like this requires a thorough and more detailed analysis and an accurate reconstruction of the traumatic event because the oppression of the individual's desire to manifest him or herself is very similar to pathologies in the Manipura chakra. Therefore, it is very important to pinpoint the cause and location of this disturbance to a person's energy flow before using any corrective programs.

A person who refuses to follow his or her intuition with assertions such as: "I won't listen to myself (intuition)" or "I will not evaluate the situation for myself" is a very good example of a person with a blocked sixth chakra.

As with cases where the functioning of the Vishuddha has been affected, the condition of the Ajna (and, indeed with all the chakras in general) needs to be analyzed very carefully. When making a "diagnosis" of disturbances inflicted on a person's energy flows, it is very important to pay close attention to even the most seemingly insignificant events in a person's life. The higher the chakra is located relative to the physical body then the wider the range its biofield's vibrations will be; the more stretched and thin its shell becomes and the more complex and unstable the state of these chakras and the pathologies they experience will be.

The creation of a blockage in the Sahasrara can only really occur when it has been subjected to the gravest negative energy from another source. In this situation, everything works along much the same principles as with the deformation of the energy flow in a chakra when it has been breached. An example of this would be the use of magic aimed at destroying another person's spiritual condition. To put this in simpler layman's terms, this all involves the use of the same energy rituals that are used in applied magic. It is important to remember that the strength of the broadcasting source will have had to be sufficiently powerful to overcome the energy of the person being attacked and prevent them from resisting and defending themselves.

At first glance, the two very different pathologies of a breach and blockage of the Sahasrara appear very similar. In order to avoid confusion and determine an accurate description of the 'health' of the chakra, you will need to analyze and observe the nature of the behavior of the energy in the individual for some time and find the correlation between these indicators and the main characteristics and markers that indicate the peculiarities of a particular pathology.

In rare cases, people with developed crown chakras are able to place a block on them themselves. This needs to be facilitated by the application of a shock that is stronger than that, which led to the blockage in the first place. As a rule, the level of a person's spiritual development whose Sahasrara is functioning normally is always going to be high. Because unfortunately, the vast majority of adults have barely developed their energy levels in the seventh chakra at all since childhood.

LIGHT AND DARK CHAKRAS

There is day and there is night, people believe in good and evil and periods in life can be good and bad. Human life is full of contrasts. So, in the same way, the chakras can differ in terms of their essence and there are Light and Dark ones. It is precisely the nature of these energy centers that we will be discussing in this section.

The Light chakras are the energy funnels in the body's biofield that radiate energy. Dark chakras, on the contrary, absorb it. The direction of the flow of the energy vortex is a distinctive factor that determines the nature of the chakra. It's probably worth recalling that when energy moves clockwise — you have a Light chakra and when it moves in a counter-clockwise direction — it is a Dark one.

At birth, a person's chakras are endowed with a single essence, which is either Dark or Light. However, over the course of life, things can change. Light can become Dark and vice versa. This occurs as the result of the influence of external factors, as well as from the desire of individuals to change their essence themselves. To understand more clearly how and why such a transformation occurs, we will need to take a look at some specific examples.

When you've had a good look at a person's behavior, their actions and their attitudes to certain things in life, it is easy to analyze the essence of their energies and determine their type.

Dark chakras are characterized by an excessive need for energy. And it is on the basis of this that the nature of their behavior is formed. Thus, Dark Chakras are constantly in search of an external source of energy to absorb the shortfall that it lacks. Light chakras, on the contrary, have plenty of energy, since they themselves generate the energy they need and even excess to radiate out to the outside world.

People who are obsessed with their appearance, being physically superior, having the ideal body and attracting the attention of the crowd to themselves as a physical specimen, have a Dark Muladhara Chakra. Vivid examples of this type can be found in social media with its fashion models, bodybuilders, diet and nutrition fanatics, plastic surgery devotees and professional celebrity 'domestic goddesses'. These people attract additional sources of energy to themselves in the form of followers, subscribers and fans, who obligingly feed them with their attention, thus providing them with the vital energy they need.

As a rule, people with a Light Muladhara do not focus too much attention on their appearance, health or how they go about bearing children. For them, these aspects of their lives are a natural part of the life process. Such people accept things as they are and do not bother themselves over things that do not contribute meaning to their lives. Indeed, as a rule, Light Muladhara people specifically prefer not to focus too much attention on these matters and often even deliberately avoid too much attention.

The most striking indicator that a person has a Dark Svadhisthana chakra is their excessive sexuality. When sexual attractiveness is used as a tool to achieve an individual's desires, a means of manipulation and a way to draw attention to one's personality. An equally striking feature of the Dark second chakra is an excessive desire to show off and an uncontrollable need for luxury items, branded clothing, jewelry and other expensive items of property, regardless of the individual's ability to afford them. A Dark Svadhisthana tends to surround itself with sources of energy from which the chakra will take strength. Therefore, Dark second chakra people are very sociable, they need to be surrounded by Light sources of energy. Naturally, the most striking example of this are women and men who flaunt their sexuality as a source of pride, as an object of adoration and a means of attracting attention to themselves. Although I might be jumping the gun, it is worth pointing out here that people with Dark Chakras act in this way unconsciously, for them this mode of behavior is the norm and a perfectly natural way of expressing themselves. It is important to understand at this point that this is the only way that their Dark Chakras can compensate for the energy that they lack.

Likewise, on the contrary, when you encounter individuals whose gender is only mildly pronounced, whose sexuality is weakly expressed or absent altogether, who have a cautious and unobtrusive attitude towards other people without any particular need to attract attention to themselves using their appearance or behavior — you can be fairly confident that their Svadhisthana will be of the Light variety.

Dark Manipura manifests itself strongly in the sort of people who insist on taking the credit for all their works, deeds and gifts. These types of individuals do not like to share their things, often they even mark and somehow find a way of labelling their things as their own. Their dark third chakra literally forces them to 'shout out' to the world: "This is what I did!", "I deserve the credit for this!", thus absorbing the energy they need in order to function normally. It is very important for people with a Dark Manipura to be 'busy', they need to be constantly doing things and attributing everything to themselves, to their personal 'Self'. It's important to remember this behavior is unconscious and stems from a perfectly natural need.

People with a Light Manipura, on the contrary, are ready to give up their work to others without directing their attention or the attention of others towards their own personal achievements. Often it is precisely these people who quietly work "for others", without ever performing great deeds in their own name, who build, create and achieve many of the things that change the world around us.

There are only a couple of precise but telling facts that can be said about Dark and Light Anahata Chakras: The Dark Anahata is the source of jealousy and the Light Anahata — the source of unconditional love. A good example of this phenomenon is when one member of a couple (with a Light Anahata) burns with an unconditional love that is sufficient for the two of them. While the second member (with a Dark heart chakra) is filled with a jealousy that can feed on the unconditional feelings of their partner without affecting or leaving a trace on them as a result.

A sure sign of the presence of a Dark Vishuddha is evident in those people who always have something to say when a problem needs solving. People like this are always 'reinventing the wheel' (regardless of the seriousness of the situation). They are obsessed with the originality and novelty of their ideas, it is very important for them to be constantly coming up with something unique, something that only they have invented.

However, those endowed with a Light Vishuddha prefer to follow the "the road well-travelled". It doesn't matter to them whether they themselves have come up with the idea or not, the main thing, as far as they are concerned, is the result achieved.

Having one's own way of looking at a question and a unique perception of the world and original theory about the special structure of the Universe are all, unsurprisingly, characteristics of people endowed with a Dark Ajna. People like this are completely absorbed in their personal thoughts and ideas and often impose their perceptions on others.

People with Light Ajnas seek out like-minded people and happily adhere to the same ideas as them. The most important thing for 'Light Ajna people' is that they initially get a general understanding of an idea and after that, it doesn't matter to them whose Word they follow.

What can be said about the essential nature of the Sahasrara? Everything here is so subtle that a very deep analysis would be required. However, in order to understand the methodology of the Destiny Code described in this book, this depth of knowledge will not be required. Therefore, we can skip providing examples that shed light on the features and nature of the Dark and Light seventh chakra and move on.

I propose talking next about how all the chakras are essentially different in much the same way that individual people also differ from each other.

LIGHT AND DARK PEOPLE

People can be considered Dark or Light, depending on the predominance of the one or the other in the total number of a person's chakras. For example, an individual with two Light chakras and five Dark chakras can safely be considered a Dark person. Whereas an individual with four Light chakras and three Dark ones can be considered a Light person.

All humans are considered equal, despite the different color of their skin, eyes, hair, culture and place of residence. There is no such thing as fundamentally 'bad' or 'good' people — everyone is equally precious to the Universe. The same applies to people's chakras. The term 'Dark' here does not have any negative connotations whatsoever. As a rule, it is people with a predominance of the Dark Chakras who become bright, unique personalities and it is they who leave a mark on history and push mankind's progress forwards. But it is difficult for people like this to get by because their energy demand is so high that their physical body cannot cope with the volume of energy flow that they require. It is of fundamental importance that they are allowed to reach their potential in various areas of life, but in other respects, they are often very unhappy. This occurs because they simply do not always get the energy they require.

'Light' people play a hugely significant role, and each of them is a vital element in the finely tuned mechanism of the Universe. 'Light' people help uphold balance by acting as a deterrent, to hold back the excesses of the people of the 'Dark'. However, at the same time, Light people feed Dark people with their self-generated energy in return for development and progress.

Based on the theory of 'Dark and Light' people, it has been calculated that there is a 94% to 6% split between Light and Dark people respectively. These are the most common figures quoted by various different spiritual practitioners and esoteric movements.

There are several indicators, which can easily help you learn to analyze the shade of a particular Chakra, and therefore understand a person's character as a whole. For example, there is a certain pattern that dictates that Dark people are always slim (thin) and do not put on weight, whereas Light people, as a rule, have an average or plump physique. This can be explained by the fact that 'Dark people' do not produce energy and are always in a state of 'energy hunger'. 'Light people' have as much energy as they need, and sometimes even more. When a group of 'Light people' endowed with a particular abundance of excess energy do not have a 'Dark person' in their midst, they process this energy at the physical level and actually gain excess weight — in other words, their excess energy is deposited in their bodies in the form of extra pounds.

Dark people are always trying to attract the attention of Light people, and the latter are drawn to the former at a subconscious level. 'Dark people' are predators, the personification of what the majority of 'Light people' aspire to be, both outwardly, inwardly and in their entirety. This is known as the magic mirror effect: Dark people act as an ideal reflection, attracting 'Light people' to 'admire' themselves, in return for providing them with the sustenance of their excess energy.

Throughout the history of mankind, one regularly observes antagonism everywhere and in everything: between day and night, good and evil, good and bad, Yin and Yang, white and black. It is important to always bear in mind that one cannot exist without the other. Balance is a matter of vital importance. And that one extreme without the other would not be possible.

The Muladhara manifests itself in 'Dark people' in their appearance. These people are physically very attractive. However, they don't do anything special to make themselves beautiful. As a rule, these people catch the eye of others, clearly standing out in the crowd. Very often 'Dark people' have very beautiful children or, conversely, children with some sort of defect. Thus, by caring for their unusual children, 'Dark people' take energy from others via their children who attract attention (in both cases).

Dark people are very sexy. Others are drawn to them like a magnet. Women with a Dark second chakra often have a boyish figure and are very angular.

Their sexuality, despite being concealed, is easy to decipher. Not only men but also women are drawn to them by an intangible animal instinct.

The Manipura chakra manifests itself in 'Dark people' brightly, clearly and is easy to spot. They are egocentric by nature, people of action and deeds. They are 'doers' — and don't they know it — as does everyone else they come into contact with. It is important to grasp the magnitude of actions undertaken by 'Dark people' in the progress of their development and not to confuse the ruthlessness and rigidity of this type of 'Dark person' with the desires of a 'Light person' with an ambitious Manipura.

The Anahata in 'Dark people' manifests itself in the way that it attracts love to itself. 'Dark people' with a dark Anahata are loved for no discernible reason. 'Light individuals' strive to get as close as possible to this particular type of Dark individual because they sense a oneness with them and the need to transfer the energy of their feelings to these people, thereby nourishing them. Many preachers and ministers of religious movements who succeed in uniting hundreds and thousands of people around themselves, have a very pronounced and active Anahata. Sometimes, these Dark individuals have little desire to communicate with others and seek solitude, but other people are ineluctably drawn to them, determined to unburden their feelings, they fly like moths to a flame, eventually burning themselves out with their outpouring of energy.

'Dark people' with an active Vishuddha are inventors. They come up with ideas and disseminate them. When others benefit from the fruits of their invention, they receive strength and energy in return. These are the sort of people who launch global processes that exploit Light people and make them their energy slaves.

The unique inherent quality of being able to see through everything, reading and accepting even the most subtle streams of information is a sign of a Dark Ajna. Of course, it is possible to develop these skills if you have a Light Sixth chakra, but, all the same, we are talking here about the superpower to "read" and "interpret". A Dark Ajna provides the person that has one with the ability to perceive a wide range of information, to take it in at high speed, as well as a exquisite ability to see the truth hidden from the majority of people. A Dark Ajna keeps its owner constantly hungry for information and completely absorbed with an obsessive thirst for new knowledge.

A very high level of energy development can be observed in a Dark individual who lives by means of his or her Sahasrara. When they share the Truth and their followers are guided by their teachings, these Dark individuals feed off their energy and convert it into ever more new ideas. These people are thinkers, sages, philosophers, opinion shapers and spiritual teachers. These are truly rare people.

WHEN LIGHT PEOPLE WANT TO BE DARK AND VICE VERSA

The task of every individual from the moment they are born to their final breath is the spiritual development of the personality: the recognition and harmonization of their Dark and Light Energies. The key element of this process is both the transformation of the 'shade' of their chakras over the course of their lives into their native shade and the desire to return them to the state they were endowed with at birth, in other words, the search for and acquisition of their true state in order to fulfil their personal Destiny. People often consciously strive to change the essence of their chakras by either darkening or brightening them.

A common example of the darkening of the Muladhara is when a woman gives birth and becomes unhappy at the resultant depletion of her energy levels. Her First Chakra might have originally been Light. But under the influence of external factors and finding herself in an unstable position, this woman might intentionally or subconsciously seek to obscure her undeveloped Muladhara by trying to find an additional source of energy. In these instances, she might manipulate those around her using phrases such as: "I had my baby for my husband's sake", "All my relatives persuaded me to have a baby", "I wanted to have a child to change my life", to attract energy with her darkened chakra from those around her who give her their attention. This is because, in theory, this woman's Dark Chakra needs to attract energy and in her normal state she wouldn't be able to satisfy the needs of her chakra not only to give energy to others (in this case, her child) but for herself. This is most likely caused by the presence of serious pathologies in the Muladhara.

People often 'darken' their Svadhisthana by, for example, having plastic surgery, simulating orgasm or wearing a lot of make-up in their everyday lives They change their image in order to leave their comfort zones. Insincere and over-the-top sexual allure or a feigned obsession with their social lives are also signs of an artificially 'darkened' chakra as well.

As a rule, dark people find it easy to show off their achievements and do so without a great deal of regard for the opinions of others because, for the most part, they themselves don't see the value of their actions. They pump up their 'Self' and inflate their own importance naturally. Their goal isn't to prove anything but to attract attention to themselves and bathe in the energy they need. At first glance, it is difficult to immediately tell whether a person's Manipura is naturally dark or has been deliberately 'darkened', you have to assess it in a complex way. A good example of people with a darkened Third Chakra are the sorts of individuals who create a lot of confusion, noise and chaos around themselves, who try to create something as a result of their behavior, but are completely unable to attract the attention of those around and garner an audience for themselves. Outwardly a 'darkened' Manipura often manifests itself literally and physically in a large puffed-up and distended belly. People at all levels of spiritual development appear to inflate themselves and, in fact, generate much more energy than they are able to dissipate. The energy thus created accumulates in their physical bodies. I have already mentioned a large belly as an example of one of the pathologies of the chakras and it is important here to be as accurate and detailed in your analysis of the state of the energy flows in the human body's biofield as possible before coming to a 'verdict'.

Have you ever been in a situation when someone has given you support and assistance and then goes on to remind you of this at every possible opportunity? If the answer is yes? Then you have encountered someone who is a typical example of a person with a darkened Anahata. Their obsessive care for others, accompanied by such phrases as: "Well, I didn't really have any choice in the matter, did I?" as well as intrusive and inappropriate demonstrations of love or insincere words of concern. This sort of behavior can subsequently cause cardiovascular disorders for these people at a physical level. They also often imagine experiences they have been through but these 'fantasies' nevertheless manifest themselves into very real consequences. Another tell-tale factor that a person has a 'darkened' Anahata is the constant desire to give 'pointless and meaningless' gifts such as mugs no one needs, little figurines or even unwanted presents that they themselves have received previously from someone else.

The Anahata can become 'darkened' either as a result of an individual deliberately wanting to, or as a part of a larger process of deformation in this chakra. In order to work out which of the above scenarios is the correct one, you will need to observe the behavior and nature of a given person's energy in the Fourth Chakra at some length and only then come to your final conclusion.

People often end up 'darkening' their Vishuddha with false threats and lies, or when their words and assertions are not substantiated. A phrase that 'darkened' Vishuddha people love to come out with is: "Just do what you've been told and that's the end of it!" People like this can often be identified by their extremely unusual voices or manner of speaking. Likewise, as a rule, they often have bad teeth. These physical signs are a consequence of the artificial darkening of the Fifth Chakra. Although admittedly, sometimes this process can in fact be necessary and justified in order to balance a person's overall energy flow.

People who are constantly defending an alternative opinion and contradicting others without any idea of what this opinion should be (for them the key word is "alternative"), are very likely to be deliberately 'darkening' their Ajna. These people 'hoover up' information and have a lot of knowledge at their fingertips but there is no structure, understanding, and most importantly, application of this knowledge in their lives. As a rule, these people have unusually large heads and very low or vice versa, very high foreheads. They may also suffer problems with their eyesight because their Ajna is unable to cope with the excess energy.

It is almost impossible to voluntarily 'darken' the Sahasrara. However, if 'darkening' does occur, then the individual in question could well be on the verge of mental derangement and insanity. He or she will become a danger not only to him or herself but also to those around them.

It could hypothetically be suggested that a blindness to one's true nature and passionate desire to see oneself as the source of faith can lead to someone wanting to darken their Seventh Chakra. In theory, a person who sincerely believes that they are the incarnation of God on earth or the Messiah could be an example of a 'darkened' Sahasrara.

A SHORT LEGEND ABOUT YIN AND YANG

At this stage, you're probably asking yourself the question: why do we need Dark and Light people at all? And where did this division into opposites come from in the first place?

I am confident that the majority of my readers are familiar with the famous black and white Yin and Yang symbol, the symbol depicting the balance between all types of energy. There are many different interpretations and stories regarding the origin and meaning of this image. The symbolism it encapsulates is used in various fields engaged in the development of spirituality, self-knowledge and the balance of energies. And each of these branches has a special theory regarding the origin of this sign. Personally, the legend 'About the People of the Light and Dark' is the one that is closest to me.

The white side, 'Yang' is the world of the living, the physical world in which a person resides during his or her lifetime. The black dot on the white half symbolizes the 6% of the population who are 'Dark People' who have been sent by the Higher Powers to explore life in this world. The "Yin" world illustrates the other world — the world of the Highest order, the world of the energetic transformation of the Soul, in which 6% of the population are 'People of the Light' who have ended up there by chance.

At the beginning of time, the Higher Powers created a wonderful universe in order to draw fresh energy from it, and divided it into two equal halves. To distinguish the boundaries of these two worlds, each half received its own special material essence. One half consists of the material essence of Light, the other of Darkness. Over time, these halves divided into hundreds and thousands of conglomerations and this material essence acquired a special form. The conglomerations of Light became people and those of the Dark took the form of souls. Both the form and the essence of the material changed. The Dark conglomerations became absorbers of energy, while the Light Ones became generators.

In the struggle for supremacy, the Light and the Dark fought for thousands of years, each defending their right to power and pre-eminence. And there was no way they could come to an agreement, their essence being inertly and statically stuck in the same state. Energy began to fade and almost completely disappeared from both worlds. Then the higher powers decided to show both the Dark and the Light how the other half lived in their opposite worlds, and sent a handful of Dark people to the world of the Light. Having disturbed the balance, energy was set in motion and created chaos within each world. So, the higher powers took an equal handful of Light people and placed them in the world of the Dark. Thus, the balance of energy was restored.

In this way, the people of the Light learned that it is possible not only to produce energy and give it to the Universe but also to take something from the higher powers for themselves. In turn, the people of the Dark became fascinated with the opportunity to invent and create something physical, in the same way as the people of the Light do and the people of the Dark wanted to embrace these skills for themselves.

And so, the people of the Dark became explorers. Travelling to the world of the Light Ones, the Dark Ones strived to create things in order to leave their mark on the physical world. And to maintain balance, an equal number of the people of the Light were sent into their world. But it turned out that the people of the Dark lacked the ability to produce life force in the world of the Light and the period that they could stay was limited. The people of the Light began to share their energy with their guests and enabled the people of the Dark to comfortably co-exist in their world. Out of a sense of justice and the chance to continue their exploration and research, the people of the Dark began to influence and shape the physical world, applying their skills for the benefit of the people of the Light.

Of course, there are no official statistics on this matter, but if you look at the biographies of famous people who have left a significant mark on the history of mankind throughout the ages, you will be saddened and amazed to find that the majority of them have left this world at an early age. Which, in turn, partly confirms and verifies the story about the people of the Dark and Light that I have just recounted to you.

People of the Dark always surround themselves with other people, ingesting the flow of energy they provide. Everything comes quickly and easily to them and their lives are bright and eventful. The people of the dark are the touchstones against which others measure their desires, the epicenters of power. But inside, in terms of their personal consciousness, they are deeply unhappy people who are eternally searching for meaning, in a constant state of tension, consumed with the desire to act upon and absorb what this world has to offer. Sometimes, a Dark person's mission in the world remains hidden from them, and the enormous flows of energy inherent in them overcomes and overwhelms them causing them often to leave this world at an early age. The time comes for them to 'report back on the work they've done' and to give up their place to those who follow them.

The people of the Light are the foundation, the very Essence of Life. It is their job to preserve the human bloodline and progress towards the attainment of perfection. Life for the people of the Light is rather uneventful in comparison. They are set tasks that they need to complete. Everyone has their own role, and at times it may seem monotonous and meaningless, but in fact, their significance is key to the life of society and fundamental to the existence of the universal flow of energy.

Sensing the need for Dark energy, the people of the Light often begin to pretend to be what they aren't and obscure their essential nature, passing off their wishful desires for reality. Often these people become energy vampires. They absorb energy without further transferring it onto the Universe. Sometimes it is not possible to understand this at first glance and perceive where truth and falsehood lies.

When people of the Light copy 'Dark people', their behavior appears unnatural. Quite often in our world, these people seem overly self-confident and their behavior elicits antipathy rather than opprobrium and recognition for their superiority. After socializing with people like these, one often even feels a certain aversion to them at a physical level. There are many such deluded and 'fake' people in life. They often create a false illusion of activity; impose philosophical principles on others but do not adhere to them themselves and they are often manipulative using pity or pressure to demand love from others. Care should be taken not to react emotionally to these provocations because this is how people with darkened chakras suck out other people's energy, which consequently goes nowhere and loses its strength, being unable to serve the greater universal good.

One can learn to distinguish between 'Dark people' and people who have become 'Darkened' by looking at practical examples.

People of the Dark will never beg others to keep them company — people in their orbit tend to be drawn to them and stay near to them naturally. 'Darkened people' will often beg and search out reasons for others to stay with them: "I'm so lonely, keep me company for a bit". People of the Dark prefer to live in densely populated cities, use public transport or occupy a high position in society, where they are constantly surrounded by other people. Dark people are not nature lovers. Finding themselves in deserted unpopulated places leads them to become physically exhausted, they find it difficult to breathe, they tend to sleep long and wake up extremely hungry, which is easily explained by the fact that if there are no people around they lack the source of energy they require.

During their childhoods, many 'Dark people' are forced to 'lighten' their Manipura. 'Dark children' do not like to share their toys or follow instructions and their parents often forcefully persuade them to change their innately Dark Manipura to a light one. Later on, it is difficult to correct this state of affairs and return the chakra to its initial natural state. Exhortations to conform such as: "You're no different from others, you have to live like everyone else", "you have to do the right thing", "keep your head down and don't draw attention to yourself" often end up 'lightening' Dark people's true natures, whereas Light people, on the contrary, are happy to apply these attitudes in their lives to help them realize their true nature, which also makes them feel like they are "not like everyone else", just like a true person of the Dark.

CHAKRAS IN CHILDREN

Many an answer to an adult's problems can be found in their childhood. Thus, having analyzed the general concepts of the Chakra system and having determined and defined the characteristics of Light and Dark people, now would be a good time to take a closer look at people's childhoods to find out what happens to the chakras when a person's personality is being formed and how external factors can affect the growing and developing spiritual organism.

From the outset, I think it is worth clarifying that everything I am about to describe is already well known and accepted knowledge for the most part. Many of you will have come across similar situations and examples of child-parent relationships in your lives as the ones described below. And perhaps some of you will even see reflections of your own relationships with your children, making the case studies described in this book even more personal.

By observing childhood through the filters of the chakra system, it is possible to identify the reasons for negative and difficult scenarios that are likely happen to a person throughout his or her life. This is a very useful and important tool when selecting and applying corrective programs using the methodology of the Destiny Code. An integrated approach allows you to take a broader view of the overall picture, spot all the nuances and appreciate the pros and cons of what is going on.

THE MULADHARA IN CHILDREN

A person's Muladhara begins to form from the day they are born until the age of three. During this period, children become aware of their existence and that they are a living organism. The main functions of the root chakra are sleep, food, a sense of security and the concept and awareness of "one's place" in the universe. These are all basic needs. It is during this period up to the age of three that a person lays the foundations that will govern how energy will behave in the First Chakra in the future. In most cases, people perceive this as a natural and arbitrary developmental process. And in adulthood, they intuitively adhere to the prescriptions received in childhood. And only a very few come to realize that a person's quality of life is directly dependent on the foundations forged in their early childhood, which go on to influence and affect them throughout their lives.

In order for the Muladhara to be healthy and well-functioning, it is important to encourage and strengthen it from childhood. The child needs to be encouraged to engage in physical activity and helped to explore the world. Their innate striving for independence should be prompted, the necessary conditions should be created to allow for the development of perseverance, diligence, hard work, domesticity and the desire for order and cleanliness in their environment. For example, from early childhood, a child should learn to tidy up their toys, keep everything around them in order, wash their hands, brush their teeth, and wash the dishes after themselves so that they might better know where and what their things are and understand the concepts of their "place", "home" and "family". They should also learn to satisfy their personal everyday needs independently and invent their own games and activities and have their own, albeit small, duties.

Let's take a look at what has a negative influence on the first chakra. First and foremost, this is, of course, physical violence. Under no circumstances should physical aggression and violence be used against a child. Likewise, small people should not be set multiple tasks to do all at once. For example, you shouldn't tell them to put their toys away, go to bed and not to forget to do this and that. This will disrupt their unformed energy flows and only end up distracting and draining them. Everything needs to be done step by step, and most importantly, with a healthy respect for the pace of the child's development.

When children are spoon-fed and their toys tidied away and chores completed for them, their Muladhara is not given the opportunity to develop properly. By letting a child do these things for themselves, parents encourage and support their character and personality, thereby developing and strengthening their other chakras. Later on, when the child matures, he or she will have the ability to act for him or herself and gain self-confidence, because his or her Manipura will have received the attention due to it. For example, he or she might open a business with a successful working concept but he or she may encounter difficulties running it: how to manage their company, how to maintain its structure, how to establish order and stability — how to be the true master of their own business. And it is precisely these functions that a healthily functioning Muladhara is responsible for.

THE SVADHISTANA IN CHILDREN

From the age of three to eight years old, the second chakra — the Svadhisthana is formed. It is during this period that children begin to realize that other people exist around them, that there is community and society and that there is a huge world out there that needs to be understood and explored. Children at this age show sympathy, identify gender, show interest in hobbies and form their preferences in terms of food, clothes and toys.

To strengthen and harmoniously develop the Svadhisthana, parents should express positive feelings in a tactile way by regularly hugging, kissing and cuddling their children. It is very important that during this period the child has physical contact with its parents, since it is parental love, care and guardianship that provide the pure energy, which is so vital for the fundamental development of the Pleasure Chakra.

It is important for a child to receive approval, treats and gifts. It is at this age that people first acquaint themselves with feelings of pleasure and comfort. Incidentally, it is worth mentioning here that according to statistics, a person's taste, sense of style and understanding of beauty and harmony are all largely instilled in them before the age of eight.

At this age, it is important to teach children how to socialize with others in society and the rules governing that socialization. Spend time with your child, talk to them, get them to meet different people, go to public places, and travel. It is at this age that children should feel how much active energy they have in the Svadhisthana, realize their role in society and how they should behave in relation to those around them: whether they absorb energy or radiate it.

The second chakra is also responsible for the Energy of wealth and all monetary and material wealth passes through it. Therefore, it is important to learn in childhood how to appreciate life and enjoy it. Harmony and balance in the Svadhisthana elicit a productive flow of monetary energy. A person who knows how to reap the fruits of their activity and appreciates the pleasures of life always finds the ways and additional means to satisfy the needs of his or her Second Chakra. If you take a look at the rich and wealthy you will see an interesting pattern in their lives. Those who, at first glance, spend their money like there's no tomorrow, forever relaxing on yachts and private islands in the middle of the ocean, are more successful and prosperous in the development of their capital in terms of their quality of life than other equally wealthy people who in contrast are always immersed in their work and failing to pay due attention to the needs of their Svadhisthana. The latter are much more likely to be stuck in a rut or may even lose their wealth without being able to restore the former quality of life they had become used to. And this may be because they were simply not taught to love life and allowed to let their Second chakra develop as it should have in their early childhood.

The Svadhisthana in children is very vulnerable to the sort of aggressive attitudes expressed in phrases such as: "You can't afford it!", "If you want something, you'll only want more of it!", "That's not funny! Stop clowning around". And these prescriptions can end up not just inhibiting the development of the child's chakra, but also creating a pathology in its energy flow.

THE MANIPURA IN CHILDREN

Opinions vary regarding the exact period and age that a person's Manipura develops. Some sources state that the third chakra is already fully formed and developed at birth and that it is only during the course of a person's life under the influence of various external and internal factors that it changes and acquires its subsequent pathologies. Many experts on chakras and energy believe that the most active period of the Manipura's development is in the period between the age of eight and fourteen.

The Manipura is always tricky to deal with. In the overwhelming majority of people, the third chakra is the most difficult to analyze. When using the Destiny Code to select and apply corrective programs, nearly all the main tasks are initially and specifically aimed at restoring and strengthening the subject's Manipura, because in the context of the methodology used to read the Destiny Code the Third Chakra is the most important one — it is the Arcanum of a person's Character, the Arcanum person that determines his or her true "Self".

When the Manipura becomes breached, it is as if the person no longer exists. Naturally, he or she exists in the physical sense, of course, and can, for example, even enjoy life thanks to the Second Chakra and continue to ensure his or her actual existence, but as a person, as a spiritual unit, he or she ceases to exist. He or she fails to do anything useful. A person with a non-functioning Manipura becomes invisible on the radars of this world. People like this do not realize their potential in life. The Universe fails to provide them with the resources they need because it cannot see them in its field of perception.

The Manipura is responsible for maturity. If the chakra is weak, then its owner will behave in an infantile manner until old age, avoiding all responsibility for their deeds and actions.

It is very important to acknowledge the victories that children achieve and to support and encourage them when they fail. To encourage independent decision-making and discuss the results of their decisions with them. In accordance with the calculations that can be made using a person's Destiny Code, children should be supported to develop the strong qualities and personal abilities that correspond to the Arcana located in the Manipura chakra. Do not force children to be active in and develop areas of activity that are alien to them. Each person has their specific goals and objectives and, by deviating from their intended path, they fail to reach their designated goal and find their place in life.

It is important for everyone to have a sense of their own authority and self-confidence and thus realize their own significance. And the sooner a person comes to understand the needs of their third chakra and embarks on the path towards developing it, the more robust their Manipura will become and the more productive their lives will be.

The most important task facing any parent is to adapt their children to life as it really is, to explain to them that every action has consequences. It is important not to raise children in a cocoon, protecting them from the wind, because one day they will have to go out into the world and follow their own path, which might very well lead them into the teeth of the wind. In life, a person needs to be independently responsible for their words, deeds and actions — to work out their personal Karma. All parents must provide their beloved children with the true knowledge they need in a timely manner.

However, people's destinies differ and the scenarios governing the course they follow do so too. Sometimes the opposite can happen. Sometimes parents try to raise their child as a 'Spartan' who is ready to slay any enemy, move any mountain and overcome any difficulty. But creating excessive pressure on children by placing too much responsibility on their shoulders can artificially create difficult situations in their lives and a fear that "everything in life is dangerous and difficult" and this can cause much more harm to them. In a situation like this, a person either consciously diverges away from the true manifestation of themselves and ends up blocking their Manipura, or diverts all their energy flows to the first and second chakras and prioritizes providing them with their needs thus becoming cowardly, unreliable and, as a rule, unhappy later in life.

Perhaps the most negative impact that can be exerted on the Manipura in childhood is committed by parents who force their children into a position of unquestioning obedience: "Do as I say!", "Sit quietly until I tell you, you can move". If one is coarse and unbending when communicating with a child this often causes a blockage in the chakra or even causes it to become breached. The following phrases should never be said to a child and are totally unacceptable: "You are not important!", "You are a nobody!", "You can forget about ever having any significance in this life!", "Who told you that you could do that!" In some societies, these attitudes are even directed at adults. It is important to be aware that this is never acceptable behavior towards an adult and all the more so towards a child.

THE ANAHATA IN CHILDREN

The Anahata begins to stir, strengthen and develop in children at the age of fourteen when a person starts to discover new meanings for him or herself. It is at this stage that children come to know things not just from other people's words but to feel it for themselves.

It is during this period that the most important feeling of all is discovered — unconditional love. If a child grows up in an atmosphere of love, tenderness and care, he or she will be able to perceive what a healthy heart chakra is and to develop his or her own. If a child is subjected to insensitive social interactions and if it is not customary in his or her family to show their emotions — this can harm the Anahata, creating blockages and pathologies in the process.

My dear readers, we can't even imagine the inherent power that lies in words of love. It is extraordinarily, I would even say, vitally important to talk to other human beings about love. And even more so, when children are growing and developing, it is vital to instil and nourish them with a sense of beauty, kindness and love. A human being who is growing is like the soil of the earth — in the end it will only yield what you have put into it.

Everyone knows that it is at around the age of 12-14 that people have their first experience of love. The strongest and even the brightest love of a person's life. Feelings of good or evil, allegiance or antipathy also make their mark at this time. I can state with absolute confidence that between the age of 12-25 years is the period when that Anahata is at its most active in a person's life.

So, therefore, tell your children that you love them! And not just for any specific reason, but simply because love exists! It is important to encourage the development and functioning of the Anahata because this is how children develop their feelings. The same is also vital and necessary for adults. By releasing the energy of love, a person builds up the strength of his or her Heart Chakra, while carrying out useful work on him or herself.

While we're talking about the energy of feelings, it is worth pointing out that it is equally important to let go of negative emotions. Energy needs to be in constant motion. If a person accumulates large amounts of negative energy inside themselves, this can lead to a pathology in the chakra, and this energy will nevertheless seek a way for it to release itself. Often, this sort of accumulated negative energy can manifest itself at the physical level and result in actual diseases and disorders in the human body.

At the age of fourteen, the Anahata is at its most vulnerable and the biggest paradox is that the heart chakra often gets damaged precisely by love or because of love.

When Love comes on the scene — teenagers begin to experience strong feelings. Parents need to be there to support their children at the right time, and not discourage them from the path of love. Of course, this is a difficult thing to adopt and put into practice, because it's very difficult to control yourself and you never know what a teenager is going to come up with next! But do not rush to set limits on or quarrel with your children or force them to make choices. You have to accept their interests and experiences as their own. It is important to allow them to open up, to listen to them, to sense how they are feeling and not to give advice unless they request it themselves. There is no point teaching a teenager how they should live!

It is important for any person at any age to be given support, and even more so at a period when they are just setting out on their own path. Parents should remember that they do not have the right to make decisions for their children, even if they themselves are unable to understand and work out their own feelings. Everyone has their own life to live, their own karmic trials to face and their own path to follow.

Parents openly arguing in front of their children, in-fighting in the family, shifting responsibility for the child from one parent to another, parents getting divorced, indifference about showing feelings and a lack of appreciation when children show their love (be it a drawing or something they've bought with their pocket money) — all these things can end up deforming the Anahata and hinders its development. It is inexcusable to compare your child with others, like for example when a parent says: "I know all children are meant to be alike, but I don't know where you get it from?" Even the most loving parents sometimes allow themselves to do and say such things that have a very negative effect on a child's Anahata.

Now let's take a look at the consequences of the above scenarios. A person whose Anahata has been damaged in childhood may in the future exhibit callousness, be afraid to enter into relationships, experience fear, and be afraid to reveal his or her feelings to others. Taken as a whole, they might not be able to love but will enter into relationships out of a sense of convenience and will not allow others to show their feelings to them. On the whole, it does not make for a rosy picture.

If we can make a small generalization about ensuring that a child develops a healthy Anahata, then it is worth saying that without a doubt the most significant factor here is the way the parents behave towards their child. I can say with a good degree of confidence that it is the parents (the environment in which the child grows up) that determines how he or she will receive and give the energy of love in their adulthood. As they say, children are like a garden: if you sow them with onions, don't expect buttercups in spring.

THE VISHUDDHA IN CHILDREN

As it turns out, everything is fairly straightforward with the Vishuddha in children. This chakra is much easier to develop than the others. Here, the most important thing is to support any signs of creativity your children might have and create the necessary conditions under which they might begin to use their imagination and creative thinking and allow them to express themselves. It is important to facilitate their ability to form opinions by giving them the floor and the opportunity to defend these opinions.

There are a number of different points of view about the age range that the Vishuddha begins to develop. It is generally believed that the throat chakra begins to open up at the age of 16-18. But personally, based on my own practical experience, I have come to the conclusion that the Vishuddha becomes active from early childhood. Accordingly, I have become increasingly convinced by the theory that all the chakras, including the throat, are probably active from birth, it's just that their character can become more pronounced or oppressed at certain different ages.

Perhaps the most obvious and common example of the oppression of the throat chakra in life is when a child is not given the opportunity to speak. "Who asked you?!", "Children should be seen and not heard, you need to listen to what your elders and betters say!", "Silence\Shut up!", "No one asked for your opinion!" Constantly telling a child not to sing or talk loudly also injures the Vishuddha. If the way that a child expresses itself is completely unbearable for the parents (they are very loud or endlessly chattering), then it's worth seeking a way to get around the situation, for example, by sending the child to singing or acting classes or suggesting that they prepare a show in another room, but if the child is just loud by nature, then you simply need to play games with him or her that requires the players to be quiet. But under no circumstances should you forbid a child to speak.

With regards telling children not to do things in general, there are so many examples and they are so common that everyone will have come across at least one of them at one stage of their lives. For example, when an adult criticizes a child's comic antics or their appearance: "You're getting all excited, and you're beginning to show off!", "Just take a look at yourself. What do you look like!", "Have you seen yourself in the mirror recently?".

And, perhaps, the most powerful thing that will traumatize the Vishuddha in childhood is any criticism of a child's self-expression, a negative assessment of something they have created, and even worse, any expression of indifference to the development of the child's imagination.

All of these actions can damage the Vishuddha. Of course, as with the other chakras, the degree of impact can vary, some will not cause a great change, while others might cause a pathology in the chakra. It is important to remember that even a single phrase spat out in a fit of anger can cause irreparable harm to the future of the child.

THE AJNA IN CHILDREN

The sixth chakra is responsible for the mind, intellect, intuition, memory, logic and, in general, for the activity of the brain. And of course, it is the Ajna that opens up our psychic abilities. What can be detected even at a very early age is that the Ajna develops slowly. It needs time to mature. It might be that it's not possible to define a specific age at which it grows and matures because sometimes even a one-year-old child can actively be alive to it. But it often happens that the Ajna only reveals itself at a fairly mature age. The Ajna needs to be developed consciously and intentionally. Parents need to make every effort to engage in its development in their children from early childhood. The sixth chakra gains sustenance and training by playing intellectual games and inventing fairy tales and stories. It is important from childhood to teach a child to look at problems from different angles. Setting riddles that use logic, fortune telling and searching for things that are hidden help develop logic and inner vision.

The Ajna needs to grow and develop slowly and its activity may not be immediately noticed, but it is very easy to harm and adversely affect it. And no matter how sad it may sound, situations where the sixth chakra is badly impacted can very often happen during every person's childhood.

"Don't touch that!", "Stop, you'll break it!", "Don't climb up there! You might fall!" Do these phrases sound familiar to you? Or perhaps you've heard these ones: "Do it as I told you to!", "Don't be a smart Alec!", "Follow the rules, and do it by the book!" All of these prescriptions and prohibitions block the flow of energy to the Ajna, weakening it and leading to pathologies. In situations where a parent finds themself about to say something like this to a child, it is important to pause and try to open your own chakra to increase the flow of your own energy. For example, you could draw the child's attention to the consequences of its actions and give him or her the opportunity to develop their logic: "Look, this tree is very tall. If you climb up it, how are you going to get back down to the ground?", "Look how fragile that is. We need to be very careful with it!", "What do you think we should do?", "Think for yourself!" In cases such as these, the child should be encouraged to try to think before doing something. If the parent works together with the child to try to resolve the issue, it can be a very productive exercise. And in this way, the adult can themselves engage in the complex development of their own chakras as well as those of the child.

It is important to give the child the opportunity to explore the world. Do not restrict him or her when he or she is learning and discovering about himself, new objects and people. Expanding a child's boundaries contributes to the discovery and opening up of the child's potential internal energy capabilities. It is a very productive exercise to visit new places and share new information when developing your children's Ajna. You should try to be sensitive to those things that the child is more interested in.

During a child's education in kindergarten and at school, parents often do their homework for them with the good intentions of helping their child get to the top of the class. But if you are a parent who does this, stop doing so! Ask yourself the question: who is going to solve their problems for them in adult life? However, do not scold your child for bad grades. It is much better to analyze why he or she is finding it hard to keep up with the program. It is important to allow the child to reveal and open up the energies residing in their Ajna according to their abilities. It is in situations such as these that the ability to analyze the Destiny Code comes in very handy. A person's attitudes, abilities and challenges are evident from the moment they are born and it is clear even at this early stage, which of them needs to be developed and improved.

Here, as with the Vishuddha: it is important to bolster and encourage the child's unique nature and under no circumstances to compare him or her with others. There is no point in becoming obsessed with the latest trends (the same applies for personal development as much as fashion), it is important to strengthen the child's individuality of thinking and their personality as a whole. Otherwise, from their earliest childhood, a person will block the energies in the Ajna (Vishuddha and Manipura) and won't be able to develop their own opinions, let alone defend them and follow their own personal convictions. Such a person will become an unquestioning and obedient member of the masses blindly following the orders of others.

THE SAHASRARA IN CHILDREN

The Seventh Chakra is both simple and complex at the same time. This is the most subtle chakra and is extremely sensitive to external influences. However, at the same time, it is the most resonant and powerful in terms of the strength of its energy flow and the most important and fundamental overall. It is all about faith, the power of thought, the connection between an individual and their higher 'Self'. This is the engine of life, and, as such, it is something that can stall and stop running for good. And of course, its condition, reinforcement and development are directly related to the place an individual will occupy in the Universe.

It is the Sahasrara that bears within itself the fateful implications and challenges of the current incarnation of a person's life. And the better the energy flow is regulated in this chakra, the more productive the individual's self-realization will be.

The Sahasrara shatters the notion of atheism and the absence of idealism and faith and, in general, the absence of symbols and symbolism in a person's life. We are not just talking about a religious upbringing, which might be a questionable notion in its own right, but about the Faith needed to understand and see the cause-and-effect of the relationships that govern the Universe, to perceive and fully understand oneself, one's path in life and the significance of life as a whole.

The reason why I have repeatedly made mention of the healthy functioning of the Sahasrara in our conversation about children's chakras is that from the moment a person is born, it is very important to expand the energy flows in the Seventh chakra and lay the foundations that will give him or her the wherewithal to immediately embark on his or her own path in life. And no matter how scary and responsible all this may sound, this is precisely the most important task any parent faces.

In order to better understand how to develop and how not to harm the Sahasrara in childhood, let's take a look at some practical examples.

An atmosphere of faith and religion is a favorable influence in the development of the Seventh chakra. When a family shares a common faith and observes the traditions, customs and rules of a particular religious doctrine — the structure and algorithms necessary for the perception (acceptance) of the world in which a person finds him or herself all begin to form and develop. It is important for a child to believe in a higher being: A Creator, a Supreme Force, Fate or the Universe. Believing in magic is also incredibly important in childhood for the formation of the Sahasrara. Children really do need to believe in Santa Claus, the Tooth Fairy, unicorns, mermaids and dragons. This helps them establish the path to finding their own unique meaning in life.

Destroying a child's faith in these things hits the Sahasrara hard. When parents think it a bit of a joke to dress dad up as Santa thus revealing to their children that he doesn't exist, they fail to appreciate the full tragedy of the situation that the child is experiencing at that moment. A trauma of this sort can have a profoundly negative impact on the child's later life. When people lose faith, they lose the meaning of life, because without faith (no matter what it is in) it is impossible to determine the touchstones and benchmarks in their lives, understand themselves and who they are and where they should be going.

Dangerous phrases such as: "People are not important! We are all just a part of the blind masses", "Life has no meaning", "You are a nobody in this world!" — are all extremely harmful to the seventh chakra, reducing and closing off energy flows and causing people to become blind to their destiny.

In general, it is very important to develop and open up the Sahasrara in children and it doesn't matter when the process begins. Unfortunately, the seventh chakra in the majority of people is often weak or atrophied altogether. However, people born in the early 2000s are changing the picture drastically. From my many years of practice, I can conclude and confidently assert that the latest post-millennial generations have arrived in the world with a higher level of spiritual development. Much fewer of them now have been set the humdrum life challenge of simply breeding and preserving the status quo, and already a much larger percentage of these new generations have been sent to perceive and realize the deeper meanings of the universe. For this new generation, the question "Why have we come into this world?" is much more acute than "How can I make life better and more fruitful?".

Once the Destiny Code's matrix has been calculated and with a good general knowledge of the chakras and energy flows, one can not only analyze the life of any individual (yourself, your relatives and friends), but also draw up and immediately apply corrective programs that can be applied to certain situations in people's lives.

By learning the finer details of the Arcana located in the matrix of the Destiny Code and by making your own calculation of the formulas or using an automatic calculator to calculate it for you, you can get a fairly detailed description of the person whose Destiny Code is being looked at. And you might be forgiven for thinking that all the facets of this individual will have been revealed. But this is not the case! This is not all that a person who has embarked on the path of studying the Destiny Code will need to know.

Before learning how to calculate the Destiny Code's formulas and before studying the characteristics of the Arcana and considering in detail what this unique tool has to offer, there is one more additional, but closely related topic that you will need to understand before practising and using this method. So, in the next chapter, we will discuss and look into the concept of Castes.

CHAPTER II. CASTES

GENERAL CONCEPT

Historically, humanity has always divided itself up into various groups at the subconscious level and in actual life. There have been hundreds, if not thousands, of classification systems. People can be divided according to many factors: by race, nationality, star sign, external qualities or even the loudness of their voice.

One way or another, people are essentially not equal. And they never have been. In esotericism, a special classification of people is used, based on a system of dividing people into castes described many millennia ago in the Indian Vedas.

The caste system is the oldest system for dividing society into social and spiritual categories. My readers will recall from their school history lessons that ancient Indian society was divided into groups (castes) consisting of workers, merchants, warriors and sages. A person born into a certain caste, could not move from one caste to another during their lifetime, and the meaning of their entire existence in this world was to prove themself as worthy as possible in their designated place, to be useful to their society, to complete their karmic tasks and provide the soul with the chance to be reborn in the next incarnation at a new level of spiritual development and become a member of the next caste.

While learning how to interpret the Destiny Code, it is important to become acquainted with the castes in the context of esotericism. Therefore, henceforth it would be helpful if you try to ignore the historical aspect of the caste concept and instead see it in a broader context. Knowledge of the system of caste division provides us with a clear idea of a person's spiritual growth after their rebirth and it is important to be able to do this when interpreting the Destiny Code matrix. It's like having additional layers of personality, which when separated can act like filters allowing us to see the particular features of each.

People are born and die. The soul moves from one body to another, traveling from one life to the next. On its arrival into this world, the soul acquires skills, goes through karmic lessons, performs certain tasks and fulfills its destiny, thereby accumulating energy and gaining spiritual experience. The soul is an integral unit. It is unique and inimitable. Its experience is transferred to other, younger souls and settles in the form of karmic programs of the past in the matrices of our descendants.

The life cycles of the soul can differ from one individual to another. Some need only to go through one rebirth, learn the lessons they need and mature to the next level, while others need to live several human lives in order to learn and accept what the Universe has prescribed for them.

In my personal practice, I have abandoned the generally accepted terminology of castes. I do not use the titles "workers", "merchants", "warriors" or "sages". It is much more convenient for the sake of understanding to simply talk about the "First", "Second", "Third" and "Fourth" castes.

In spiritual practice, determining the age of a soul is one of the important factors when carrying out most rituals and corrective programs. The age of the soul indicates many factors that allow us to analyze a person's physical and spiritual state. Terms such as "young" and "old" souls are often used as a part of applied esotericism.

Young souls are the people of the First Caste. They have only just come into this world and are getting the hang of living in it. During the first stages, Ones learn to understand life's certainties, accumulate the experience of how to survive such as finding a home, food and security. These souls are only just learning to stand on their own two feet, their main challenge is to learn to stand firmly and confidently on the ground in order to be able to progress and take their first steps.

Old souls — the Second, Third and Fourth castes are people who, having already experienced previous incarnations, have set themselves higher goals. And the more experience an individual has, the more global their goals and the higher their caste.

The soul lives many lives, accumulates unique experience, collects knowledge and is filled with energy. The soul is like a vessel that can be filled to different levels: just a little, half full or right to the brim.

All castes are equally important. The caste that a person belongs to merely demonstrates the level of energy accumulated and the range of tasks facing them and under no circumstances gives the member of any caste the right to look down on someone in a caste below them. Each person has their own role in this life, each is connected with others through the single energy of the Universe, each is equally important for the harmonious development of the world and the implementation of the overall task facing all.

THE ASSEMBLAGE POINT

Where is the Soul located in the human body? This is a highly complex and controversial question. In accordance with esotericism's generally accepted perception of the soul as the source of strength, many adhere to the theory that the soul is something that fills a person's entire physical body from the tips of their toes to the tips of the hair follicles on their heads. Others take a slightly different approach to this question and argue that the spirit moves freely from one position to another, thereby traveling through a person's physical body and releasing energy forces depending on the needs and tasks facing an individual at a particular stage of life.

The current trends in esotericism, including the study of the Destiny Code, have no hard rules stating that one or the other theory should be strictly adhered to. There are schools of the Destiny Code, which base their studies on the notion that energy is not concentrated in a single center and that its flows change and behave chaotically depending on what physical affairs an individual is engaged in at any given moment. For example, if this person is eating their favorite food, then the center of their energy will be concentrated in the Svadhisthana, but as soon as a person begins to clean their house, this energy passes to the Muladhara in accordance with the functions of the chakras.

Personally, I like to allow myself to see things in a different light and support a theory that is closer to me personally based on the large body of evidence that I have accumulated over many years of practice and, which importantly, has its roots in other spiritual teachings outside the context of the Destiny Code.

I believe that when calculating the Destiny Code, you can address negative karmic programs by deliberately moving the concentration of energy from one position (chakra) in the human body to another, thereby using these actions as a tool to correct your energy balance. This allows you to change a person's life and raise the level of their soul, in other words, you can change the position of the Point of Integration.

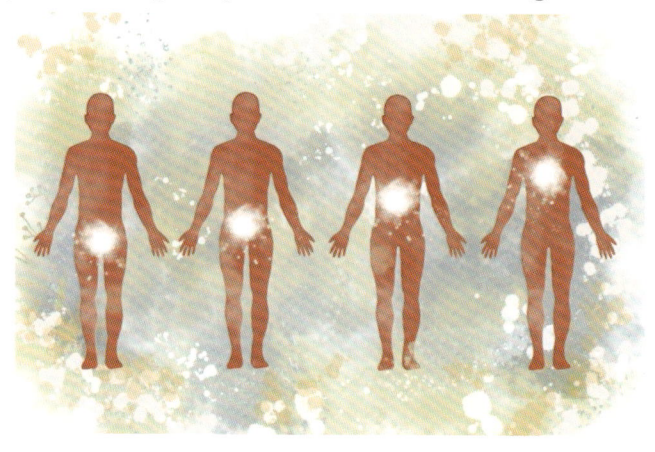

The concept of "the Assemblage Point" was first introduced by Carlos Castaneda. It is generally accepted that the Assemblage Point is a term passed on to Castaneda by his spiritual teacher, an ancient Native American Indian shaman.

The Assemblage Point is the place where the greatest amount of energy is collected, the window through which a person looks onto this world. According to the works of Carlos Castaneda, the Assemblage Point is located within the energy cocoon (biofield) at about the distance of a fist from the human physical body, at the level of the shoulder blades. When practising the Destiny Code, one should still adhere to the notion that the localization of energies is located in the chakras. Accordingly, the concept of the "Assemblage Point" should also be used in a way that departs slightly from the original source, and this term should be understood in the context of the key relationship between the position of Energy and the chakras.

In shamanism, it is believed that the Assemblage Point is the place where the soul resides. It doesn't matter if a person takes this into account in their own life. It doesn't matter how it is formulated by any given individual: whether as the soul or a conglomeration of energy, or something else. The assemblage point is the place where life force is concentrated. And its location is a fundamental factor influencing a person's life in any case.

Shamans are able to shift the Assemblage Point with the power of magic: whether that be through rituals, the use of sacred plants, or physical actions. In Hindu and Buddhist practices, there are similar ideas about the centralization of energetic forces, which can be shifted or moved using meditation and other spiritual and physical practices.

What is the point of doing this? First of all, it allows you to realign the energy flows that might have been disturbed in an individual for some reason. Secondly, it makes it possible to gain a different level of perception of the world, discover new facets of reality and look at the world from alternative sides. Thirdly, it is an important process that facilitates spiritual growth and an increase in energy levels in general. When investigating the Assemblage Point during an analysis of the Destiny Code, it is important to learn how to correctly locate its position, because this determines a person's caste and indicates the level of their soul's development. By knowing the karmic tasks in a particular person's Destiny Code, having determined his or her Assemblage Point and formulated the question for which a person is seeking an explanation or wants to receive specific recommendations, it is possible to create a corrective program and work on his or her personal Assemblage Point by changing his or her everyday and socio-psychological behavior. At the initial level, there is a uniform distribution of energies according to personal strong and weak characteristics (corresponding to the Arcana in the matrix of the Destiny), which leads to the harmonious infusion of a person into the life stream of the Universe. Or, in other words, a person finds their true path by accepting their own tasks and personal destiny. At the second stage, a personal corrective program stimulates the need for a person's spiritual growth and, consequent to them honestly working to implement the recommendations received, a person moves their Assemblage Point subconsciously (and sometimes consciously), thus moving to a higher level of spiritual experience.

Many times in this book, I talk (and will talk further) about the paramount task — to grasp the connection between everyone and everything in the universe. Anyone who wishes to learn how to interpret the Destiny Code must accept this as the first and fundamental rule. You cannot separate one concept from the other. And even now, when talking about castes, I cannot help but return to the subject of chakras again. This is simply for the reason that these concepts are inseparable from each other, especially in the context of any discussion about a person's Destiny Code.

CHAKRAS AND CASTES

The Assemblage Point is the place where the soul resides. The chakra on which the Assemblage Point is located acts like a window onto the world. This works in different ways for all people. That's why people's views are so different. Sometimes during a conversation with another person, you get the impression that you are from totally different planets and speak totally different languages, unable to understand each other even when conversing about the simplest everyday things. The thing is that people's Assemblage Points are located at different levels, they are representatives of different castes and sometimes simply cannot understand each other. Not everyone likes haute cuisine and art house movies and not everyone understands classical music and is able to listen to opera or hard rock. People are at different levels of spiritual development and consequently, the limits of their perception are also different. The important thing to understand here is that this is how things should be – this is balance.

In order to better unde rstand any information, visualization is often very helpful, so let's imagine the caste system in the form of a four-storey house.

The residents on the first floor can see the bushes and trees growing under their windows. They are satisfied with this view because it gives them peace of mind and confidence that they are stable and safe. Those who live on the second floor can already see not only the bushes and trees but also a playground. Which makes them extremely happy because they know that they can always unwind and have fun if they wish. The residents on the third floor can see that there is a road beyond the trees and the playground. This means that beyond the borders of their territory there are opportunities to expand their holdings and the prospect of setting off on new adventures. And as for the people on the fourth floor, they can see the whole picture and know that beyond the road, is the ocean, which stretches to the very horizon. The world is limitless.

This example helps us to more easily understand the values that people of different castes are guided by. Who cares about being safe, who is interested in having the opportunity to get more out of life, who is looking for new ways to develop themselves and who is reaching beyond the limits of what is available?

A person uses all seven of their chakras and tries to fully satisfy the needs of each. Nevertheless, he or she lives to a greater degree in the one where his or her Assemblage Point is located. It is within the range of this chakra that people see the world, themselves and their primary tasks. The functions of the chakras determine the meaning of existence. And the caste that a person belongs to can easily be determined by their lifestyle, interests and preferences.

THE FIRST CASTE

Ones are workers. They are young souls. They have come into the world in their first incarnation to gain basic skills. They are like children. They can be attributed the age of zero to twelve years old. They are born children and leave the world as children. Their main goal is to learn how to survive and be useful in fulfilling the universe's overall plans. Life would be impossible without young souls. They are like a foundation, a base and support. The first caste does not bring anything new to life, they are not going to write poetry or reinvent the wheel while they are here. The members of this caste are like worker ants — they do not change anything, but everything depends on them. The first caste is very important, as these young souls are the foundation on which the preservation of life in the world rests. Because all the processes that make up the mechanism of the Universal flow of energy are carried out by members of the First Caste, one should never be dismissive of young souls. It is foolish to think that if a person is not interested in art or has not written a book, they have no value. It is precisely Ones who make our life safe and stable, and also resilient in the face of the antics of the members of other castes.

Interests

First Caste people are interested in those things that are characteristic and typical of the Muladhara. For them, the acquisition, ownership and improvement of their homes are the most important criteria in life. Ones' range of interests are linked to worldly affairs, work is seen as a source of livelihood and family as a vital building block for society. They consider the status of being "married" as being more important than having feelings for one's partner. People like this place great value on family and clan but not the individual.

Ones generally do not have a great deal of time for esotericism and spirituality, since they simply lack the necessary energy and strength to perceive things that are not physical. They might pretend they are interested in these activities, but this is most likely to be because it is the "done" thing in their circle, or they think that it might provide them with a promising way of ensuring their primary needs (for example as a source of income). But these people do not seek the depth of meanings for themselves, it is enough for them to learn, know and follow the algorithms. It is precisely for members of the First Caste that religion has been invented and the rules governing behavior in society formulated in the form of laws and constitutions.

External appearances

As a rule, members of the First Caste are not too bothered about their appearance. It is important for them to comply with the basic principles of society and not differ from generally accepted norms and rules, but that's about it. They accept themselves as they are. As far as trends set by society go (fashion, celebrity lifestyles), they tend towards imitation rather than individuality.

People of the First Caste are 100% Light. They are capable of darkening their chakras but their true essence is invariably Light.

Friendship

Imagine a kindergarten, playground, or elementary school. Ones make friends as children do — whoever is close at hand can be a friend. The strength of their feelings of friendship is intense and often perceived as being "truly heartfelt". But if a friend offends them then they are immediately perceived as an enemy. They make up just as quickly and easily as they quarrel. As a rule, the company they keep appears motley and disparate, ones tend to stick together for the sake of having company as much as anything else. They have friends from school, university and work but no more than that.

Family

People of the First Caste marry and start a family, as an inevitable part of life: at a certain age ("It's time") and according to the generally accepted principles in society ("You should really have a family by thirty"). Members of the First Caste marry for love. The choice of a partner follows generally accepted criteria: the groom should be worthy and responsible, and the bride should be beautiful, a good housewife and in future a wonderful mother.

The first caste places extreme importance on having their passports stamped and their contracts and debts in order. Relationships within the close family circle and with more distant relatives are maintained solely on the basis that they share a common family and clan. They do not consider it pertinent to have any feelings or personal relations or opinions towards this or that member of their family circle. Marriages must be preserved regardless of any sympathy between the partners.

Ones sincerely value family ties as one of those things that have to be borne in life. All their relations are considered relatives, and they must be loved because they are family. And that's all there is to it.

Attitudes towards children

Children for Ones are, first and foremost, the living continuation of the family line and clan. Children are planned for and born because that is what is required. If you are married that means you must have children. Members of the First Caste do not see their children as separate individuals. Children are the continuation of the family line, they must obey their parents, be their pride and joy and support them in their old age. As a rule, their relations with their children are guided by the concept of duty: "We gave you life, and now you owe us".

Attitudes towards parents

Relationships with parents for the First Caste are also based on a sense of duty. Regardless of the interpersonal relationships in the family, or the presence or absence of harmony and peace, Ones take their parents for granted: "Your parents are always your parents! You don't get to choose them".

Unfortunately, Ones often perceive their relationships with their parents as a heavy burden and responsibility. When the time comes, and the parents pass on to another world, members of the First Caste, as a rule, take over the reins of the family and start the cycle all over again. If, as a result of this process, a person fails to realize their personal karmic challenges and takes over the reins and follows the course their parents have set, then sometimes they end up abandoning their personal destiny and their karmic duties will be set aside to be worked out on their next incarnation.

Sex and love

Love for the First Caste is first and foremost a question of habit. Relationships are initially built on the principle of what is "proper" and "commonly accepted". Ones believe that love comes with time, through working together and acceptance, through the complexities and difficulties of life: "To fall in love is to endure". They do not allow themselves to manifest their true feelings and follow their desires.

Relations with one's spouse are built and based on a sense of duty. In general, the concept of duty is a highly typical characteristic of Ones and it relates to absolutely every area of their lives. Marriages last because people should support each other no matter what, because there are obligations to the family, you need to raise children and bear common financial responsibility (loans, mortgages, debts).

Sexual relations are for the most part seen as a marital obligation necessary for procreation. To a large extent, sexual needs are suppressed and primarily by female Ones. It often happens that First Caste women experience little pleasure from sexual intercourse with their partner at all. And at the same time, they are expected to channel this accumulated energy into other areas of their lives (for example, children, work, everyday chores), thereby forming blocks in their Svadhisthanas. Which, of course, leads to an imbalance in relations with their partners and a lack of harmony in their perceptions of themselves and their self-esteem.

Work

Work for people of the First caste is simply a given. Like family, children and a roof over your head — it is an unquestionable must. Ones cannot perceive carrying out an occupation without having a specific list of obligations, an exact and regular schedule and the promise of stability (at least apparent stability). They find it very difficult to adapt to freelance work and jobs that require a degree of responsibility when making decisions. They are quick to criticise other people for their lack of work.

In most cases, Ones are people who perform duties and are hired hands. They engage in activities that require a clear program of actions and the sharpening of their skills. The greater the person's compliance with professional requirements, the greater their professional recognition and their satisfaction in their own sense of usefulness. They have no need for career growth and no professional ambitions.

When they are in a positive state, Ones are true professionals in their field. Performing their duties with outstanding excellence. When they are in a negative state, they do their jobs from shift to shift as if it were hard labor, and always complain about their pay and the severity of their work conditions, while completing their duties very badly.

Money

Ones do not know how to "make money", but they do know how to earn money as a hired hand. As a rule, when they do become entrepreneurs, they tend to behave like small children in a sandbox. They are unable to build their own independent strategies for their businesses due to their inability to see beyond the end of their nose and their narrow view of the way the world works. Quite often they occupy high positions in society — exclusively as an important cog in the mechanism of the machine. This, as a rule, is allowed to happen when it is in the interests of members of the Second or Third Caste, when they need to have a well-functioning and well-run mechanism without the risk of someone taking things over for themselves, which (for the most part) can be guaranteed when you're dealing with a One.

"It's good to have money, but if we don't, then we'll get by somehow," is the working motto of the First Caste.

Professions

Ones carry out the widest range of professions. Primarily, these are in specializations where the work is done by hand and a living earned by physical labor. As mentioned above, a specific program of activities and a clearly regulated range of responsibilities are extremely important for Ones.

Depending on the person's individual energy embedded in their Destiny Code (in the Talent and Finance zones), it is easy to adjust and sort out a One's productivity in their professional field and therefore their income. By acquainting themselves with their individual programs, a person can adjust the balance between their opportunities and desires. After all, if a person understands where they will be most comfortable, interested and effective, then their professional activities will always contribute to their development and growth in the specialization and path they have chosen and, accordingly, guarantee the realization of their personal destiny.

There is a vast list of professions in which Ones can realize their potential, but in general, they choose jobs in the service sectors such as builders, cooks, factory and production workers, plumbers, electricians, police officers, office clerks, accountants, salesmen, shoemakers, hairdressers and manicurists to name just a few.

As previously mentioned, it is possible that a One may occupy a high position in society. Therefore, Ones can be active members of political parties or large organizations and hold responsible positions in large companies or corporations, as long as their roles are functional and do not involve making important decisions. When occupying any position, a person must first and foremost perform the specific function he or she has been assigned. As a rule, in the hierarchy of power Ones are supervisors guaranteeing the smooth running of operations, on the condition that the upper echelons of management are confident that they will not usurp the reins of power from them — after all, they are simply not yet capable of seeing the overall integrity and interconnectivity of operations and processes. However, in the unlikely event that a One begins to assert their rights and decides to change their position, they can easily be pacified simply by dealing with them in much the same way as an adult would deal with a naughty child.

Personal goals

For the First Caste, the most important thing in life is to satisfy their primary needs. It is worth recalling the role the Muladhara Chakra plays here and what functions it is responsible for. It is precisely these things that Ones consider to be their personal goals in life.

It is very important for Ones to be able to eat, sleep, get an education, have a job, build a house, plant a tree and raise a child. Success in life is assessed in terms of boxes ticked on a list of everyday domestic requirements. Ones barely give a thought to spirituality, romance, esotericism and other things of that nature. But lunch should always be on the table at the right time, there is no room for compromise here!

Thinking

As a rule, Ones do not think independently. More often than not, they are guided by the wise words of older, more authoritative people or advice from trusted sources.

With Ones, you should always remember that they are young souls without a great deal of knowledge and experience. Ones are like sponges, they absorb all the information transmitted to them in its pure form, without filtering or further analyzing it. If the news says that this year winter is going to start in July, then that's as it should be.

Their unique ability to accept reality as a given provides Ones with a huge advantage in life. Members of the first caste do not bother themselves or complicate their path in life. It is important that Ones do not torment themselves with the injustices of life and do not expend too much energy on realizing their own egos. For the first caste, life is important as it is. Of course, there are exceptions, but only in those cases when a person is able to independently maintain their personal energy balance. Despite the simplicity of accepting and perceiving reality as it is, many members of the First Caste are prone to negativity and aggression, which, of course, is due to the dissonance between their personal needs and their life priorities. This behavior is especially characteristic nowadays when people find themselves trapped in a web of addiction, dependency and social pressure. Excessive demands, competition and the expectations of their environment force people to play roles that are alien to them. And here, it is more important than ever to correctly set and define one's personal priorities and values, to abandon the imposed "proper and correct ways of doing things" and, of course, to discover truths that can lead you back onto the right path and help you realize your destiny.

Interests and hobbies

The First Caste does not, as a rule, have time for hobbies and interests, but if they do get a free minute, Ones will devote it to improving their everyday life: fixing, cleaning and ironing things or removing a stain from a shirt that has not been worn for ages. Alternatively, they sometimes go fishing or out to the forest, or grow vegetables and fruit in an allotment or take care of animals.   Ones rarely read books, preferring newspapers and magazines. But if they have become accustomed to reading from childhood, then, as a rule, they choose books with light plots.

When it comes to TV, Ones love watching the news, ratings-boosting TV shows and popular light drama series. And with music, they prefer what is being played on the radio, or whatever their circle is used to listening to.

In many ways, Ones are influenced by trends and fashions. Therefore, it is quite possible that Ones can engage in whatever they want to. But their interests are short-term and, as a rule, do not seriously or sincerely preoccupy them. They can get quite involved in football, yoga or learning to play the guitar and they might even buy themselves a deck of tarot cards. Although here, much will depend on the individual's personal energies as set out in the Destiny Code and how these energies are actualized.

Politics

Ones are convinced that they understand politics better than anyone else. Broadcasting the ideas of an authoritative source (usually from the TV or a neighbor who is privy to some "secret" inside information), Ones will defend a dearly held position to the death and will be unshaken by any counter-arguments. In most cases, their political preferences are cardinal: either they have complete faith and support for the current government, or they are totally dissatisfied with it.

Ones tend to vote for flashy populist candidates. Ones are very susceptible to promises about simple things such as money, work, the availability of housing and medicine – these are the sort of "sugar-coated rewards" that will attract the votes of the First Caste. And since there are more Ones in percentage terms than any other section of the population, it is on the basis of precisely these sort of simple short-term promises that loud-mouthed spin doctors operate when promoting their candidates for power.

Religion

To be absolutely honest, it could be suggested that religion was created specifically with Ones in mind. This is because it is more important for Ones to have strict behavioral guidelines than any of the other castes. Religion provides them with specific instructions on how to live, where everything has come from, what to strive for, what is possible and what is not, what is good and what is bad. Ones are essentially children (young souls), it is important for them to have a set of laws and rules to make it easier for them to navigate this world as they take their first steps. Ones do not care so much about whether a statement or assertion contains the truth as whether the statement or assertion is considered a fact.

Knowledge

What we are talking about here is academic knowledge, and here we can say with a good degree of confidence that Ones are not greatly drawn to education on the whole. Ones do go to colleges and universities but only because it is the accepted thing to do in society. As a rule, Ones do not give much thought to their choice of special subjects, or their parents choose them for them. Ones place much more emphasis on experience gained in everyday life. For members of the First Caste, the statement that life is the best teacher is absolutely true for them.

Speech and thoughts

Ones can be silent types or very verbose, it all depends on the person's individual qualities. But whatever the case, the specific nature of their way of thinking and talking is based on an emotional component. Like children, Ones are fairly random and chaotic thinkers. Their speech is not structured and lacks complex lexical constructions, epithets and turns of speech.

Ones are marked by their tendency to use filler words like "um" and expletives, which are their 'go-to' tools when expressing their personal relations and emotional state in a given situation.

Development

It is not terribly important to Ones whether there is much development in their lives or not. For members of the First Caste, stability is more fundamentally important. Of course, if we are talking about development as a process of becoming, accumulating the necessary experience to organize your everyday life and the implementation of basic tasks, then, undoubtedly, this sort of development occupies an important place in their system of values. But if we are talking about the development of the individual, an increase in one's level of knowledge, spiritual growth and the desire to look beyond the horizon, then these matters are of no great interest to members of the First Caste for the very simple reason that their horizons are limited by their specific personal karmic programs.

Life management

Ones are not the masters of their lives. From the very first, they find themselves under the sway of circumstances and factors that limit them, including personal beliefs, social and group attitudes, phobias, psychological barriers, and most of all obligations. That's right! I have deliberately singled out obligations as a factor influencing members of the First Caste. Because it is their sense of duty and obligation that force Ones to get themselves ever more entangled in a web of hopelessness and deliberately trap themselves in circumstances that encroach on their freedom of action and thinking.

Honesty

Ones find it very difficult to distinguish between truth and falsehood. Their faith is based on the authority of their source of information. This difficulty is only characteristic of the First caste because they do not understand context and hidden meanings. If they were told that the Earth is flat and shown a picture of a flat planet, they would blindly believe what they had been told without question or doubt. After all, how could it be otherwise? That's what smarter people have told them.

Food

Ones do not like expensive, fashionable restaurants, arguing that home cooking tastes better or what is the point of paying more when you can buy and cook it yourself.

But food is of great importance to First Caste people. The more of it, the better. The phrase "a comfortable life" is very indicative of Ones' values. Always having food in the house in abundant quantities is one of the main indicators of a person's quality of life and success.

If a One occupies a high position in society and is obliged to eat out because of their status, then, as a rule, they will prefer heavier, fatty, high-calorie food. The restaurant chosen will be rated on the size of the portions served and how full the One feels when they leave.

As for preferences, Ones primarily prefer heavy and filling food and they particularly like plenty of flour and meat in their diet. Regardless of their nationality and, accordingly, traditional cuisine, the most important thing for a One is that their food is filling and that there is plenty of it!

Addiction/Dependency

Like everyone else, Ones are prone to addiction to alcohol, drugs, smoking, gambling and other things.

The level of their resistance or predisposition to these temptations is determined solely by the nature of their personal energy as designated in the Destiny Code. But all the same, Ones differ from the other castes in that they are more influenced by alcohol or other bad habits as a result of the influence of external factors. In one hundred percent of cases, Ones will begin to use illegal substances, if it is accepted and the norm in their circle and environment. Ones do not have a conscious concept of what is good and what is bad. What is right for them is what the elders in their society tell them and what they see going on around them and have become accustomed to.

Therefore, an important factor when relating to Ones is to evaluate not only their personal qualities and characteristics but also to take into account the external factors that affect their lives as a whole.

The touchstone for people of the First Caste is SIMPLICITY. Simplicity in everything everywhere. The simpler life is, the happier the person.

THE SECOND CASTE

The Second Caste are merchants They are older souls, more in the 12 to 18-year-old age range. They have already accumulated experience to meet their basic needs: they know how to meet their everyday needs, and they know how to walk, eat and sleep. And now they want to enjoy life and improve and facilitate its course. Having learned certain things in their previous incarnations, they already understand that life can be comfortable and carefree, and now at this stage can set themselves the task of living for pleasure and for themselves.

Interests

Twos live in order to meet the needs of the Svadhisthana. Twos value comfort and pleasure. For them, it is important that their food tastes good and their houses are large. Things should be important not only for their functionality but their beauty and value. Sometimes it is precisely a thing's beauty and value that come to the fore when assessing its significance. Twos value influence and connections and actively seek them out. Universal opinion and status are first and foremost what affect their lifestyle choices. Socializing, meetings and conversation are as vital to them as the air they breathe. After all, these are the tools that Twos use to work out their karmic challenges.

In-crowds, parties, delicious food, owning valuable things, wealth, sex, recognition and status are the things that make up the meaning of life for Twos. In addition, it is the Second Caste, which is responsible for ensuring that the world's regulating systems and processes that control mankind's quality of life as a whole are operating properly.

External appearances

For the most part, members of the Second Caste are stylish, beautiful and striking people. They are attractive and sociable and have individuality in spades, regardless of whether it is an external or internal component of their make-up. If they have pathologies of the chakras, then, as a rule, these become a distinctive feature of their personalities (being plump or thin or having a slouch or other physical side effects). Their desire for universal attention can result in them becoming unusual or eccentric, but unlike Ones, this manifests itself in good style rather than bad taste. In addition, Twos are often sexually attractive on some deep animal level. They catch the eye in the crowd, even if they have not set out to do so.

Friendship

It's easy to work out if someone is a Two: simply borrow their phone and take look at their contacts list. Your average One will have about 50-250 names maximum. Twos will have the numbers of almost everyone they have ever met during their life journey. Although it is worth clarifying — not quite everyone's, just those that might be potentially useful to them. Next to each name, there will almost certainly be a note saying who this person is and what job they do. For example: Johnny (tow truck), Marie (organic market worker).

Mutually beneficial relationships are the cornerstone of forming friendships for Twos. Any "useful" acquaintance will automatically fall into a Two's circle of friends. And no matter where they are, they always somehow have a local connection there. You only need to have a Two in your circle of acquaintances and you can be sure that he or she will be able to connect with someone you might need.

Family

In the majority of cases, Twos have a respectful attitude towards family. For Twos — their families represent their reliable logistical backup. Their relationships often blossom from a simple infatuation in their youth into a system of family ties that becomes ever stronger and more stable over the years as a result of their common projects and business or financial obligations.

The more people they have around them, the more comfortable Twos feel. That is why they are always in touch with their relatives. Big family holidays, anniversaries, the birth of a nephew —are all very important and precious events for members of the Second Caste.

Attitudes towards children

My practice has taught me that the vast majority of Twos go through several marriages during their lives. Accordingly, they also have several different children from different marriages. For Twos, children are also connections, no matter how strange that may sound. Already at an early age, Twos see their children as potential business partners and heirs to the family empire.

It is commonplace for Twos to initially make serious mistakes when bringing up their children by making plans and life decisions for their offspring. Subsequently, these plans can often go "awry" for Two parents because the objectives and goals they set do not always coincide with those of their children, which can lead to relationship breakdowns. And this can have a very painful and destructive effect on Second Caste people.

The strategy of shifting one's unfulfilled hopes onto the shoulders of your children is obviously going to lead to failure, even if you are absolutely certain that this is the right path for them. Each soul must follow its own path, even if that involves slipping on your own personal banana skin and suffering one of life's hard knocks.

Attitudes towards parents

Here again, it is perhaps worth quoting the experience I have gained over the years. My practice has shown me that most often, Twos experience a choice of two scenarios when it comes to their relationships with their parents.

If the Two's parents are members of the First Caste, then, as a rule, the relationship will turn out well. Twos take financial care of their parents and try to help them. The Two often becomes the pride of the family and bears responsibility not only for their parents but for all their relatives in the clan.

Twos set up jobs for their nephews, solve their second cousin's husband's sister's problems and send cards (and sometimes even gifts) to all their relatives on their birthdays or other celebrations.

If the Two's parents are members of the Second or an even higher caste, then the relationship here can turn out to be more complex and ambiguous. If events develop favorably, Twos can follow in their parents' footsteps and sooner or later become the head of the family business or the family as a whole.

If disagreements arise with their parents in childhood, then Twos can break away from their families at a very early age and cut off all ties with their parents and other relatives. However, despite this, Twos value the importance of family, and over time they strive to create their own family and clan.

Sex and love

For Twos, love and sex are the same thing. Twos are prisoners to their desires, they are incapable of self-sacrifice for the sake of someone or something else, and they are not prone to moral or emotional stress. Love for Twos is all about longing, passion and desire. If there is no longing or desire for their partner, then there is no love.

Twos are the sort of people who are able to fall in love at first sight one evening and by the next morning, their feelings will have evaporated with the first rays of the sun.

Twos prefers to have relationships with beautiful, stylish and striking people. Male Twos are attracted to Instagram models or pin-up beauties — the most charming and attractive women in their circle. Female Twos, for their part, are attracted to "real", brutal and authoritative men.

Members of the Second caste have a particular passion for sex at an almost feral animal level.

Work

Twos strive to enjoy a high standard of living, regardless of what they consider that to be: be it the desire to get a regular job, taking a loan out for a car and then living happily ever after, or establishing a billion-dollar empire and building a rocket and flying off into space. Whatever the scenario, Twos will always follow the easiest path to achieve their goals.

In the majority of cases, Twos are businesspeople of one sort or another, big or small, successful or unsuccessful, it doesn't matter. What is really important to them is that they have their own business. Twos have big ambitions but do not always have the courage and character to stick to their guns to get ahead.

Members of the Second Caste can also work as hired hands but only in everyday or intermediate positions, and in this instance, they generally take up these positions to get closer to the big bosses.

Money

Money for Twos is everything. It is the means of possessing what they desire, its presence is the guarantor of status and influence in society. There should always be money around! A person without money is a nobody.

Professions

First and foremost, Twos are the most talented orators and salesmen. Twos are skilled lobbyists, diplomats, negotiators, and schemers.

The range of professions they engage in covers absolutely any kind of activity, whether it be trade, politics, entertainment or medicine. Twos tend to be most comfortable in positions where communication, advancement skills, a passion for money, and a talent for building interpersonal relationships are positives. The important thing is that the notion of labor itself is alien to members of the Second Caste, so even if it so happened that a Two is engaged in a profession that involves some kind of physical labor (plumber, builder, factory worker), his professional qualities will suffer greatly as a result of his or her constant internal struggle with his or her personal aspirations. Twos are, for the most part, not hardworking and can be careless and irresponsible. But they are determined, and their desire to make it to the top is huge.

Personal goals

Twos do not set themselves super-challenges such as building world peace, conquering new business heights, or the subjugation of the whole of humanity. Money is what interests the Second Caste most. The more money, the cooler the car, the more prestigious the house, the tastier the food and the greater their sense of self-worth.

You always need to be careful with Twos because they lack any concept of decency and moral boundaries. An attractive goal of average importance can justify any of the means they might use to achieve it, even at the expense of others.

Thinking

Second Caste people's thinking processes are idiosyncratic, sometimes strange and unpredictable, but perfectly logical and natural. Twos like to consult and collect information for analysis. But at the end of the day, they will act exclusively in their own way, sometimes even contrary to common sense.

Mentally, Twos are teenagers, their thinking processes are chaotic and ambitious, in places they appear reasoned and logical but in fact, they are spontaneous and elicit many questions.

It goes without saying that members of the Second Caste are able to think independently, analyze and draw their own conclusions. However, the opinions of others remain an important factor influencing their ability to make decisions: whether they are agreeing or disagreeing, Twos, one way or another, spurn alternative sources of information. They are always confident in the rectitude of their thinking but are still not quite ready to take full responsibility for themselves.

Interests and hobbies

What captivates the Second Caste? The answer is everything that is beautiful! Collecting, owning and enjoying luxurious or unique things is a huge source of pleasure for Twos. Even their love of shopping can be seen as a hobby or a yearning for beauty, and sometimes even the meaning of life for them.

Twos, like no one else, have a natural sense of beauty, so their longing for all things beautiful becomes an obsession in their early childhoods. Sometimes, other castes may experience certain doubts about being original or eccentric when it comes to "beauty"... But not so with Twos.

Second Caste people always strive to appear better at everything than they really are. They try to seem smarter, better-read, taller, slimmer, richer, more influential. Twos are quite likely to attend private viewings at galleries and exhibitions of contemporary art, or go to the ballet, opera and concerts. But as a rule, their interest is fairly superficial and does not coincide particularly with their true interests. Twos will watch an action movie or listen to RnB and hip-hop with equal pleasure. However, one should avoid concluding that Twos only understand things superficially, on the contrary, they can know about a lot of things. It's just that "knowing" and "understanding" are slightly different things.

Politics

Twos are not innately interested in politics but find themselves forced to understand it and figure out how it all works. Their political views are expressed on the basis of the advantage they might provide in a given situation. Without a great conflict of conscience, Twos can easily change their political views if necessary.

The Second Caste are natural swing voters and the ideal target audience for the opposition since they can always be offered something that is in their personal interests but sometimes to the detriment of the majority.

Incidentally, it is worth noting that Twos are frequent participants in political battles because they are often members of the business elite and intermediaries between large organizations. So, no matter how Twos may feign indifference to politics, they still play an important role in it.

Religion

Second Caste people have an attitude to religion that is simultaneously straightforward and complex. Twos can be completely fanatical in their expression of their Faith. And they are capable of either completely and openly immersing themselves in religion, or totally denying it. These attitudes can develop regardless of whether or not they belong to any particular denomination.

Twos are often big fans of yoga, alternative or leftfield types of spiritual development, sects or other ways of gaining self-knowledge or Faith.

The higher the caste, the greater the individual's yearning to gain greater knowledge of their spiritual condition. And it is through their Faith that Twos are subconsciously drawn to undergo the spiritual development necessary to become members of the Third Caste, although, in fact, it is through their religion that Twos strive to find themselves and bring their ego to its ideal state and subsequently improve their worldly existence. Which, of course, is an attitude that fundamentally differs from the true relationship with religion that Threes and Fours profess, where the value of spirituality and development itself are placed an order of magnitude higher than material values.

Knowledge

There is no doubting that Twos are drawn to knowledge. On their path towards mental development, Twos are more inclined to value accumulated theoretical knowledge over acquired social experience and practical skills. There will always be Twos who can solve any issue with a mentor and be on a "close footing" with the right sort of people. The Second Caste places a great value on efficiency and consequently Twos consider practical experience more useful than studied knowledge. Therefore, for them, just one conversation with the "right" person can easily compensate for studying a textbook. Twos are well aware of this and skillfully use it to their advantage.

However, if we are talking about knowledge from the point of view of collecting information, then the Second caste understands the need to update their theoretical baggage better than any caste. Twos are constantly going on refresher courses, business seminars and self-development sessions and often master additional and, at times, completely new specialisms.

When it comes to self-development and the desire to absorb new knowledge, at first sight, it is easy to make the mistake of confusing Twos with Threes or Fours. Here, it is very important to take a little more time and delve a little deeper when assessing a specific person's caste. How can one go about doing this? It's all very simple. You just need to observe the person in question and determine their true motives. Imagine, for example, a course for say, "Creating a perpetual motion machine". A Three might attract everyone's attention, broadcast their ideas on the subject, advance their personal interests and, possibly, even refute the relevance of this course. A four will disconnect themselves from reality and immerse themselves in the process completely, frantically writing down every word or asking millions of questions, as they would say, to better improve their understanding of the subject. Twos, however, will not waste any of their time in vain. They will get to know all the potentially most promising people on the course, make inquiries in advance about which parts they need to "shine" in and who they need to impress, and eventually end up with a certificate or diploma on completion of the course, having skipped much of the course's material and completed the minimum required amount of course work.

Speech and thoughts

Twos are master orators, even their usual colloquial conversation is clear, hard-hitting and eloquent. Twos are outstanding storytellers, skillful negotiators and talented flatterers.

Their speech and thoughts are rich, colorful and full of imagery. And their ability to capture the tone of a conversation when socializing often makes them the life and soul of the party. Twos have the natural ability to perceive who to pay compliments to.

Sometimes, they might refute something that they have stated earlier. Twos always say what they are thinking, and the course that their thinking takes is very changeable and chaotic. But whatever the case, Twos speak clearly and eloquently and have a lot to say, an awful lot.

Development

The second caste are, how shall I put it, forced to develop and advance themselves This is because the members of the Second Caste innately and a priori want to have more than they did at the beginning of their lives. In order to get what you want you need to do something. And any action entails constant motion, the accumulation of experience and repeated attempts at improving the actions one takes in order to achieve the goals that have been set, which, in essence, is what development is all about.

Life management

Twos have the ability to influence the lives of others, Ones, as a rule, but they cannot fully manage and organize their own lives. This is because Twos find themselves in a big spider's web of various dependencies. While arranging their path in life, Twos grow networks of connections, circumstances and obligations, and if they violate this complex mechanism, they risk losing everything that they have built up (comfort, position, money), which is unacceptable for them. Therefore, more often than not, Twos prefer to deftly adapt themselves to the system, protecting "their place in it" and playing it safe — even to the detriment of their personal ambitions.

Honesty

Twos' unique ability to "think beyond" morals and principles is a quality that, to some extent, is worthy of respect and even envy. Twos always tell the truth! Even if they are telling you an outright lie. And paradoxical as this may seem, this is the truth. Twos sincerely believe what they are saying, otherwise, their goals would not be justified.

The need for Twos to get what you want no matter the cost, every day and over many years, hones and polishes their brilliant and unique skills in the art of telling lies and practising hypocrisy and flattery from their earliest days. It is better to try to perceive these qualities as a positive thing because from the outset everything they do is done for the best. Well, for the best possible outcome for them, if someone else has to suffer as a result — then that is of secondary importance.

Food

Twos are not fussy when it comes to food, they will eat anything. Twos will happily go out for a McDonald's or a pizza. But if a convenient opportunity arises, they will never knowingly turn down an invitation to dinner at a fancy expensive restaurant.

Interesting fact: Twos are more comfortable solving business problems and negotiating over dinner. In general, they have a special relationship with food, for them — it is a real ritual. For Twos, fine cutlery, beautiful porcelain and just the right atmosphere are very important. They pay a great deal of attention to these things and understand well the powerful influence of serving good food to others can have.

Addiction/Dependency

The Assemblage Point of Twos is the Svadhisthana. Pleasure, comfort, and communication are the key pillars of life on which Twos build and arrange their lives. Twos are therefore very prone to addiction to alcohol, drugs and casual relationships. The meaning of life for members of the Second Caste is overwhelmingly concentrated on the material: money, things and people, which naturally makes Twos dependent on satisfying their needs. Perhaps the following observation might seem paradoxical, but Twos knowingly and masterfully use their destructive and evidently negative addictions to their own advantage. Hanging out with the right people helps them to network and obtain the information they need (sometimes even incriminating information) about competitors or objectionable people, which again can be very useful to them in order to achieve their aims.

Twos may be totally committed vegans or fitness fanatics, but one way or another, even on a subconscious level, they will strive to find something to become addicted to and fill their life with meaning.

The main characteristic of the Second Caste is their LACK OF PRINCIPLE. Twos do not have any clear red lines or moral principles. The ends always justify the means for Twos.

THE THIRD CASTE

The Third Caste are Warriors. These are strong mature souls, whose mental age roughly correlates to 18-60 years of age. They have already entered into the world with a great deal of experience and a high spiritual level of development. Members of the Third Caste are, first and foremost, warriors in life: strong, self-sufficient and confident in the knowledge that they have a very important task to complete in their lives. They are the sort of people who are leaders of men and able to drive progress and change the world.

Interests

The most important and significant thing for members of the Third Caste is to find their own way in life. Of course, this criterion is questionable, since finding their way in life is no less important for Ones and Twos as well.

What is the Manipura responsible for? Well, specifically: a person's character, willpower, self-realization, status and significance. Action and achievements are very important for Threes. Self-realization is more important for them than for any other caste. It is the members of the Third Caste who make a significant mark in human history, it is they who shape opinions and can change the generally accepted norms and mainsprings of society.

External appearances

People of the Third Caste do not dwell on their appearance. Nevertheless, looking neat, tidy and imposing matters to them. As far as clothes are concerned, they prefer strictly classic styles or a certain luxurious minimalism. It is important for them that they make an impression, but not in order to win the admiration and hearts of everyone they meet, as is the case with Twos, but rather to demonstrate the status and power of their personalities through the superiority of their external appearance.

Friendship

It is not easy becoming the true friend of a Three. Threes apply a strict selection process to their circle of acquaintances according to the principle: "who would I trust to go into battle with".

When socializing, Threes are careful not to reveal their true feelings even to those who are close to them. Reliability, confidence, trust and stability are the key criteria by which the Third Caste chooses its allies. They might only have one friend, but he or she will be a friend for life.

Family

The family for them is a dependable fortress, an impregnable closed private world. Relationships with a future partner are minutely tested using a combination of trials, life situations and time. Marriages are united by common interests, common goals and the common desire to achieve ambitious grand objectives. Living with a Three means living a life of principle, following a Code of Honor and observing strict rules and precepts.

The expression "to go to the ends of the earth for a loved one" is a perfect definition of a Three's relationship with their families. The total support and complete acceptance of all their personality traits on the part of their partners are key to a strong alliance with a Three.

Attitudes towards children

In my experience, Threes usually only ever have one child. In rare cases, two. Perhaps this is because Threes perceive their child as their own "achievement".

Accordingly, the process of bringing them up and caring for them is arranged in accordance with the classic norms: the best teachers, extra classes, several foreign languages, music, dancing, sports — and all this is imposed from the earliest childhood. For a three, these endless extra-curricular developmental activities and additional workload and pressure are an expression of their love and care for their children.

Attitudes towards parents

Threes treat their parents with great respect and reverence. Understanding the cohesion and influence that family has to offer, Threes strive to become a source of great pride for their parents (and indeed, this is the prism through which they go on to perceive their children in the future). Parents for Threes are always a source of authority, Threes listen carefully to their parents' words and seek the blessing of the older generation.

Sex and love

Threes are very reliable and honest partners. Relationships are built on the principle of being in the same "boat" as your partner. Only a person who can meet all their requirements, and sometimes these can be quite strict, can become a life partner for a Three. And if a Three has chosen a companion, then this innately implies the strength of their feelings for them. The most important thing is — if a Three loves someone, then they do so honestly and unconditionally. Sex for members of the Third caste is very much an intimate and personal matter. For the most part, they are not looking for casual relationships. What is important to them are the intimate heart-to-heart exchanges that take place after sex, and this is their main criterion when assessing its quality.

Also, for Threes, more than any other caste, the act of wooing and winning their partner over is likewise important, this goes as much for choosing a long-term partner as someone with whom to share a brief intimate relationship. Conquest is an additional stimulant and incentive for them, because the more difficult the goal, the stronger the desire to achieve it.

Work

Threes have the strongest flow of energy passing through their Manipura chakra. Their distinguishing characteristics are their striking leadership skills, their persistent striving for excellence, their ambition and the ability to look at the world in broad terms and to see and achieve their goals.

For a Three, their chief activity (their work usually) automatically becomes central to the meaning of their lives. Threes are often business people or politicians, people of influence and action who can persuade and lead the masses, people who sooner or later always end up occupying the highest posts.

Money

For Threes, money is simply a tool that provides them with the means to achieve what they want. For them, having money opens the door to becoming the person they want to be. You don't need a lot of money to grow spiritually, but when you do have it, it allows you to get what you want in different areas. Money is a resource that you can use for your own purposes.

Professions

When it comes to their professional activities, Threes are natural leaders. They are often businessmen, politicians, outstanding athletes or public figures. Threes are undisputed authorities and leaders in their field.

Threes can take up any profession but their main criterion when choosing an occupation is that it should offer them good prospects for development and the highest final goals.

Threes do not like physical labor or monotonous mental work. Stability and lack of mobility are two big turn-offs for Threes when considering a potential profession. They are warriors, it is vital for them to be under constant pressure and in a state of readiness for military action. Therefore, they can take on most professions as long as it involves a swift ascent up the career ladder and requires that they have to fight hard in order to do so.

Personal goals

Threes are the most important fighters and conquerors in this world. Their ambition and determination raise the bar to achieve goals on a cosmic level. To be as productive as possible and conquer everything out there in the Universe are the goals of any Three. They innately want a lot in life and a great deal more than the other castes. The greater the goal, the stronger their yearning and striving to achieve it.

For a Three, any goal is a personal goal. Their individual karmic programs determine the specific direction and form their goals take. However, everyday goals such as building a house, getting rich or going on holiday are not matters of great interest to them because they are not of a sufficient order of importance for Threes and, therefore, unworthy of a great deal of their attention. The goals that Threes are interested in are on a titanic and global scale. The main thing for them is the desire to achieve the maximum results.

Thinking

Threes are usually extremely self-sufficient. They analyze the information they receive by collecting opinions and drawing conclusions that they are precisely guided by and can unambiguously defend. Threes know how to think. The ability to look at things in broad terms gives them an advantage and allows them to form independent conclusions.

It is impossible to impose an opinion on a Three because they always have their own. They will listen to no one and always do as they see fit. However, they will listen to others with great respect if they consider their ideas logical and feel that their perception of matters is similar to theirs. Threes are the sort of people who inform and form public opinion.

Interests and hobbies

Threes are very selective when determining the range of their interests. They will not waste their time on things that will not bring them benefits.

Threes prefer to read serious books and watch films from which they can gain experience and knowledge. They don't have any particular genre preferences when it comes to music. The only thing that can be said with any confidence is that Threes prefer to listen to high-quality music that is filled with content and meaning. Threes also have a certain addiction to the latest news. It doesn't matter what source Threes get their information from (television, the Internet, or print media), they are constantly following what is going on in the world.

As warriors and conquerors, Third Caste people love trophies and more than any other caste love collecting things. They also love sports — Threes don't just see sport as a simple pastime but as an extension of the battlefield, where the main goal is to conquer the enemy and achieve results.

Politics

Threes love politics for the simple reason that this is what they do. Constructing delivery systems and defining a list of goals, formulating a strategy and defining plans — who could be better qualified than a Three to take on such exciting tasks?

Politics is the real mission for Threes and it doesn't matter to them at what level they are building these strategies be it at the global, country or local backyard level. It doesn't matter where Threes prove themselves, what does matter are the conditions and rules they create for everyone else in their circle.

Religion

Faith is a matter of great importance for Threes. But their Faith lies not so much in a higher power than their own. Threes are familiar with religion and understand and respect the system of prescriptions that this tool provides. They are happy to study religious trends and read, analyze and understand them. To take dogma on board and to use it as an additional lever of power to be used for their advantage.

Knowledge

Threes undoubtedly value knowledge and strive to acquire it. One of their key philosophies is expressed in the saying: "Knowledge is strength". Although admittedly, it would probably be more accurate to expand and reformulate this expression to: "The possession of a lot of valuable information provides you with privilege and superior advantage when it comes to achieving your goals".

Speech and thoughts

Members of the Third Caste talk mainly about their affairs. They appreciate the energy and power of words. Threes are unlikely to go to a party and start gossiping or just chatting about the weather. They love to discuss and make plans.

Threes speak in a structured manner, without unnecessary emotional charge, each word is weighed and carries a specific message. Threes never read from a pre-prepared text if its content does not coincide with their personal opinion. They always know what they want to say and how and where to say it.

Development

Self-improvement is an innate and natural need for members of the Third Caste. By acquiring new skills and knowledge, Threes know that with each step they are getting closer to their goal. Threes believe it is perfectly justifiable and necessary to improve themselves in every field they consider necessary, even if this constant studying comes at the expense of other vital needs. For Threes, increasing their level of knowledge gives them an edge and the necessary confidence to "defeat anything and everyone".

Life management

Threes are very much the architects of their fortunes. Their lives are dictated by the goals they set themselves. The freedoms governing the decisions and actions they take and the choice and setting of priorities are completely dependent on these goals. But, unlike any other caste, Threes are bound hand and foot by these very self-imposed limitations that ensure they achieve the results they desire. To achieve the goals they set themselves, Threes have to give up a great deal, including many primary human needs: comfort, family, and feelings. Of course, this might seem an extreme statement but one way or another, in practice, this assertion is confirmed in the real lives of the Threes I have worked with.

Honesty

Threes are first and foremost honest with themselves. It is no less important for them to be truthful with those who are of value to them. Honor and nobility can be interpreted in different ways depending on the context in different situations. But to say that Threes are genuinely honest to the very marrow of their bones is an easy assertion to make.

Threes have no time for superfluous actions and words and very little patience with evasion and pretense. They know exactly what is true for them and what is false, what is acceptable and what is not. And, basically, it's up to everyone else to simply make a note of this.

An interesting fact about Threes is that when it comes to themselves, they do not always consider "honesty" and "openness" to be the same thing. In their personal relationships, even if they are conducted with total honesty, a Three might never fully open up to their partner.

It is worth bearing in mind that Threes themselves determine the boundaries of honesty and the target audience that is worthy of their trust. Here, as in war: if you are a friend, you can relax, but if you are a foe, there can be no question of any justice. Although, if they find themselves in competition with a rival or they are in the process of trying to achieve a desired aim, Threes can use deceit as a tool. But they will always be honest with themselves about it.

Food

Threes are always thinking about efficiency and productivity. They perceive food as an important factor influencing the quality of life, health and the prospects of an individual's future productivity. Threes value the quality, freshness and origin of the food they eat. They love exquisite taste sensations and unusual dishes.

Threes are often healthy eaters, and most of them stick to one diet or another. Threes prefer to eat food without expending too much unnecessary energy procuring it, but at the same time, the food should be healthy and of a high quality, and also not very time-consuming to prepare. Accordingly, Threes like restaurants, food delivery companies, or preparing lunches at home. Their motto regarding food would probably go something like this: "Save time and energy — do one big cook a week".

Addiction/Dependency

Threes can very easily become dependent addicts. Because of their overwhelming desire to direct their personal energy into realizing the goals they have set themselves, (in this context, to satisfy the needs of the Manipura), their other chakras often become exhausted and try to attract additional sources of vital energy to themselves. And because the Svadhisthana, which is responsible for weaknesses and cravings for easy satisfaction (regardless of the area of need), works faster than the other chakras, sports, sex, alcohol, food and drugs can become a source of additional energy for Threes and these are all weaknesses that the Second Chakra feeds on.

Workaholics and people who are completely immersed in a particular occupation need to have a change of focus every now and then. Since Threes understand the value of time as a resource, it is much easier for them to take the quick and easy route to restore and rebalance their energy than to allow their body to genuinely rest and recover, which for them would be a waste of valuable time.

THE FOURTH CASTE

Fours are sages. Old souls. Even when they are children, Fours are considered by their circle to be old beyond their years. As a rule, Fours are not worried about earthly cares. Sages have a very fine sense of the Universe, they read the signals and tasks it sends and broadcast them to humanity. Achievements, the struggle for power, and especially material values, are of little interest to the Fourth caste. But issues of a global nature excite and greatly disturb Old Souls.

Interests

Members of the Fourth Caste seem a little otherworldly. The stream of their thoughts is so difficult for Ones and Twos to understand that they find it easier to consider Fours slightly crazy.

Fours often look rather unkempt and keep themselves apart, which bespeaks the fact that they do not perceive or accept many of society's basic principles and conventions. For them, the vain everyday affairs of the world are of no concern to them — whether they be the latest trends in clothing or the latest popular fads dictated to us. For Fours, the taste of food or the cost of things bear no importance. They care deeply about the value of those processes that they can influence thus changing the world as a whole. They seem to exist outside of time. But despite their lack of primary interest in the blessings life has to offer, it often seems to turn out that most Fours already have them in abundance. Wealth, success, and money come into the lives of Fours, as and when they need them and they use them as tools to change and improve the world.

For the Fourth Caste, global problems take first place: famine in Africa, environmental issues, the extinction of plants and animals, climate change. They are also greatly interested in creating and inventing unique devices that can change the whole world and even enslave it. But first and foremost, their minds are busy searching for the meaning of life and the system that interconnects everything in the Universe. Of course, many other people are also interested in these issues, but it is only the Fourth Caste who literally suffer as a result of what is going on in the world.

In life, sages are people of knowledge. It does not matter whether they are concerned with esotericism or not, sooner or later, they will seek alternative channels in order to sense and transmit their knowledge. It doesn't matter if they are a mage, a shaman or just a university professor, if they are a member of the Fourth Caste, then from the outset, they are already at the very highest level of development and the energy sources feeding their knowledge are not available to others. This status can easily be felt even at a physical level. All members of the Fourth Caste and above have colossally high energy levels that can even be sensed at the physical level.

External appearances

Fours don't bother themselves with their external appearance. It would simply be unthinkable for them to waste their energy bothering about outward appearances. If a Four goes out into the world, then it's frankly a good thing if they remember to put on any clothes at all. For the most part, Fours tend to dress simply and succinctly with nothing too bright or specific and nothing that might distract attention away from the more important things in the life of humanity and the universe. But sometimes one comes across a special type of Four, as a rule, a Dark Four. These are very eccentric people, whose appearance is so unconventional and provocative that you cannot but help notice them. They wear bright colors, vivid prints and combinations of incompatible elements – horror and chaos are combined to create an unforgettable and impressionable effect.

Friendship

Fours construct their relationships with other people through the Anahata, Vishuddha, Ajna and Sahasrara chakras. People of the Fourth Caste value the notion of the "unity of all souls" in their relationships and friendships above all else. When a Four understands that they are on the same wavelength as another person, that they have something to talk about and that there are common points of empathy, then they will be open to personal interaction.

People of the Fourth Caste make friends with the "heart". They are ready to open their arms to anyone in need of attention and sympathy. Fours will listen and support others. They are like a tree in the forest, to which you can come at any time and receive warmth. Provided, of course, that the person who wishes to has access to this "tree".

With Fours, a social interaction might just be a one-off. Having met by chance and exchanged a couple of phrases, two people might go their separate ways and never meet again. However, a Four will always fulfil a certain mission in the process and carry on further down their path, forgetting about the meeting they have just had. The Four's casual interlocutor, on the contrary, will remember every word of the exchange for the rest of their lives.

As an esotericist, I would say that meetings with Fours in life are "chance synchronicities". Fours only appear on the road when someone really needs them. Every person should remember that what they are looking for is always looking for them in return.

Family

Fours do not strive to have families. But if an alliance they have with another person results in children, then there is a very high probability that this marriage is a part of that Four's personal mission. Having people who are close to them is, of course, as important for Fours, as any other person. But the specifics of their perception of personal boundaries and their distinct views on the structure of the system of relationships between people add certain complexities to having a relationship with a Four.

Attitudes towards children

People of the Fourth caste perceive children as equals. And if a Four is destined to have offspring, then their children automatically become their life companions, walking side by side, with the same rights, the same rules and with the same respect for the personal needs of everyone. Children will never become an end in itself or the meaning of life for a member of the Fourth caste.

Fours love their children very much. But they don't believe they have any moral right to impose limits on them. In my experience, I would say that more often than not, the children of Fours are uncontrollable because their parents perceive them purely as they are. A four will never allow themselves to educate and teach anyone about life and consequently, their children do what they please. On the one hand, the children of Fours are lucky, since they have a teacher and mentor at hand from birth. But on the other, at the everyday level, they have to do everything for themselves.

Attitudes towards parents

Relations between Fours and their parents are built on the principle of forming interpersonal relationships. Fours do not attach much importance to blood ties, but spiritual kinship is considered precious.

On the whole, Fours either have friendly heartfelt relationships with their parents or they dissipate completely over time. As a rule, parents who have not been able to establish a spiritual contact with their Four when they are small, do not enjoy any authority over their children, and as a result, the child takes the lead when it comes to building social interactions.

Sex and love

Love is a feeling for which the Anahata is responsible. People of the Fourth caste, if they love, do so completely and unconditionally. Care, empathy, guardianship and attention are the key foundations on which Fours build their loving relationships. Here, Love is Love.

Fours can either have sex or forget its existence altogether. Everything depends on the energies of their personal Destiny Code. Fours can behave very differently with regard to their feelings and this is also based on their personal Energies.

It is worth noting that Fours are harmonious by nature and can happily enjoy solitude for long periods, which does not necessarily mean that they do not possess feelings of love. It's just that Fours look at everything around them from a global perspective, their thoughts and feelings are self-sufficient, just as they are themselves. They do not need feedback and are perfectly satisfied with love for love's sake.

Work

Fours do not aspire to occupy the boss's chair, they have no desire to be the head of a company and climb any career ladder. They feel much more comfortable at the very bottom of any hierarchy because it is much more interesting and productive to manage things and people from below. Although Fours do not really seek power, power seeks them.

People of the Fourth Caste are often gray cardinals and puppet masters. Without showing themselves in public, they are able to effectively build productive work systems within a team or collective. While someone else might hold endless discussions to get what they want, Fours will decide everything that is required and get the results they have intended. But there is one very important condition here — this only happens if the four in question is really interested in this sort of role.

For the most part, Fours prefer to serve society for its own good and not for the sake of their own pride.

Money

Money as an end in itself is not that important for members of the Fourth Caste. Of course, it is easier to get by with it, but Fours, when necessary, will always solve the challenges and tasks that are set before them.

Fours' relationships with money tend to develop along two types of scenario. As a rule, Fours are born into a situation where they have all the resources they need. Four children are often born into a wealthy family, where all their primary needs are satisfied as a matter of course. Fours do not need to waste their time and energy thinking about food, sleep, clothes, and household arrangements — everything has already been resolved and sorted out in advance. There is another scenario, when the Four is born into a poor family, in which case he or she simply does not attach any importance to everyday issues and just eats what he or she is given and sleeps wherever he or she might lay their head.

Just like Threes, money for the Fourth Caste is merely a tool (it's good when it's there, but if not, you can always find another way to resolve any issue).

Professions

People of the Fourth caste are altruists by nature. They are the bearers of ideas and seek ways to solve common universal human challenges.

Fours are thinkers, philosophers, theorists and inventors. Physical labor is alien and incomprehensible to them. Of course, according to destiny, Fours also have to work with their hands because everyone's life develops differently. But the fine-tuned structure of their souls and their high internal potential subconsciously lead Fours towards a path serving the benefit of humanity.

Fours work mostly with knowledge. They are teachers, educators, philosophers, doctors, professors and researchers. Thinkers, theorists, inventors, designers, poets and writers. Mentors, pioneers and, of course, engines of progress. Fours are magical and esoteric by nature.

Personal goals

Gaining new knowledge and experiences are the main goals for Fours. They don't have "personal" goals as such because everything they do is not so much dedicated to themselves as everyone else, humanity and the world as a whole.

Their inquisitiveness of mind and desire to work out the truth — is what drives Fours, and if the goal justifies their expectations, then a Four will do everything to achieve it.

It is worth noting that Fours are very slow by nature, and the tasks and goals that they take on in life might be so large in terms of their size and timescale that it might require more than one human life to resolve and achieve them. Fours understand this, and this suits them fine.

Thinking

People of the Fourth caste think on a global scale. But this has one important drawback: they are often unable to see what is going on right under their noses.

Fours can talk for hours about the structure of the universe, they know exactly how quantum physics works and what state the solar system is currently in now. But they find it quite difficult to organize the everyday side of their lives and think in everyday realities. Despite knowing and understanding extremely subtle matters, Fours can easily get very confused when paying for their groceries in a store.

Interests and hobbies

Garnering knowledge is what the people of the Fourth Caste do in their work and free time. Fours are happiest when they are exploring and mining seams of new information. Books should be deep, filled with meaning and with layered plots, and the same goes for films, which, by the way, Fours prefer.

Fours do not need to be entertained or distracted because the way of life they have chosen is their "interest". Therefore, we can safely say that for Fours their life and the activities they fill it with are their main hobby and passion in life.

Politics

Politics is no longer of any interest to the people of the Fourth caste. For Fours, "freedom" is all important. It's easier for them to keep silent and "not to interfere", as long as they are left to their own devices and no one interferes with them.

But the strength and weight of Fours in the make-up of the world's order are too great, so from time to time, one way or another, representatives of the Fourth Caste are forced to play a certain role on the political stage.

Religion

Fours know too much to be limited by the boundaries of religion. Fours can see the sense of religion and observe its rules, and show respect in a religious society. But they will not dissemble or put on a show of sham belief. Faith for the people of the Fourth Caste is the freedom to see everything that is possible to comprehend. Their faith is so strong that in practice the boundaries of knowledge do not exist for them. The type of faith that Fours have cannot be placed within the simple framework of "Accepting God". Their faith stretches to everything. It either exists or it doesn't.

Knowledge

For Fours, knowledge is the meaning of life. This is their air, food and water. Without knowledge, Fours would simply go crazy, without any possibility of realizing themselves.

Fours are like sponges, they absorb information, sorting it out and leaving only what is important and necessary and provide the knowledge gleaned with a form and shape. Having garnered this knowledge, it is not their aim to discover how it might be applied. This is where their powers end. What is important for them is simply the action of sorting the wheat from the chaff.

Speech and thought

Fours are economical with their words. Their speech is quiet and sometimes inarticulate. They often stray from one thought to another, and the person they are talking to simply loses the thread of the conversation.

The Vishuddha in Fours is often deformed. Fours sometimes find it difficult to put their thoughts into words and they often stutter or have various other speech defects. Perhaps this is also due to the fact that if the Four is living at the level of the Ajna or Sahasrara, then they simply lack the energy for their fifth chakra to function normally.

Development

The thirst for knowledge is, without a doubt, what stimulates development in the people of the Fourth caste. But here we are talking exclusively about spiritual development. Fours have little interest in material wealth, the clothes they wear and their quality of life. A Four would never bother developing qualities whose only use was the acquisition of material assets. But once they have entered, for example, the esoteric labyrinth Fours will be spurred on to explore ever deeper.

Incidentally, Fours are endowed with the strongest energy and the practitioners of many occult practices, they are also the wisest teachers of spirituality and sacred knowledge.

Life management

Fours are eminently capable of controlling and managing their lives. They are devotees of freedom, if external factors put limits on their needs, they are quite capable of rejecting the conditions in which they are not happy and going elsewhere. They can quite easily leave their families, quit their jobs or move to another place. The only things Fours hold sacred and dear are their inner codes and boundaries of acceptance.

Honesty

Fours do not need to deceive anyone, so honesty is a natural state of being for them. However, the environment they find themselves in sometimes creates conditions that they are uncomfortable with and they find themselves having to lie a little in order to avoid losing something more precious. Such as, for example, their free will and freedom of thought. Which is a compromise that sometimes has to be made.

Food

When it comes to Fours and the everyday side of life, their attitudes do not differ greatly from most other people's and their food preferences depend largely on their personal taste. The only thing that distinguishes Fours from other castes is that food in itself is of no great importance to them. They do not pay any particular attention to the quality of their food and how often they eat. If a Four wants to eat, he eats. If he wants something tasty – he finds something tasty. For the Fourth caste, food and its intake is a natural automatic process.

Addiction/Dependency

Unfortunately, Fours are highly susceptible to various kinds of addictions. Drugs, alcohol and altered states of consciousness — are all seen by Fours as new opportunities to open up additional channels of information. Once Fours have experienced a psychedelic experience, they want to go through it again and again. Fours often succumb to various excessive and addictive habits, for the most part as a result of wanting to escape the mundane, perceiving that a psychedelic state can offer them a lot more experience and knowledge than everyday reality can. Often, they go in search of themselves by abusing alcohol, tobacco and drugs.

But Fours can also express their addictive natures in following a particularly obsessive way of life, through abstention, asceticism and the rejection of their everyday worldly existence. Restricting oneself from certain convictions is another form of this sort of addictive behavior. It is not exactly the same as religious dogmatism, since Fours see it in a broader context than religious teachings do, it takes the form of a certain kind of fanaticism to a certain path leading to knowledge.

Any addiction can cause tremendous harm not only to an individual's physical but also spiritual health. People who have Fours in their close circle should beware and take care that the Fours they know avoid indulging in extreme behavior. Beings of a higher order also need support, attention and love. Fours, more than anyone else, need Guardian Angels.

THE CASTE PYRAMID

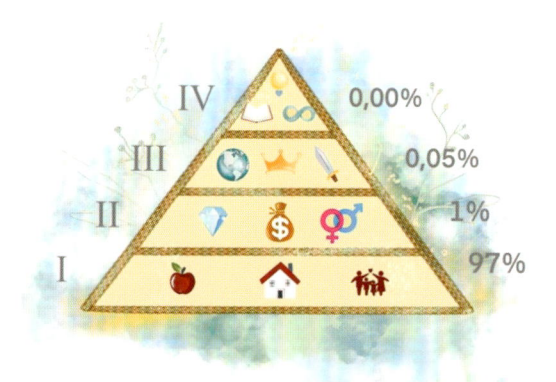

In the classic view of the caste system, it is believed that there are more Ones than any of the other castes in this world. In theory, there are 40 Threes for each Four, likewise, there are 40 Twos for each Three, and 40 Ones for each Two, respectively.

It might be easier to imagine this ratio in terms of a small town with a population of 70 thousand people, thus, in the entire population of this town you might only meet one member of the Fourth Caste, about forty Threes, plus or minus one and a half thousand Twos and the overwhelming majority of the inhabitants would be Ones, of which there would be approximately 64 thousand of the total number of townspeople. The remainder would be made up of people who are transitioning between castes (see Transitional Castes). Yes, some people do transition between castes.

Statistically, Fours avoid small towns and prefer to settle in metropolitan areas and capital cities. They are drawn to big cities as this allows them to get lost in the crowd. Fours, like black sheep, tend to stand out against the general background. The smaller the city, the more attention they receive which is something they prefer to avoid, even if their essence is Dark.

Threes occupy the majority of key positions in small towns. Governing bodies, the police and other important city structures are more often than not headed by Threes. But sooner or later, there comes a time when they also leave their small towns in an effort to satisfy their extremely active Manipuras. People of the Third caste are ever eager to climb and conquer new and higher mountains in new territories and therefore move to ever bigger cities. But this is not always the case. It sometimes turns out that Threes are able to actualize themselves without moving on, promoting the interests of their "home town" along with their own.

It makes no fundamental difference for Twos and Ones where they realize their destiny. Sometimes, they migrate and sometimes they don't. Although it is less of a trauma for Twos to move to a new place than it is for Ones. This is because Ones have just started finding their feet on this earth and it is much more traumatic for them to break away from a place they have gotten used to than it is for the other castes.

The caste pyramid can be compared to Maslow's hierarchy of needs pyramid, which simply and effectively illustrates the percentage ratio between the basic needs of every person. Only with the Caste Pyramid, we can see the distribution of these same priorities in accordance with the level of people's spiritual development and their caste.

TRANSITIONAL CASTES

Incarnation after incarnation and step by step, the Soul is reborn into new human lives, on each occasion striving to solve the karmic tasks that have been assigned to it, acquiring knowledge and skills and gradually raising its spiritual level until the soul eventually develops and evolves. How soon an individual's caste changes and how soon their soul will be set new personal programs depends on how quickly this growth takes place.

If we imagine the caste system as a series of steps, then it's clear that we need to perceive life and reality not only in terms of the horizontal step that we are standing on but also to learn to see our higher goals that are not directly accessible from our current position but at a higher potential level that is inaccessible and invisible. Important "Super-tasks" in the life of a person stimulate them to assimilate new knowledge at a higher rate and, therefore, even within the timeframe of a single human life, it is possible to get to a stage where one's soul is ready to transition from one caste to another.

As a rule, people of the Third and Fourth castes are engaged in some form of esoteric practice and spiritual development. Rarely, but occasionally it does happen that Twos show an interest in these things and try to understand themselves better and discover their spiritual path. However, when a One comes across esotericism, they simply play with it like children, without sensing the responsibility it entails and without understanding its meaning, and this can sometimes lead to them breaking their own lives and those of others as well.

FROM A ONE TO A TWO

And so, people live, develop and see different lives play out around them. They work hard, create order and a basic life for themselves and their family and their everyday life is now predictable and stable. But there comes a liberating moment when they watch something on TV or learn something through their social media and no longer see beautiful objects as things that are largely insignificant to their everyday environment and now want to possess them themselves. That's when a member of the First caste begins to latch on to the interests of the Second.

An enticing image full of beautiful luxury cars and clothing brands, tropical resorts, yachts and luxurious houses opens the eyes of the First Caste to the fact that life is not just about getting through one's everyday work and duties. They come to the realization that life has a lot more to offer than they are currently getting. They now understand they don't just need to earn money to cover their everyday expenses but need to learn how to make money. After all, they now realize that one can live a life of pleasure.

Out in society, it is easy to spot this Transitional caste. These are people who usually like to show off their achievements to the social group in which they find themselves. Material values and showing that they are in possession of them is very important to these people. For example, a person might move from a small provincial town to the capital to work or study. Seeing how the Second Caste lives, this person begins to adopt their values. Imitating and repeating the behavior of the Twos they meet, the One learns much more about the possibilities that his life has to offer than his relatives and friends could ever teach him. The time comes when our hero returns to his home town, but nothing is the same as it was before. His level of knowledge is now higher. To return to the image of the four-storey house that I used at the beginning of this chapter, this person has now learned that there is a playground beyond the hedge outside the first floor of the house he is living in. He already yearns for more than that which is accepted in his circle and environment and comes to the realization that to get what you want in life, you need something more than just work. For example, that you can get more money for your work, or that you can organize and manage a company and get others to work for you.

This transition period from the First Caste to the Second is reminiscent of the situation a child of seven or nine finds herself in when she first learns about something that is forbidden (for example, how to kiss "like a grown-up") or try beer or cigarettes for the first time, and then goes back to share this amazing knowledge of the secrets of adult life with the five-year-olds who are still playing in the sandbox. She is overwhelmed with a sense of pride and awareness of her importance, now she has become a grown-up, this naturally means that she should be in charge. The little ones in the sandbox listen to her and give her their candy as a sign of respect.

Transitional Ones possess the skills to communicate and make money and the desire to increase their levels of comfort. But for them, the concept of comfort and well-being are substituted by a perception of these things at the material level, at the level of the First Caste. If these people buy a painting by a fashionable contemporary artist, for them it is not about communing with art or making a contribution to the preservation of humanity's cultural heritage and not even just an investment. For this transitional caste, it is merely something cool and expensive that no one else from their circle and background has ever had.

This transitional caste firmly believes that there is nothing out there beyond the playground. For them, the possibilities of the Second Caste are the limit of perception.

FROM A TWO TO A THREE

The time comes when a member of the second caste reaches the summit of their development. They already have everything they need and want, they have a lot of money and a load of connections. At this stage, they understand that all these things that they have accumulated are not the main thing in life. A need for something deeper emerges. And it is then that members of the Third caste with their power, influence and global ambitions and goals begin to enter into these Twos' field of vision. The world view of these Twos begins to change and the metamorphosis from a Two to a Three commences.

Incidentally, when I talk about the Second Caste, I am not exclusively talking about people on the Forbes rich list. I am talking about the spiritual level of a person's development. A simple farmer can be a Two, and he may not have a great deal of capital, and his income may be considerably less than that of the city dweller, but at his own level, in his own town, he is considered a significant figure, everyone knows him and is trying to copy his success. But when this farmer decides to run for, say, the mayor of his home town, this is a good example of his transition from a Two to a Three.

The main distinguishing feature of the Transitional Two is that for Twos, money and connections still remain everything. Despite wanting to become a Three, they don't usually have their own ideology and the ability to defend their position and basically try to "buy" everything and everyone to achieve their ends.

FROM A TRHEE TO A FOUR

Threes are strong, charismatic people. They are leaders and individuals, sometimes distinguished for their cruelty and aggression. But these seemingly negative personal characteristics are, in this instance, effective tools that they use to achieve their goals, and interestingly, their use does not negatively affect the karma of the individual wielding them but works to their benefit on their path to development.

Having money, power, influence and control, these people sooner or later begin to ask themselves questions about the way the systems of the world are structured. It becomes important for them to know: "Why is everything happening like this?", "How is everything organised?", "Where have we come from and where are we going?" And this is already a sign of their new stage of growth — their transition from being a Three to becoming a Four.

At this stage, this person wants to find someone who can provide them with answers to their spiritual questions. For these Warriors embarking on the path of Knowledge, it is important to have a mentor or sage who can guide them to the truth. It often happens that when Threes are transitioning "from Three to Four", they are forced to live at the level of a One, not yet having found the justification for their spiritual torment, which is a very characteristic state for people of the Third caste and above. These people no longer care about their comfort, their everyday environment, earthly joys, money and power. Threes and above are birds of a different feather. And if it happens that when a person who is transitioning "from a Three to a Four" is forced to return to the bottom of the pile and work, study and conform to the conventions of the social group in which they find themselves without any possibility of self-actualization, then, unfortunately, this person might become psychologically unstable, renounce society entirely or even go crazy without reaching their full potential.

Transitional Threes often become hermits, go on a journey around the world, or a retreat to a monastery or the forest and give up everything they have for the sake of an idea, a global goal, or simply their search for the truth. It often happens that millionaires or very rich heirs give up everything they have and discover a new path for themselves by throwing themselves into the depths of self-knowledge.

Visually, Transitional Threes can look very different from each other. But what they do have in common is that their appearance is always very memorable and sticks in the minds of those whom they have met on the way. They have very high energy levels that can be felt at the physical level, which attracts people to these personalities but also alarms them at the same time.

The main difference between a transitional Three and other Threes is the presence within them of the realization that power and one's own ego are no longer key aspects of life. The understanding that strength does not lie in one's ambition blurs the lines between good and evil. White and black are now revealed in their hundreds of different shades. Aggression is replaced with moderation, acceptance and humility.

CHAPTER III. THE DESTINY CODE MATRIX

A UNIQUE TOOL

The universe opens up opportunities for people to the extent that they are ready to accept them. When a child in the womb is developing and preparing for its independent life, it miraculously takes the decision to be born. The time comes to walk — the child begins to crawl, stand up, take the first step, and one fine day he or she is already running after adventures, discovering the world and enthusiastically making new discoveries, developing, exploring, creating.

Sooner or later, the time comes for every person to reveal their true potential. To focus on what is truly precious in life. To understand the meaning and tasks of one's existence by revealing one's personal significance to oneself, society, and the wider world. Having embarked on the path of development, a person strives to become better. Thus, the process of transformation is launched, where, after making personal changes, everything around that person changes. By starting with him or herself, a person changes the world.

Having gained a general notion of the chakras and the system of caste division, having accepted new knowledge and expanded our understanding about energies and the indicators of the levels of spiritual development, it is finally time to get acquainted with the practical part of the Destiny Code's methodology, which, is essentially what this book is all about.

So, let's work out what the Destiny Code is, how to build a matrix, how to calculate a person's Destiny and their compatibility with each other. We will define and learn the zones and points of the matrix, find out what meanings and tasks are embedded in them and discuss how the energies located in one or another part of the matrix can radically change a person's life. So, let's start by acquainting ourselves with what the Destiny Code looks like.

WHAT THE DESTINY CODE LOOKS LIKE

The Destiny Code consists of several elements. Firstly, it's a matrix. Secondly, it has a table setting out the three Destinations during the course of a person's life. Thirdly, it contains the Health Map. To start off with, let's look at the Destiny Code Matrix.

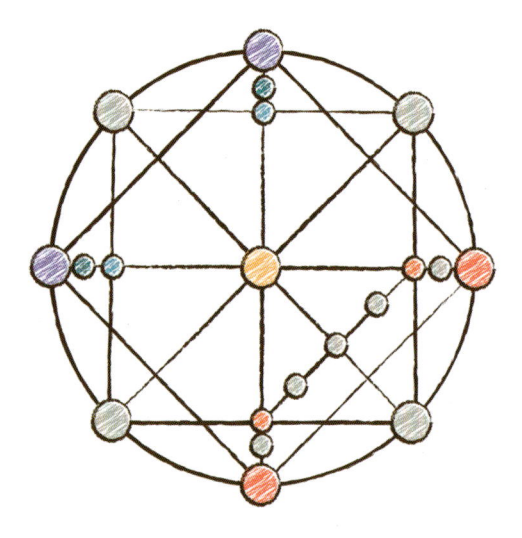

The Destiny Code Matrix looks like an octagram, consisting of a square and a rhombus, superimposed over each other. The square is connected using horizontal and diagonal lines that traverse the middle and corners of the square and rhombus respectively. For the sake of clarity, the central point of the matrix is highlighted with the small yellow circle and marks the intersection of the lines connecting all the vertices to each other.

CALCULATION

The Destiny Code Matrix is calculated using a person's date of birth. It is very important to remember that because the technique for using the Destiny Code originally came from Europe, the date of birth should be recorded in the following order: day, month, year.

In order to understand the algorithm, where each number should be placed, I propose that you make a copy of the image of the empty Destiny Code matrix, below. The letter markers will help you understand the order that the calculation needs to be carried out and clearly illustrate the route through each of the zones and points.

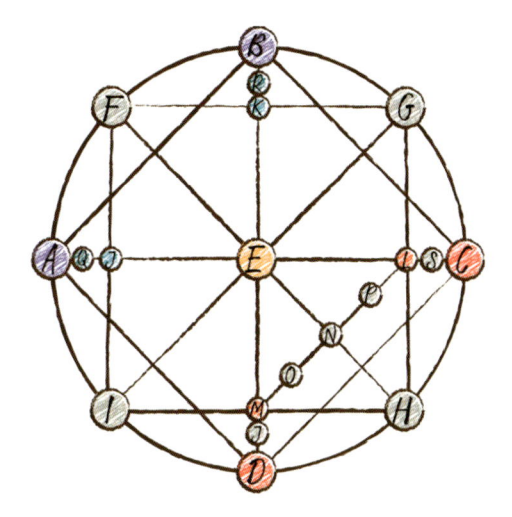

In order to calculate the Destiny Code, we will need the subject's date of birth. Suppose we are interested in a person born on January 7, 1987.

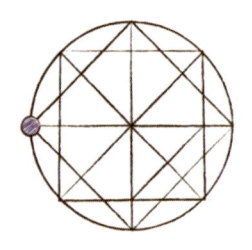

The first number we will use is the day of birth. So, we will write the number 7 at point A (the leftmost horizontal corner).

No number in the Destiny Code matrix can exceed 22. If the date of birth of a person, for example, is 23, 24, 25 or more, then the two constituent numbers in this figure should be added together. For example, if a person was born on the 23rd of a given month, we can calculate their point value as follows: 2 + 3 = 5, and we should therefore enter the number 5 in point A. If their birthday is on the 31st, then we add 3 + 1 = 4 and enter the number 4 in the Destiny Code matrix.

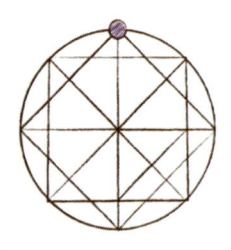

Next, we use the number of the subject's month of birth. In our case, if the person was born in January that means we enter the number 1 in point B (the highest vertical point in the Destiny Code Matrix). As you have probably already guessed, only numbers between 1 and 12 can be placed on this point, as per the total number of the months of the year. If you get a number greater than 12, then you will need to recalculate because a mistake has clearly been made in this instance.

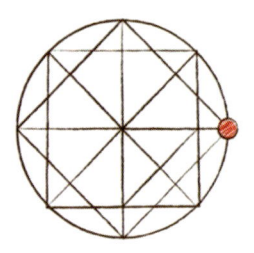

The next step is to calculate the number that needs to be inputted into point C (the rightmost horizontal point in the Destiny Code Matrix). Here, we simply add up the numbers that make up the subject's year of birth. Therefore, using our example, we will need to add 1 + 9 + 8 + 7 = 25. Then we simplify this figure as follows: 2 + 5 = 7 — and input the number 7 into point C.

Next, we will need to calculate the lowest vertical point in the matrix — this is point D. This is done by simply adding together all the numbers inputted into the previous points using the formula A + B + C = D. Based on the numbers we have in our example, this works out as 7 + 1 + 7 = 15. We then take 15 and enter this number into Point D.

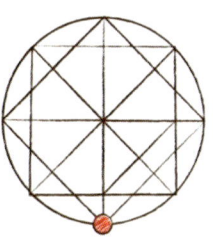

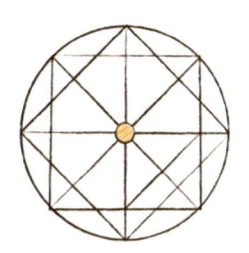

One of the key considerations when calculating the Destiny Code is the definition of the subject's personal energy. The process for calculating the center point of the matrix is likewise very simple — simply add the numbers obtained that have been entered into the four vertices of the rhombus using the formula A + B + C + D = E. So, let's calculate what number we would get in our example: 7 + 1 + 7 = 15 = 30 and 3 + 0 = 3. Therefore, the main energy tally for the person whose date of birth we took as our example will come to 3. Now, enter 3 in the center circle of the Destiny Code Matrix.

Points A, B, C and D (the four corners of the rhombus) are the quartet of personal energies that determine the individual characteristics of a person. We will talk about this a little later when we come to analyze the values of zones and points in more detail, but for now, let's get back to our calculation process.

Now, we need to calculate the corner points of the Square (later referred to as the Ancestral Square). Let's start from Point F, which is located at 10 o'clock on the Destiny Code Matrix between points A and B and is the top left-hand corner of the square. This figure is calculated using the formula A + B = F. Using the numbers from our example, we would add 7 + 1 = 8, and therefore we input 8 into Point F.

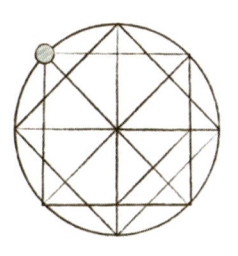

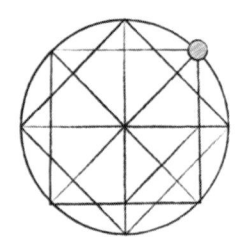

Next, we calculate the corners of the square clockwise by adding the two values of the corners of the rhombus that pass through the corner of the square in question. Therefore, point G on the square will be obtained by adding Points B + C of the rhombus, in our example, this is 1 + 7 = 8.

We then get the value of Point H by adding the values of C + D = H. In our example, we would get the following calculation: 7 + 15 = 22. We will then enter 22 in the lower right-hand corner of the square (point H).

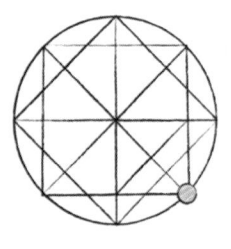

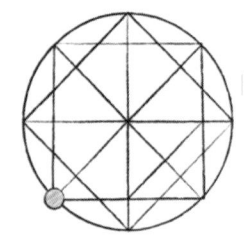

And finally, we work out the value of point I by using the formula D + A = I: 15 + 7 = 22 — consequently enter "22" in the lower left-hand corner of the square.

So, this is how we calculate the Major Points in the Destiny Code Matrix for a person who was born on January 7, 1987. Even with such basic initial data, already quite a lot can be gauged about the subject individual. Various character traits are evident, it is possible to evaluate the subject's virtues and faults, to correlate the probabilities of their external and internal qualities and understand what inspires this person and what can lead him or her into depression. You will be able to determine what difficulties this person will face in life. And at this stage, the karmic tasks assigned to this person in this life will also be discernible.

Next, we need to calculate the other points in the Destiny Code Matrix that are no less important and, which will reveal additional information about a subject and the energies they possess in more narrowed-down areas of their life.

In order to work out the value of Points J, K, L, and M, we need to calculate the sum of the subject's personal energy (character) points and the values of points located on the Rhombus's right angles. Therefore, to get the value for Point J, we need to add up our data using the formula A + E = J and do the same for other points in the matrix square going clockwise: B + E = K, C + E = L, D + E = M.

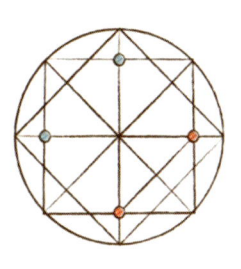

If we substitute the numbers from our example. Point J comes to: 7 + 3 = 10, Point K: 1 + 3 = 4 Point L: 7 + 3 = 10 and Point M: 15 + 3 = 18 We then enter the values received into their corresponding points in the Destiny Code Matrix.

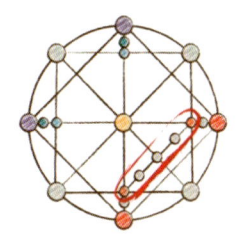

Next, we will need to calculate the Prosperity Line and the three points indicated in this zone.

The Prosperity Line is located on the lower right-hand part of the Destiny Code Matrix and runs from point M to point L. The Prosperity Line contains five points.

We already have a couple of the values that we calculated a little earlier (Point M and Point L). We now need to determine the value of Point N. To do this, we need to add the outer points of the Prosperity Line (i.e. The values of points M and L that we have already calculated). We can do this using the formula M + L = N, which gives us: 18 + 10 = 28, and then simplify it to get: 2 + 8 = 10.

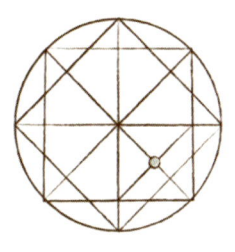

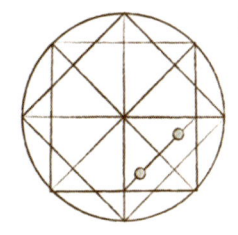

The next values that we need to determine are Points O and P. This is also straightforward. We can do this calculation by using the formula M + N = O: 18 + 10 = 10, and L + N = P: 10 + 10 = 20 This is how the energy value of 10 is determined for Point O and the energy value of 20 for point P, respectively.

Now, we need to learn how to calculate Points Q, R, S, T. And it is easy to do this using the same principle as the previous calculations, you just need to add up the end points of the side lengths of the rhombus (this time) with the point opposite, on the line of the Square). We can do this using the formulas: A + J = Q, B + K = R, C + L = S, D + M = T.

If we substitute the numbers from our example, we get: 7 + 10 = 17, 1 + 4 = 5, 7 + 10 = 17, 15 + 18 = 33, which we need to simplify, because this number should not be more than 22 and thus we get: 3 + 3 = 6 The resulting values of these points should be entered into the Destiny Code Matrix.

So, now you should have before you the main points of the Destiny Code Matrix. These values should provide you with sufficient data to make an initial analysis of a person's personality and start working on his or her karmic programs.

I propose looking at the calculations necessary to work out a person's Destination using the Destiny Code in more detail a little later. After we have learned a little bit more about the zones and points. This is vital to help us understand the meanings embedded in the combinations of the energies of all three Destinations. When calculating them, it is important to have at least initially familiarized yourself with the significance of the zones and understand what they are responsible for.

This book provides an introduction on how to read the Destiny Code. This is the initial level — the process of getting "acquainted" with this tool. The Destiny Code Matrix contains many more zones and points that reveal the characteristics and tasks of a person's personality with hundreds of shades at intermediate points, which we will not touch upon for now in the calculations. In order to discover the full possibilities that this technique has to offer, you will need to move on to the next stage of studying the Destiny Code. But that's another story and a great idea for my next book.

At this initial stage, I recommend doing the calculations manually, independently counting and entering the numbers into the matrix. In addition, to help you understand how energies are linked, you will be able to open additional channels, which will provide you with a wider range and shade of information. It's hard to describe exactly how it works, but when you do the calculations many times and compare this with how it feels using a calculator, you'll get to see exactly what I mean.

However, if you want to do a quick calculation, you can use my free calculator on my official website www.ajgollov.com. This calculator calculates the Destiny Code for specific individuals, as well as the compatibility matrix for couples.

THE SIGNIFICANCE OF THE ZONES AND POINTS

Each zone in the Destiny Code Matrix is responsible for certain areas of human life. In these zones, there are points in which various energies are located — the Arcana. The main task is to determine which Arcana are present in an individual's Destiny Code Matrix and to understand how these energies affect this individual.

I should remind you that the significance of the numbers in the Destiny Code Matrix corresponds to one of the 22 major Arcana in the Tarot deck. Each energy has an interpretation that corresponds to the characteristics of the personality archetypes for each of the Arcana. It is important to understand and learn to get a feel for the specific nature of the Arcana in order to unravel causes and suggest consequences, to highlight the features and general characteristics of each of the energies and to find out their specifics as a whole and the strength of their influence together and on each other.

Energies can be in a "+" state and in a "-" state. These states can be easily represented on a scale from 1 (negative, fully "-" state) to 10 (good, fully "+"). Ideally, a person should strive to find balance and work to bring their energies closer to "+", but they don't need to be fanatical about it. Sometimes, being hyper-positive can do more harm than suffering from a chronic negative condition.

An analysis of the state of a person's energies and an understanding of their characteristics allows us to correct the influence of these energies in a particular area of human life and bring them into a "+" state. As soon as the process is begun, the Universe will begin to open up new doors and lead this person in the right direction, along the path to their true Destiny.

CHARACTER (COMFORT ZONE)

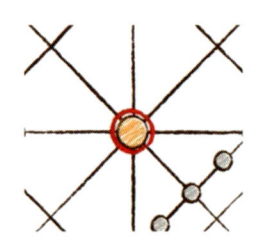

Defining Character is the main way of answering the questions: "Who am I?", "What do I imagine myself to be?", "What am I?", "What makes me different from others?" and "What makes me akin to others?". This is the most important point of the Destiny Code Matrix and the energy contained in it has the strongest influence on a person. It determines his or her personal qualities, the structure of his or her inner world and undoubtedly has an impact on every other area of his or her life.

The Character is located in the center of the Destiny Code Matrix and corresponds to the Manipura Chakra (point E). This is where an individual's true Ego resides, which possibly may be hidden from the eyes of those around them but is the true embodiment of their personality.

The center point in the Destiny Code Matrix is also called the Comfort Zone. The energy residing in this point is the most convenient and comfortable state that this individual can be in. Consciously or unconsciously, a person's soul strives towards those conditions that are characteristic of the energies residing in this zone. These are the most important characteristics for that person. The Arcana, located at this point, will help describe an individual's main personality traits, features, pluses and minuses, strengths and weaknesses, form their principles for life and indicate the causal relationships of certain events in their lives.

It is by working on the energy located in the Comfort Zone that an individual can begin the path of correction. Having accepted their life bonuses and realizing the aggravating circumstances inherent in the Universe in these energies, an individual can learn to use them both for the good, to avoid risks and deftly use their features to unlock the full potential of these energies.

Only the following Arcana can be placed in the Character Zone: 3, 4, 5, 6, 7, 8, 9, 10, 11, 12, 13, 14, 16, 18, 20, 22

According to statistics, Arcana 5, 6, and 8 are most often found in the Character Zone of the Destiny Code Matrix. These are the most common energies found in people.

Arcanas 13, 14, 16, 18, 20, 22 are considered rare. The people whose personal energy is determined by these Arcana are unique. They can be confidently considered very special. Often, global karmic tasks are embedded in the matrix of people such as these, and these people have been born to change the world.

The Character Zone can never have Arcanas 1, 2, 15, 17, 19, or 21.

PORTRAIT

Point A is the person's Portrait. This point is located along the line of the Earth and is located in the extreme left corner of the rhombus of personal energies. The Portrait is one of the most important zones in the Destiny Code Matrix and is considered a Major Point — it is the second one that is considered during analysis.

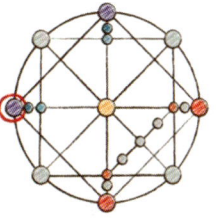

The Portrait is how the individual's environment sees that individual. The way that the world sees him or her on the radar of life. And to a greater extent — what role a person plays in his or her environment, the mask under which his or her true Ego is hidden. It is the way others see him or her. It is important to remember that the Portrait does not really define the person. It characterizes how a person is seen by his or her environment. This is his or her mask, his or her role.

An analysis and description of the characteristics of the Portrait makes it possible to identify the features of a person's behavior in society (in the community), to evaluate his or her "reflection in the mirror", which, as it were, indicates to us the requirements of life. A person will be what others want to see him as — this is what the Portrait shows us. The program of this or that energy will also be played out on a subconscious level, provoking a person to follow certain models of behavior — the activity or passivity of the individual. This is how temperament is determined and even the features of a person's appearance can be divined in this way.

THE HIGHER ESSENCE

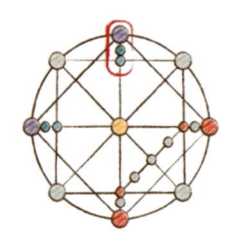

The Zone of the Higher Essence includes three Arcana, located on points B, K and R. Every master has their own way of interpreting this zone. Some call it the energies of the Guardian Angel, others call it a personal resource, while other masters state that this is the program of the Vision of the path and the way to find God. Essentially, they are all correct! Because the energies located in this zone of the Destiny Code are primarily responsible for spirituality and indicate the easiest path that an individual can follow, using the talents and other life bonuses given to them by the Universe.

Point B — the spiritual source of energy. The Arcana located in it indicates the highest spiritual idea a person might have about the good and the ideal manifestation of his or her perfect happiness — the thing that makes a person truly happy and which fills his or her life with color.

The energy of Point B indicates the path, which you can follow in order to get pleasure from the process and replenish your energy reserves. Subject to observing the recommendations that are characterized in the Arcana located in a given point, a person will always have "personal resources" and the productivity of their activities and actions will help develop that person. This individual will always receive the fruits of their labor in the here and now.

The energy of point B helps you throughout life, it gets you out of difficult situations and magically always returns you to the right path.

Point K — the skills and abilities accumulated in the past incarnations of the soul. This is the experience that the soul has received previously, those lessons that have been learned and the accumulated knowledge from which it is now time to apply in its current life. This is not something that a person has studied specifically but applies on a subconscious level, using the memory of the previous incarnations of their Soul.

Among other things, the energy of Point K indicates the lessons that a person should learn from their relationships with their Family. These may be tasks that are important for them to solve, elicited by certain life circumstances relating to this person's relatives (parents, brothers and sisters, ancestors). The Arcana at point K indicates exactly how a person behaves in circumstances they have set out and what role they need to take in their relations with their Family.

Point R — human talents. These are the talents that the Universe has decided to endow a person with at their birth.

At first glance, it may seem that the values of the K and R points are very similar. And indeed, the energies contained in these points are considered superpowers — life bonuses. However, how these skills are realized differs in that one is given to the person already and automatically developed — it is simply there to be taken and used (Point K), while the second is something that you need to work towards, to develop and only then it will begin to bring benefit to that person (Point R).

The Arcana of the R point also indicates which path you need to follow in order to make things easier and more comfortable in life. By analyzing the specifics of this energy, it is easy to determine those activities in life that you need to be more active in. These are the favorable fields of an individual's interests, through which they can replenish their energy reserves and, as a result, actualize themselves.

The Higher Essence reveals to an individual where their sources of energy and talents lie and intimates to them which superpowers they can easily develop.

When the energies of the Higher Essence are in a positive state, a person can move mountains, he or she is full of strength and has the inspiration required to accomplish great things. When the energies in this zone are negative, the individual is exhausted, falls into a state of apathy and depression and their source of strength is depleted and empty.

In order to replenish this energy reserve, you need to know the nature of the energy located in this zone, identify its key features and adjust your behavior in accordance with the recommendations made to you.

These simple actions can dramatically change your life in the here and now. As soon as an individual begins to implement these adjustments, they will immediately feel the effectiveness of the Destiny Code technique.

CHILD-PARENT KARMA

Points A, J and Q form the zone of the Destiny Code Matrix, which is commonly called Child-Parent Karma. This zone is responsible for the connection between an individual and their parents (ancestors) and their children (descendants). The purpose of the energies located in the points of the Child-Parent Karma Zone is to provide a picture of the individual's relationships and show them their role in society with their parents and children. And also to define tasks and point out the peculiar traits that need to be taken into account in order to build harmonious and strong relationships.

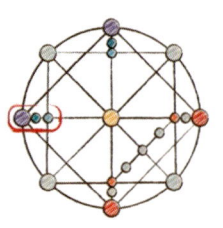

Child-Parent Karma is located on the horizontal line of the Earth in the Destiny Code Matrix and consists of the three points on the far left.

The Portrait of a person (point A) that we looked at earlier is a little higher. It has been highlighted separately because this is a Major Point in Destiny Code Matrix and its characteristics need to be considered first and separately from the zone in which it is located.

By analyzing the Child-Parent Karma, it is easy to trace the route of an individual's personality development. The way an individual is viewed by society directly determines their relationship with their parents and vice versa.

The Portrait is, for the most part, the image that an individual has received, arising out of the conditions created for them by their parents, the result of the actions that the parents have committed in relation to that person. Regardless of the nature of the actions committed, the Arcana, located at point A, reveals exactly what has happened as a result of the efforts of the parents. As a result of their expectations and requirements. As a result of their assessment of conformity. As a result of "side effects".

The relationships that an individual develops with their parents form their ideas about what kind of relationship they should have with their children. The energies in this zone provide clues and answers as to why and according to which principles the connections between parents and their children are built, they reveal the secrets, motives and reasons behind the state an individual finds themselves in relation to their parents and children.

The energy in Point J reveals the nature of the individual's relations with their parents and describes the situations they found themselves in when they were growing up. This point also describes where and from which kind of family and wider ancestral family line that a person comes from. It indicates an individual's value systems (or their lack thereof), which have been promoted in their family.

Sometimes connections with parents have been lost for one reason or another. But whatever the case, it still has an impact on the individual's perceptions of the system of child-parent relationships. Everything develops according to the law of karma.

Point Q indicates the nature of an individual's relationship with their children (and attitudes to their children). This energy reveals the motives, values and reasons for certain attitudes towards them. The Arcana, located in this point, primarily reveals the relevance of this theme to an individual's life, the nature of their feelings, the level of their communication with their children and, of course, describes the expectations and hopes that this person has (or has not) entrusted to the next generations.

The energies of the Child-Parent Karma can help find the causes and establish the primary sources out of which certain scenarios have arisen. Each of the 22 Arcana help to recreate snapshots of the past and present, and having examined them it is possible to identify various connections and begin to correct the relationship between parents and their children.

MATERIAL KARMA

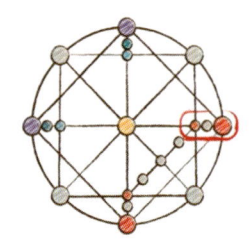

The Material Karma Zone is located on the right-hand side of the Earth line and comprises the three Points C, L and S. When working with this zone, it is important to remember that the energies inherent in these positions are responsible for the material aspects of an individual's life. For their physical reality, for what they have, how they get it, and what is hindering or helping a person in their material life.

Material Karma energies are closely connected with the Finance Zone, which is located on the Prosperity Line. When working with the Destiny Code, as in life, it is important to remember the interconnection between everyone and everything.

Thus, point L, being at the junction of both zones, reveals not only the experience that the soul has been through in past incarnations with regard to its material values, but also describes the factors that influence the formation of the financial potential (cash flow) of an individual in their current life. The energy of this point indicates how and by what an individual's income can be increased and what it is that might block a person's material possibilities.

The characteristics of the Arcana in this position should not simply be interpreted in terms of their general descriptive qualities, but rather as specific working tools.

If we evaluate the weight of the influence of the energies of the Material Karma Zone as a percentage, then we can provisionally determine that the energy of Point L has approximately a 25% impact on a person's professional activities, in contrast, for example, to Point P, which determines 50% of what an individual should be doing to get themselves a good income and increase their level of well-being.

In other words, if we recommend engaging in a certain professional activity within the framework of the energies located in Point L and Point P, it is possible to say the following: the energy in Point P indicates which area and profession will suit you best, and the energy in Point L will tell you which actions and tools are best suited to achieve this purpose.

In addition, it is possible to draw an analogy between the given values of Point L and the functions of Point K. In both points, the energy present there will tell you what a person can use from the experience gained by their soul in their previous incarnations. If in the Higher Essence this is the ability to know "how to think", but in Material Karma this is the ability to know "how to act".

Point C is responsible for earthly prosperity. The energy located here reveals the specifics of the relationship an individual has with what he or she possesses in the material and physical sense. These are such things as housing, property, and family (as a physical factor). These also include the requirements necessary to maintain a certain standard of living — a rider or extra piece of information so to speak.

The energy in Point C also describes the material karmic program. In other words, it determines the nature of the events in a person's life in relation to their material sphere.

The energy of Point S provides us with clues as to how to activate cash flow and shows what can block it. The characteristics of a particular Arcana in a given position should be analyzed in terms of its strengths and weaknesses. For example, if the 18th energy is located on Point S, then this indicates that a person should, first of all, listen to their intuition, perhaps even contrary to their common sense. Moreover, the 18th Arcana indicates that in a completely incomprehensible way a person might be in the right place at the right time. Therefore, this person always succeeds in taking more than others can (provided that this energy is positive in that person).

The energies of the Material Karma Zone can not only be interpreted separately by analyzing the characteristics of each Arcana, but also by taking all three together by forming them into a karmic program. This will allow you to look into the past and understand where the complications that are creating difficulties in this life might come from.

THE PROSPERITY LINE

There is one special line in the lower right part of the Destiny Code Matrix. The curiosity devouring the majority of people to decipher these particular energies is difficult to overestimate. And this is all because this is the part of the Destiny Code Matrix, which provides answers to the most tremulous questions in life regarding their personal happiness and wealth.

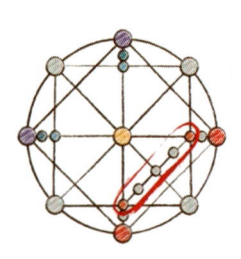

The Prosperity Line runs from point M to point L and is divided into two parts: The Relationship Zone (love) and the Finance Zone (vocation).

The Relationship Zone includes points M, N and O, which are responsible for everything related to the feelings and relationships a person experiences in life. This is above all the zone of love and partnership. So, if there are questions in this regard, then the energies located here will reveal the meanings of the cards and provide the necessary answers.

Point O is the main energy located in the Relations Zone. It describes the type of partner that is most suitable for a given individual, and what qualities the person who becomes their life partner should have. The energy in this point indicates an individual's personal happiness. And it is precisely personal happiness that is considered to be the foundation of life for the majority of people. For most people, but by no means all.

The energy in point O reveals the specifics of an individual's preferences. The Arcana located in this point draws a precise portrait of the person that the individual in question really wants to have beside them in life. Often the Arcana number of an individual's Point O coincides with the birth number of their partner.

Next comes point M, which is a part of the Karmic Tail. The energy located in it is initially given to a person in a negative state. It reveals the special features of the development of an individual's relationships with other people, it reveals the causes of difficulties and indicates those factors that affect the eventfulness of that person's life. If a person cannot manage to build any relationship with their partners and does not understand why this is happening, then it is the energy located in Point M that will provide the answers and identify the causes of these difficulties.

The energy in Point M tells us how a person has behaved in relationships with other people in their past lives — it precisely reveals the negative side of their behavior. This is where a person has made mistakes, and what he or she has transferred into their current incarnation to be worked out.

Point N is located on the intersection between relationships and finances and is a very interesting one when it comes to analyzing an individual's personality. This is the Compromise Zone. It reveals the peculiar features of a person's personal priority system. It indicates the principles that align the connections between personal (self-realization) and partner (marriage, family) values. The energy of the N point describes how a person maneuvers between their relationships and professional activities. This point acts as a kind of scales in its own way, where love and feelings sit on one tray, and career and money on the other. The Arcana located in this position describes in detail and nuance the specifics of human behavior in relation to these two aspects of life. The characteristics of this Arcana will tell you why a person is behaving this way and not otherwise, according to which principles he or she is building his system of priorities, and also indicates what the consequences might be if this energy is in a negative state.

Regardless of the depth of feelings experienced, especially when a person is building relationships, their personal tasks are important. Here everything is cumulative and is built according to the law of karma. Every person in life, every relationship with anyone — is an action taken that has consequences. The consequences can be both favorable (warm memories, emotions, marriage, positive experiences) and dramatic (a hard lesson, a test of fidelity, loss, etc.). For every person, these tasks are individual and are given depending on the personal Destiny that that person is heading towards. Therefore, the energies in the Relationship Zone not only describe what a partner should be like and how the connection will develop with him or her, but also determine the tasks (lessons) that need to be undergone through the prism of an individual's personal relationships.

The Finance Zone is responsible for the individual's professional realization, their vocation, and reveals the idiosyncrasies of their relationships with money, success and prosperity.

Point P helps us to find the answer to perhaps the most frequently asked question: what is a person's calling in life? The energy of this point helps us to find the most comfortable, and most importantly, promising areas for a person's professional realization. The characteristics of the Arcana will suggest which profession choices are suitable to a person and the specific features of their nature regarding specific types of professional activities.

It is important to remember that you should not just go through a list of professions, attaching to them the characteristics of a certain energy. There is no need to be limited by the framework of the Arcana — you need to transfer the specifics of the energy to the activity that a person is already engaged in or would like to be engaged in. Bearing in mind the special features and idiosyncrasies of all the major energies in the Destiny Code Matrix, it is important not to fall into the mistake of restricting yourself to the conditions set forth by this or that piece of advice given by any single given zone. It is important to remember that everything is built on a system of interconnected relationships, where one thing will undoubtedly have an effect on another. The Point P Arcana primarily provides us with pointers about the tones and shades that should be present in the picture, and not about the style or manner of its execution.

Point L is responsible for those things that reveal or block a person's potential personal actualization in life. Its energy describes the possible scenarios where the use of certain tools should be considered in a person's professional and business activities. This energy can provide suggestions regarding the most favorable target audience or behavioral scenario for an individual and the most effective image they can project.

THE SKY LINE AND THE EARTH LINE

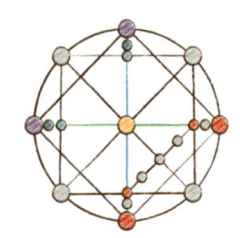

The rhombus of the personal energies of the Destiny Code Matrix is divided by two perpendicular lines. The vertical line is called the Sky Line. The horizontal line is called the Earth Line. The energies located along these lines can be analyzed separately and together in the context of the zones where they are located and are read within the framework of the general specifics of a separate Line (the Earth or the Sky).

The Earth line relates to the material world. Everything you can see, touch, hear, feel. Everything that is connected with the earthly (physical) reality. These include: the individual's dwelling place, the things they own, the money they receive. The following zones are located on the Earth Line:

The Portrait zone (point A) — an individual's image. Their appearance and how they are seen by the world;

The Child-Parent Karma zone — the places in a person's life for their parents (Point J) and children (Point Q);

The Material Karma zone —indicates the individual's prosperity and the level of material wealth (Point C), those things that open up or block a person's cash flow (Point L) and the Karma of Finance, the soul's material experiences from its previous incarnations (Point S).

The Sky Line relates to mentality. It is spirituality, the connection between a person and the Higher powers (God, Guardian Angel, the Universe, etc.). It is intuition, memory, thoughts, the psyche. It is the inner energy and strength of man.

The energies located on the Sky Line, as is the case with the Earth Line, can be interpreted individually and within a specific zone, depending on the request formulated by the subject in question.

The Sky Line includes the following points and zones:

The Higher Essence — the source of life force. This is what gives us energy and takes it away (Point B), these are our human talents, skills and abilities gained from previous incarnations (Point K) and those superpowers bestowed on us by the universe as a bonus in this life (Point R):

The Karmic Tail — the difficulties and trials that a person has to go through to atone for the debts of their previous lives. It is the Personal Karmic Program: Spiritual (Point D), Social (Point M), Event-related (point T).

The energies of the Earth and Sky Lines mould the individual's general outlook on life. It is their personal code of perception. It is on the basis of the characteristics of the energies located on the Earth and Sky lines that a person forms an image of the world, a picture that he or she will interpret and perceive throughout his or her life.

THE ANCESTRAL SQUARE

The Destiny Code Matrix is a complex system. When we look at its shape, we can see that it consists of two main figures: a square and a rhombus. You will recall that the rhombus is the Zone of Personal Energies and we will examine the meanings of this zone in more detail a little earlier. But for now, let's analyze further what the Square is about and what the energies located within it describe.

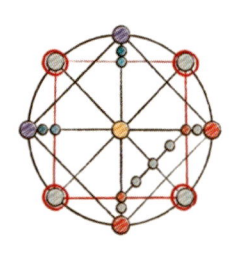

Each individual is physically and spiritually connected with their wider family, with their ancestors. From one incarnation to the next, the soul accumulates and stores the memories of its ancestors, it gains experience and knowledge and by passing these on it undergoes and completes its ancestral karmic programs.

Ancestral programs are predefined scenarios for the development of events within the framework of a single human life or several generations, or a whole family line. Ancestral programs consist of a set of specific features, conditions, restrictions, lessons, tasks and goals through which an individual will have to pass. Alternatively, you could say that they are those external factors that affect a person and their life, regardless of their personal qualities: their habits, their way of perceiving and accepting the outside world and the way that the world itself impacts this person. It is a combination of circumstances and the course of events that will have to be faced.

The energies located along the perimeter of the Ancestral Square describe the kind of tasks an individual has had passed on to them in their current life by the ancestors in their family line, and they indicate the special idiosyncratic expectations the outside world will be demanding of them. They provide clues about a person's strengths thanks to their ancestors' achievements, and an indication of the burden they will need to bear and issues resolve as a result of their "failings".

The top line of the Generic square is called the family line's Zone of Strength. The energies located in it (Points F and G) provide us with an indication of what the ancestors want from us and what hopes the family line has placed on the individual. The Arcana of the family line's Strength also provides us with clues about what bonuses and talents (Point K) a person might use thanks to the memory of their ancestors.

The bottom line of the Ancestral Square is the Zone of the Failings of the Past. The energies located in it (Points I and H) reveal those moments in a person's life when they have been weak due to the "failings" of their ancestors. At one time, someone in their family line committed some action that they shouldn't have or failed to do one that they should have... Therefore, there is a process that has not been completed that remains due on the wider family's account and has been postponed as a personal debt that an individual in this incarnation is duty-bound to complete.

Point J (parents), as you can see, is a part of the Ancestral Square, which indicates an inextricable link with the past. The energy of this point reminds the individual why it is they are the way they are and calls upon them to figure out exactly who they are.

Point L (Financial Karma) is also a part of the Ancestral Square, and it is within the framework of this zone that the material experience of an individual's ancestors is revealed. It helps the individual to use the memory of the soul's previous incarnations to help them with material matters. It indicates what a person can safely use in their current life, based on the experience that is already available to them. The energy in this point also indicates those aspects of the material world that an individual should be more wary of, knowing that their ancestors might have had difficulties with them.

THE LINE OF MEN AND THE LINE OF WOMEN

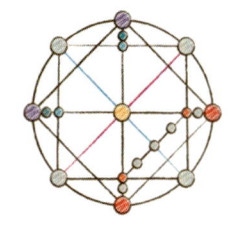

There are two additional zones in the Destiny Code Matrix, which are part of the Ancestral Square. These are the Line of Men and the Line of Women.

The Line of Men traverses the Ancestral Square from top to bottom, from point F to point H. The energies in the line reveal the pertinent features relevant to human interactions with men. Here we are talking about the scenario for communicating with and perceiving the male sex as a whole (regardless of the gender of the person doing the communicating or perceiving).

Every person radiates and absorbs energy. Depending on their personal characteristics and needs, these processes are very individual. One person will understand the energy of another on the basis of their perceived needs in relation to the object of their attention. This formula is relevant both in the particular and in the general sense. Therefore, it is important to be able to analyze how an individual will be perceived by those around them, to be able to predetermine what is expected of them, to know in advance what, perhaps they should give to those around them, taking into account the characteristics of the energies that indicate these factors to them.

The energy of point F reveals the specific nature of the spiritual task assigned to the current incarnation of the soul by the Ancestal Family line. This is something the individual needs to learn to do; needs to go through, and the experience gained from the process needs to be added to the treasury of the memory of the individual's ancestors. In addition, the Arcana located in this position provides hints about what the individual needs to learn, what tools they need to use and what principles they need to follow in order to get the most productive result out of any situation in life. It is like the "pass key that opens all doors".

The energy in this point provides a lot of information regarding an individual's relationship with their father — this is the paternal karma. The Arcana located in this position, reveals the specifics of the relationship between the child and the father, describes how this connection with the father affects the individual and the important things that need to be done to work out an individual's paternal karma.

Point H is the Material karma for the male line of the Family line. These are the things that our ancestors did not learn, what they did not understand in the past in terms of everyday material life and what the individual will have to master on their own from scratch.

The energy of this point reveals the moments in a person's life where they might be vulnerable on the material (physical) level. The point provides an indication of the kind of person this individual is in their everyday material life, what their habits are, and how they behave on the physical level and in terms of their behavior.

The Arcana for Point H describes how a person behaves in relation to all things material in their lives. It indicates how this individual might approach things such as their home, clothes and so on. How they solve domestic issues, how good they are at organizing the actualization of their primary needs in life.

The energy of point H provides information on the individual's ability to accept life's gifts. In other words, the Arcana for this point describes the specific nature of this person's attitudes and perceptions that are characteristic to him or her when new material objects and opportunities appear in his or her life. The energy in this point determines a person's attitude to receiving gifts from others, to their purchases, and also indicates the specific nature of their reactions and behavior when faced with new opportunities.

The energy in Point H also specifies the important things that an individual must do in relation to his or her father. And, of course, all the energies located on the Line of Men in one way or another affect the individual's relationship with their father. And it is important to remember this. I would like to add that the energy in Point H often provides a clear indication of how important it is to the individual in question to prove him or herself with regard to their relationship with their father. How to behave, what to do, what gifts to give, what moves to make.

Each person is unique, and accordingly, it is worth bearing in mind that not all of these aspects work according to a single scheme. For one person, it might be enough to simply understand the specific features of their relationship with their father, without making any changes. Whereas others may require precise instructions to take certain actions.

The Line of Women crosses the Ancestral Square from top to bottom, from point G to point I. The energies of this zone reveal the features of a person's interaction with women as a whole and define how the female gender will perceive this person in this incarnation of their soul. The energies in the Line of Women reveal those factors that are important for a person to consider when communicating with any woman that they might meet on their way in life. It is important to understand these factors so that any communication will bring positive emotions, guarantee productive results and help the individual to realize the karmic programs set forth by the female Family line on their way to fulfilling their Destiny.

Point G is located at the top of the Destiny Code Matrix on the right diagonal. It is responsible for the spiritual programs of the Ancestral Family line on the female line. It is primarily about those things that a person will have to deal with on their way to the goal that has been set for them. It is not really about overcoming tests or difficulties but rather, it is what makes the individual reach their goal. It is about the state of their spirit and will and, if I may say so, the level of their endurance.

The energy located in this zone describes what it is that can help a person accomplish more in their life. The Arcana located at Point G, provides clear indications of the tools that need to be used. The difference between the significance of point F and point G is that the former is more of a case of "what would be great to learn" and then use, and the thrust of the latter point is how one needs to act in order to achieve the result.

If we analyze the energy of this zone from the point of view of the Family Line Karmic program, the energy located in point G reveals the influence of the mother. This is the connection with the mother, the karma of maternal care. And, of course, the energy of this point explains the female karma of the Family line and the important tasks that need to be resolved in relation to the mother.

Point I is the material karma of the female family line. The energy in this point reveals the individual's needs and desires. What they want, but are just unable to possess or complete. These are those states that a person periodically wants to immerse themselves in completely. This point is located in a zone where the energies are inherently in a negative state, therefore, the Arcana located at Point I should be analyzed primarily from the negative side. In my own practise, I prefer to call this point the Zone of Weaknesses, vices, obsessions and bad behavior.

The function of Point I coincides with the task of point H, where the Arcana in this position, reveals the specific nature of the Karmic debt in relation to the father, only in this case it is the karmic debt owed to the mother. Accordingly, this energy indicates what needs to be done in relation to the mother, what filters the relationship with her will need to pass through and what needs to be given to her in this life in order for the individual to work out their Maternal Karma.

The lesson to be learned from the energies located on the Line of Women and the Line of Men is that it is very important to understand one simple truth: everything that a person succeeds in taking from the world at any given moment is nothing more than the result of how much they have given to it.

THE KARMIC TAIL

The Karmic Tail represents the programs of the past that an individual has to go through in this life as a result of mistakes made in previous incarnations of their soul. These are lessons that need to be completed in any case — today, tomorrow, yesterday, in this life or the next. The energies located in this zone are initially given to a person in a state of minus, and the characteristics corresponding to them should be considered those difficulties that a person will have to face in his life.

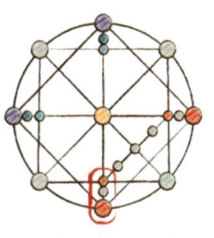

The Karmic Tail is located at the bottom of the Destiny Code Matrix and consists of the three lower points of the Sky Line — Point D, Point M and Point T.

The Karmic Tail can be interpreted in three ways.
- ◉ Using the Arcana — when the characteristics of the energy are revealed exclusively within the framework of the point in which it is located, and the answers to questions are given to a defined sphere and aspect of life.
- ◉ Using a Double up — when a combination of two energies indicates a cause and effect relationship between certain life situations.

- Using a Triple up — when three energies can be read as a karmic program of the past incarnations of the Soul.

All three ways of interpreting the Karmic Tail can be applied in practice simultaneously or separately, depending on the depth of the important information that you are trying to obtain. The deeper the request, the more methods that can be used in the analysis.

It sometimes happens that the Karmic Tail has a mirror reflection when the energies of the Karmic Tail coincide with the energies located in other zones of the Destiny Code Matrix.

For example, when the Karmic Tail coincides with the Zone of the Higher Essence, which indicates that it is important for the individual in question not to make the same mistakes in their current incarnation that they did in their past ones. The energies indicate that back in a past life an individual could have realized their programs, but for some reason got stuck in the process of doing so and was unable to complete the tasks set them. Everything will repeat itself, and this time the individual must listen to their intuition and the memory of their soul.

Perhaps the most difficult thing to work out is a case when the Karmic Tail coincides with the Relationship Zone. In this situation, the individual will come up against all the "temptations" of the mistakes of the past in the sphere of their relations with other people. And since relationships are the most emotional part of an individual's life, difficulties such as these are the most painful to work through.

It is very rare to meet people whose Karmic Tail completely coincides with the three Destinations in the Destiny Code Matrix. These individuals are only to be congratulated because they have been given a unique opportunity to have a precise map for self-realization. The program of the Karmic Tail describes the difficult things that an individual has had to bear in the past, and the Destinations coordinate the individual and indicate where they should eventually come to and how.

When analyzing the Karmic Tail in the Destiny Code Matrix, it is important to keep one key point in mind. This is the fact that the individual needs to be prepared in advance for how the information received will affect his current life. Knowledge about the karmic debts of the previous incarnations of the soul, first and foremost, calls for the individual to ponder how they might change the situation and correct the mistakes of the past in the here and now in order to improve their present life and improve their spiritual and material level. How they might learn their lessons, pass their tests and pay off their debts in order to develop and move on.

But only a very few people are ready to accept the truth about themselves. Therefore, when revealing and describing the characteristics of a person's energies and the karmic programs of the Destiny Code Matrix, the master should be very careful with the person to whom he or she is revealing this knowledge. And if an individual resists or refuses to accept the characteristics of the programs, it means that their time has not yet come to take on and go through these lessons in life. It is impossible to limit or impose something on a person within the framework of their reality because they will begin to play an alternative role and in this way end up failing to follow their path to their Destiny.

Now, let's take a look at each of the three points included in the Karmic Tail Zone in more detail. This is the most important zone in terms of the work that needs to be done on it. The points located in this zone are considered Major Points.

Point D is perhaps the most complex area of the Destiny Code Matrix. Its meaning needs to be analyzed very precisely and carefully because this zone is responsible for the personality's deep and negative programs, its characteristics need to be interpreted carefully and subtly. The Arcana located in this point, reveals fears, injuries and the concealed psychic states of the Soul

The energy located here indicates what a person was like in their past incarnations. It describes their personality, their state of mind and their place in the world of that time. But all these descriptions will be negative and read as mistakes made in the past. The energy located in Point D describes the debts owed by the individual and not the merits due to it. What they need to go through and complete in this incarnation, in this current life. The program of karmic debt that has been assigned to this individual. The Arcana located in this point, indicates the most difficult moments in life, the crisis situations and the difficulties that a person will face, and the most problematic aspects of their life.

But at the same time, the energy in this point demonstrates the hidden potential of the individual's Soul. Although this is the program of Karmic debt, the very thing that a person could not cope with in their past life, it is precisely the program that has been assigned to them to complete today and which will finally allow them to move on.

The energy in Point D indicates the individual's weaknesses. It is important to highlight one thing here: if a person has a certain Arcanum in Point D, the difficulties corresponding to this Arcanum will arise. When a person knows in advance what they don't have an aptitude for, it is much easier to understand how to build a life strategy and direct his or her efforts towards getting through this lesson.

Point M is the unresolved relationships program. It tells us how the individual behaved with other people in their past incarnations. This is the memory of the soul, which has brought into the individual's life those things that still need to be worked on, which the Soul was unable or did not have time to deal with in the past. And as a rule, the energy located in this point indicates the most difficult moments that this person has had to face in their current life in the sphere of their relationships.

Like all the other energies of the Karmic Tail, the energy of this point is in a state of negative minus. It is important that this program is undergone in this incarnation. And once acquainted with the Arcana located in this position, it is important for the individual to create a correct strategy of behavior with other people in their environment in the here and now. It is important for them to correctly determine their place in the chain of their relations with their environment, in accordance with the "debt" that they need to give back to this environment. And naturally, the energy in Point M reveals difficulties in the individual's personal relationships and indicates those aspects that they need to be ready for when entering into a love affair. The Arcana in the Relationship Zone indicate the reasons and circumstances under which a couple might get together, as well as the risks that such a union might face.

Point T reveals information about the Karmic program of the personality at the "physical" level. This might be something that a person has not done but needed to do. Or something they have done but shouldn't have. Something global that broke their life in one of their past incarnations. The thing that is important now is to correct and pass through this test in this life.

DESTINATIONS

The Destiny Code Matrix can provide a huge amount of information about a person: it describes their character, it shows the image they project in society, and it provides an indication of the good and bad things that they will face throughout their life. This alone makes it a very valuable resource, but perhaps the main goal of this approach to the Destiny Code is to reveal to people the true nature of their Destiny, the meanings that determine the route they need to take through life, the final end point or destination that a person needs to strive for.

The Destiny Code not only reveals to the individual what their Destiny is but also determines intermediate guidelines regarding certain periods of their life and the implementation of the tasks they have been set. In the technique we are using, they are called Intermediate Destinations. There are two of them.

As a rule, the Destinations, are written down just below or next to the Destiny Code Matrix for ease of calculation and interpretation. The Destinations are also written down in a specific order as a table:

THE FIRST DESTINATION
0–40 "FOR THE SELF"

The first Destination — "For the Self" — covers the first forty years of life from 0 to 40 years of age. This is the period when the personality is formed, the individual is filled with knowledge, corrects their energies and forms their system of values and their relationships. It is the time when the individual takes things from the world and concentrates their efforts for the good of themselves without giving anything back and accumulates experience. The things that an individual can take in this period of his life will serve him or her in the future to get through the next stage.

The Arcana located in the Zone of the First Intermediate Destination, indicates how the individual will behave, what will appeal to them and what lessons they should learn at this stage of life.

The First Destination indicates what will affect the formation of their moral and material values. Using the Sky Line, one can determine how a person sees the world around them, how they will think and what behavior strategies they will follow. This is when the Spiritual path and the formation of personality are determined. In other words, everything that is connected with thinking, the psyche, fantasies and everything spiritual: the intellect, intuition, self-expression, feelings in all their manifestations, compassion, charity, love, aggression, and fears. In addition, the Energy of the Sky indicates the lessons that are important to learn in this period of life, and how to pass the tests related to them.

Earth energy is responsible for all earthly things. This is everything that is tangible, material and physical that a person will encounter in this period of their life. Everything that they will acquire, everything they will lose, everything they aspire to, everything they like, and everything that will affect them on the physical level. The Arcana located at this Destination point also provides an indication of the eventful lessons that they need to go through at this stage of life.

In order to determine the First Intermediate Destination, you need to calculate the energies of the Sky and Earth. To begin with, you will need to add the two end points of the Sky Line (the vertical vertices of the rhombus/diagonal square in the Destiny Code Matrix) using the formula B + D = SKY. So, returning to our example, it comes to: 1 + 15 = 16. Then, we enter 16 onto the Sky Destiny Point.

Next, we will need to calculate the Earth Point using the formula A + C = EARTH, which we get by adding the end points of the Earth Line together. If we take the numbers from our previous example we get: 7 + 7 = 14 and then we enter it at the value of the Earth Point in the First Intermediate Destination.

No matter how obvious it may sound, a person's experience is formed as a result of their spiritual experiences, physical sensations and life lessons learned. And the same applies to a person's Destiny. Having come through various tests, having experienced emotional outbursts, having learned lessons in moral and physical endurance, the personality is formed and comes to perceive what is of true value (of course this is the ideal, but nevertheless!), acquires valuable experience and the opportunity to move on, having determined what is the right direction.

Thus, in order to determine what the energy of the First Destination is, you will need to add the energy of the Sky and the energy of the Earth to understand why, and for what purpose everything happens this way and not otherwise. In order to determine what is important to take with you on your journey.

The energy of the First Destination will be the sum of the numbers calculated for the Sky and the Earth. We can calculate it using the formula: SKY + EARTH = DESTINATION "For the Self". If we return to our example, we get: 16 + 14 = 30, 3 + 0 = 3. Therefore, the number for the energy that will inform us about the First Destiny of the person whose date of birth we have taken as an example is the number 3.

After passing through the first stage of life, regardless of whether the individual has passed all the tests and life lessons that have been prescribed for them, maturity and a new stage of development arrives. This is the period of the Second Destination — "For the World".

THE SECOND DESTINATION: 40–60 "FOR THE WORLD"

When we talk about the First Intermediate Destination "For the Self", we are talking about what the individual takes from life, what experience they have accumulated, what trials they have faced, and what they have done for themselves. When we talk about the "For the World" Destination, we learn what the individual needs to give back, and what contribution they need to make for the order of the world as a whole. This happens when the individual passes on their experience, or by having children or through the activities that they have dedicated themselves to. It is important to understand that this is the stage of giving back.

The individual passes through the Second Intermediate Destiny between the ages of 40-60. During this period, they put the experience they have accumulated into practise, they check their value systems and the resilience of their personalities and they change the world. It is during this time that they pay off the debts they owe. If something at some stage has happened, then it is during this period that the "boomerang" will fly back.

In order to calculate the Second Destination, we need to take a look at the Ancestral Square and use the numbers located on its end points.

The Second Destination sets the individual the task of establishing a connection with the world, becoming a part of it and pouring themselves into the universal flow of energy. Building relationships and connections is key. In order to calculate the energy that characterizes the ideas and tasks of the Second Destination, it is important to understand the energies of the male and female Ancestral Family Lines.

We can make this calculation using the following formulas: F + H = MALE, G + I = FEMALE Using the data from our example this comes to: 8 + 22 = 30, which we then simplify as follows: 3 + 0 = 3, 8 + 22 = 30, which is then further simplified: 3 + 0 = 3 So, we have ended up with two threes (3), which we enter in the "MALE" and "FEMALE" Points.

The energy of the male family line ("MALE") indicates what the men living in this world require from you, how your relationships with them will develop, what important lessons are to be learned at the Second Destination stage, and what experiences can be gained from men. The concept of "men" here includes not only the idea of one's social relations with men by gender but also ancestral family line programs with ancestors in the male family line. The most important of these, of course, is the relationship with the father and the development of relationships with male relatives.

If you look at it on the surface, then the energy of the male ancestral line also indicates how social relationships with men develop in general (it does not matter what the gender of the individual whose matrix is being considered is). It is possible to analyze what behavior strategies will be used for the formation of relationships with men in a given person, to identify the advice and life bonuses that can be used when relating with men, and to see the weaknesses that prevent an individual building productive relationships with them.

The energies of the Feminine Line ("WOMEN"), accordingly reveal the characteristics of relationships with women and indicate the tasks that need to be worked out on the female ancestral family line. The Arcana reveals the specifics of building relationships with women and provides clues as to which life bonuses you can use and what things you need to be more careful about regarding the energy in a given zone of the Destiny Code Matrix.

The energies of the "HUSBAND" and "WIFE" will tell you how to build relationships, taking into account the specific characteristics of the Arcana, and will help to determine exactly how a male or female audience responds to this person. This can be used to build personal relationships, in the search for love and to promote an individual's personality to the wider masses, if necessary. For example, if a person wants to become popular and famous, then you will need to analyze the Arcana for "WIFE" and "HUSBAND" and use the recommendations provided by these energies to build a strategy to promote this person.

In order to calculate the energy of the Second Destination, you need to add the total values of the Line of the male ancestral family line and the Line of the female ancestral family line using the formula HUSBAND + WIFE = Second Destination "For the World". When we enter the numbers from our example, we get: 3 + 3 = 6. The energy of the Second Destination in this case will be equal to 6.

In both Intermediate Destinations, all the Arcana can be used, from the 3rd to the 22nd.

THE OVERALL DESTINY

From their birth to their death, an individual travels from one point to another. A person's destiny is the main task of their whole life. If "Character" is the answer to the question "Who are you?", then Destiny is the answer to the question "Where are you going?"

When a person has learned the lessons that have been set for them, solved their spiritual and material tasks, has been able to realize him or herself as a person and become useful to the world, the time comes when he or she needs to understand: what all this is for? And at this stage, the individual is left to their own devices and the time comes for them to understand their raison d'etre and accept their personal Destiny.

Any experience consists of a certain amount of knowledge and practise, and therefore a person's Destiny is reduced to a common denominator, based on the experience gained during their passage through the stages of their formation. The difficulty or ease with which an individual comes to find the main meaning of their life depends on how well they have utilized their energies and how diligently they have completed the lessons of their life.

So, now let's complete the calculation of the Destiny Code Matrix for a person born on January 7, 1987, and see what their completed Destiny Code Matrix looks like.

In order to get the number for an individual's Overall Destiny, we need to add the figures for the First and Second Destinations using the formula FIRST + SECOND = OVERALL. We can substitute the numbers from our example 3 + 6 = 9.

The energy of the Overall Destinty is indicated at the final point that every person must come to sooner or later, whether they want to or not. A person's destiny is predetermined, but how a person travels towards it is a matter of choice. And by making this or that choice in life and by changing their preferences and taking actions, a person can only correct the route, where in the end the Truth will invariably be waiting for him or her.

Only the 3rd, 6th, 9th, 12th, 15th, 18th and 21st Arcana can be located in the Overall Destiny.

THE HEALTH CHART

When energy has not been implemented, one way or another it seeks an outlet and, when it can't find it, it settles down on the individual's "physical" aspect and begins to affect their health. Unrealized energy is more often than not the cause of the onset of illness, disease and poor health in humans. Often an illness is the final warning aimed at showing an individual that it's time to change something in their lives.

All health disorders initially occur at the energy level. But these subtle changes are not always possible to detect in a timely manner with the naked eye. The next stage is a malfunction in an individual's physical condition.

When an individual uses the Destiny Code, it provides them with the opportunity to find out which energies are affecting them with regard to this or that issue in life. And a person's health is also influenced by certain determined factors. Each person has a unique Destiny Code and, accordingly, the programs embedded in it are unique. The Health Map in our Destiny Code technique reveals which energies affect a person's physical and mental health and how.

According to the Destiny Code technique we are using, when calculating and analyzing Health Maps, the chakras and their place on the body are used to denote which energy centers are responsible for which specific organ or system of organs are used as designations.

The Health Map is recorded in a separate table consisting of four columns. As a rule, the first column is responsible for the physical manifestation of energy (the biosphere) — here the Arcanum is recorded in accordance with its position on the chakra and is located in the Destiny

Code Matrix on the Earth Line. The second column is responsible for the energy impact of the Arcanum on the overall flow of energy and is recorded in accordance with the location of the Arcanum on the Sky Line. The third column is the sum, the total influence of energies on the individual's health in accordance with the functions of the chakras in which these energies are located. Likewise, it is this zone that provides insights on how to influence the health of a specific organ in a person's body in accordance with the recommendations provided by a specific Arcanum in a specific chakra. The fourth column contains the name of the chakra to make it easier to read and interpret the Health Map.

The Arcana that are located at certain positions in the Destiny Code Matrix in accordance with the chakras are the energies that cause these chakras to vibrate. The result (the last line of the table) is the general field, the energy contained in the individual's biofield, its outer shell. In order to correct or strengthen an individual's overall physical and mental health, initially, they need to work with the resulting energies set down in the Health Map, but first, they will need to stabilize their condition and only then can they start working with each energy on each chakra separately.

THE COMPATIBILITY FORMULA

The Compatibility Formula is calculated by superimposing the individual matrices of the two partners and adding the Major Arcana of the rhombus and square together using the principle of matching the location of these Arcana relative to each other. Then, secondary zones can be calculated in this new compatibility matrix using the principle of adding the figures located next to them (in the same way the calculations are done in the personal Destiny Code Matrix.

The first thing you should do is take a look at the combined matrices is the Character Zone since this zone is the Compatibility Formula and specifies the nature of the relationship between partners. Next, you will need to take look at the Portrait Zone to see how the couple are viewed by those around them. In order to find out what unites partners, where and from what they can draw strength in order to reinforce their union and identify any possible causes of contention, you will need to carefully analyze the three Arcana of the Higher Essence. For deeper work on the relationships between partners and in order to determine their common karmic program, attention should be paid to the compatibility matrix's Karmic Tail.

The Compatibility Formula can be studied in the context of the relations between married or unmarried partners. The Compatibility Formula helps you to assess the nature of relationships with anyone: children, parents, friends, colleagues or just with a potential acquaintance. It is a unique and versatile tool that can be used for various purposes in different areas of life.

CHAPTER IV. ENERGIES

THE 22 ARCANA OF DESTINY

Each number or value in the Destiny Code Matrix bears a unique energy. Each point in the matrix defines specific areas of a person's life, and the energies represented by the numbers in these zones affect those areas of life, respectively. Each of the energies is special and unlike any of the others, having certain plus and minus points, each energy makes each individual person different from other individuals, and their unique combinations in the matrix make each person's destiny totally unique.

The energies used in the Destiny Code technique are interpreted by using the Major Arcana Tarot cards. The classic Tarot deck's features and characteristics are extremely metaphorical and, at first glance, it may seem difficult to transpose their meanings when reading and interpreting the Destiny Code. But first appearances can be deceptive. It is worth noting here that our methodology and technique are systematic and based on a specific structure. In order to understand what tasks have been assigned to an individual in their current incarnation, it is important to be able to perceive the essential features of the Arcana and their main messages. Advanced practitioners learn to get a feeling for the energies, to understand their essence and to catch their vibrations.

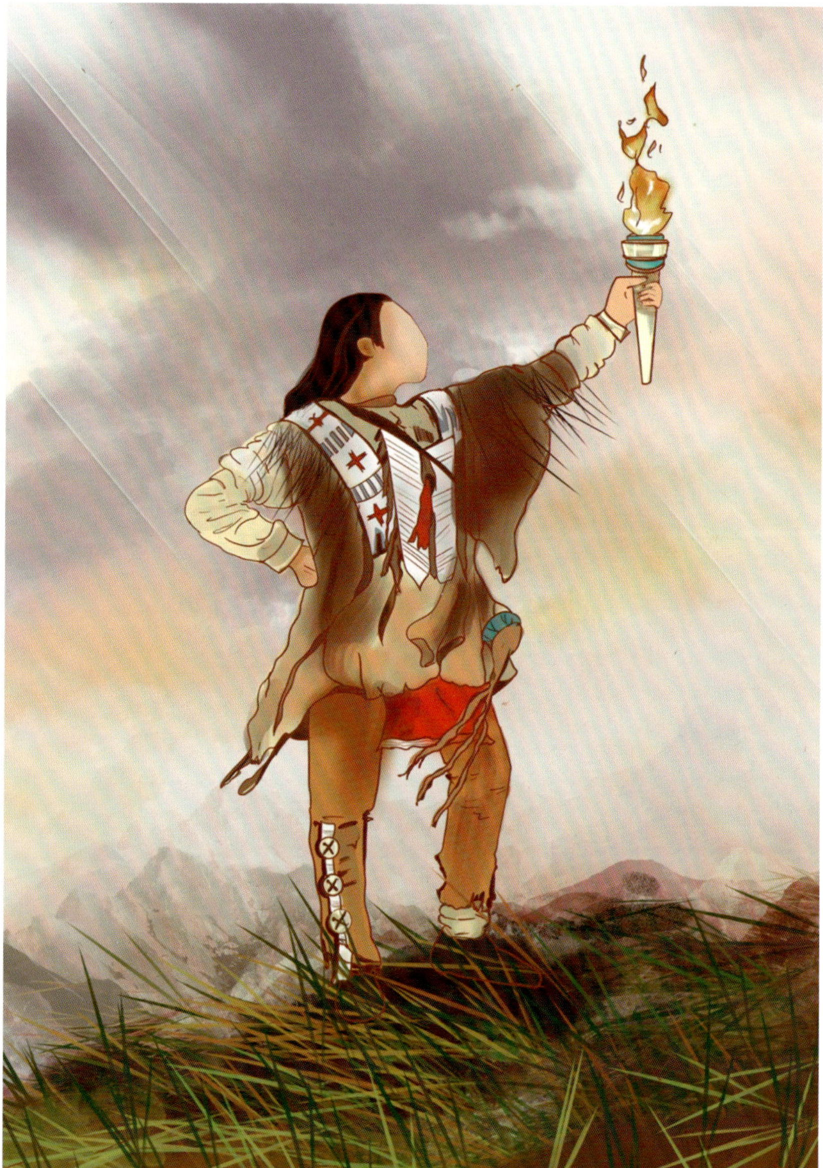

ARCANUM 1. THE PIONEER

The Great Spirit has not yet flown past that place —
Which lacks the Spark of the Fire of Wisdom,
Only they will go
Beyond the horizon and distant parts
Who have found Their Way in the presence of the Spirit.
Who in the dark, without moonlight,
Pass through the road of slumber
Holding the Fire in their outstretched hand.
A Great Warrior, the brave son of the Eagle.
The Chosen One
Who is the first to see the Essence.

POWER – IDEAS – DISCOVERIES

In the Destiny Code Matrix, it is extremely rare to encounter the energy of the first card in the Major Arcana. As a rule, individuals who are born on the first day of the month or in January possess it. The only zones in the matrix that the energy of the First Arcanum can be located in are the Portrait, the Higher Essence zones or the Health Map.

Individuals who possess the First Arcanum are explorers and pioneers. They have the ability to come up with and promote unique ideas and unusual ways of implementing them. Pioneers are first and foremost the sort of people who strive to always be first in everything they do and everywhere they are.

In the Tree of the Sephiroth, this is the pinnacle of human spiritual development. A soul that is endowed with the first energy is no longer a young one, and in its previous incarnations, it will have passed through the lessons of the 21st Arcana and mastered the tasks set. In this incarnation, the Soul is called upon to realize all the experience it has accumulated and become a leader, a king (queen), open up new boundaries, invent, exceed expectations and make the impossible possible.

Everyone who possesses Pioneer Energy in the Destiny Code Matrix must first of all understand and accept the following important features of their lives: A Pioneer is a person of unique abilities and talents, it is important for them to actualize their power and strength, they tend to take risks lightly and with ease and whatever endeavor they undertake will be successful, Pioneers define the limits of their possibilities for themselves.

If the First Arcanum is located in the Inspiration zone, then this person is endowed with a trump card in life, so to speak. For people like this, their possibilities depend only on their desires and they can achieve everything they want.

If the First Energy is in the Portrait zone, then this indicates that these individuals' circle and the World as a whole see them as all-powerful, a risk-taker, courageous and fearless, although in fact, they may be nothing of the sort. These individuals' inner "I" may doubt their abilities. The weaker the faith they have in themselves and the stronger the fear of possible failure, the more the First Arcanum will enter into a state of negativity, and the influence and strength of spirit may turn out to be only an illusion and mask. But one way or another, those around these individuals will sense their potential even when they have yet to come to realize it themselves.

The card of the First Arcanum in the Tarot deck is a man depicted with a torch in his hands, standing above and in front of everyone. He is endowed with a strong will, broad views and has the ability to generate important and much-needed ideas. Ingenuity, genius and an infinity of possibilities are inherently bestowed on this person from above.

WATCHWORDS

- Nothing is impossible!
- Give yourself permission to be allowed.
- You are on top of everything: your opportunities, your circumstances and the people around you.
- Just take the first step and success will follow.

Those with the First Arcanum in their Destiny Code occupy an active position in life. One of the characteristic features of people with Pioneer energy is their self-confidence and healthy egotism, regardless of the Arcana located in their Character zone.

Without exception, everyone endowed with the First Energy feels forever young, regardless of their age. They are drawn to young people and tend to socialize with them.

It is important to know that Ones always need to strive to realize their ideas. Otherwise, their energy can become negative and their strengths become weaknesses. If an idea comes into their heads, they really need to make it a reality.

FINANCES

Because the First Arcanum cannot be located in the Finance or Material Karma zone, this energy cannot be used to adjust and improve an individual's financial situation. Nevertheless, the energy of the Pioneer provides its owner with one extra trump card. Amazingly, Ones are never in want of money and always have just as much as they need!

Ones are highly professional whatever their field of activity and their professional development is solely dependent on their success as an individual. At the same time, publicity is an integral part of these people's careers. Regardless of their chosen profession, much of their work depends on their ability to speak well and keep their audience's attention. As a rule, people with this energy become lawyers, politicians, managers at various levels, entrepreneurs, doctors of sciences and sales representatives for exclusive goods and services.

People endowed with the First Energy in the Inspiration Zone could easily set up and successfully promote a master class on a book having only read it once. Those who, in addition to having the First Energy, have a Major Fifth Energy in the Destiny Code matrix would also benefit from this kind of professional strategy model.

Ones will always strive to work for a special audience and create special things. These people are pioneers in every sense of the notion of being "First". The uniqueness and novelty of an idea is more important for people with a One in their matrix than for anyone else. And indeed, what do they need to be modest about — after all, it is they who the universe has endowed with superpowers to create something special and innovative in this life.

Ones try to keep the secrets of their skills and talents close to their chest and not reveal them to anyone. And this is perfectly normal. The exceptions to this rule are those individuals who, in addition to the First Arcanum, possess a Major Ninth energy in their matrix, whose specific set task is to transfer knowledge to the World. In this instance, it is important to recognize this and bring their Hermit's Arcanum to a "+" state, by getting them to work through their karmic program.

HEALTH

First Arcanum people have the ability to heal others using various forms of alternative medicine, and when treating their own ailments they have a tendency to use these methods on themselves. They can sense other people's energy well and have the ability to cleanse it of negativity. This can be done using magical rituals (provided that they have discovered these abilities in themselves) or on an intuitive level (for example, initiating heart-to-heart talks and providing support in the form of a friendly touch or an arm around the shoulder).

A person with th e First Arcanum in their Destiny Code Matrix will often be well-versed in the properties of medicinal herbs and have a strong sense of the power of nature.

First Energy people have a high risk of developing problems with their eyes and vision. From a karmic point of view, this is because these souls have passed through all the lessons of each of the 21 Arcana in their previous incarnations and their eyes have become overloaded by the sheer volume of what they have seen and have now simply become tired of looking and observing. But practice shows that as their First Energy is actuated, their vision becomes restored with age. All they need to do is fulfill the task that has been set them by the Universe.

All illnesses and diseases are derived by the head and come from them. When the energy of an individual's internal potential is not realized, that energy passes into their physical body.

People with the First Energy in their Health Chart correspondingly suffer primarily from problems with the head, the brain, blood vessels, vision and hearing. The vulnerability of these organs for these individuals can often cause all sorts of illnesses and diseases.

RELATIONSHIPS

The energy of the First Arcanum is a very special one and is endowed by the Universe to allow the individual to accumulate and work out their experience to increase their self-knowledge. The first energy cannot be located on the Prosperity Line or the Relationship and Partnership Zone. However, people with the First Arcanum in their Destiny Code Matrix are endowed with certain qualities that are clearly manifested in their love and partnership relationships.

INDICATIONS THAT THIS ENERGY IS IN A –

- An inflated sense of their self-importance — when a person puts himself above others to their detriment.
- A tendency to be harsh and rude.
- A lack of confidence and self-doubt (this can have a catastrophically destructive effect, with a high risk of manifesting itself on the physical level).

- Avoiding all publicity and society in general (thus leaving the main karmic tasks designated for this First Energy unfulfilled and unrealized).
- A tendency to concentrate their attention on the boundaries of what is permitted (instead of the opposite, thereby blocking their development paths).
- Being weak-willed when it comes to discipline and endurance.
- A refusal to realize themselves to improve other areas of their lives (for example, regarding their relationships, family and children but, in this instance, it is important to take look at the Destiny Code holistically and take into account the influence and tasks imposed by the other energies in the individual's matrix).

INDICATIONS THAT THIS ENERGY IS IN A +

- Faith in yourself and your abilities.
- Communication and openness.
- The birth of ideas and the effectiveness and energy with which they are implemented.
- A comprehension of the unique and significant contribution they can make to their professional field (the individual understands the potential weight of their contribution to the development of their chosen career and takes responsibility for this).
- An innovative view of the world (the individual develops the abilities endowed to him or her by the Universe to invent and discover something new).
- A healthy egotism.
- A persistence in advancing their position (regardless of the opinions of others).

KARMIC TASKS

- To realize their strength and capabilities;
- To learn to take responsibility;
- To keep their egotism and sense of superiority under control;
- To be open to everything new, to be creative;
- To take risks and get themselves out of their comfort zone;
- To learn to forgive the mistakes and misdeeds of others;

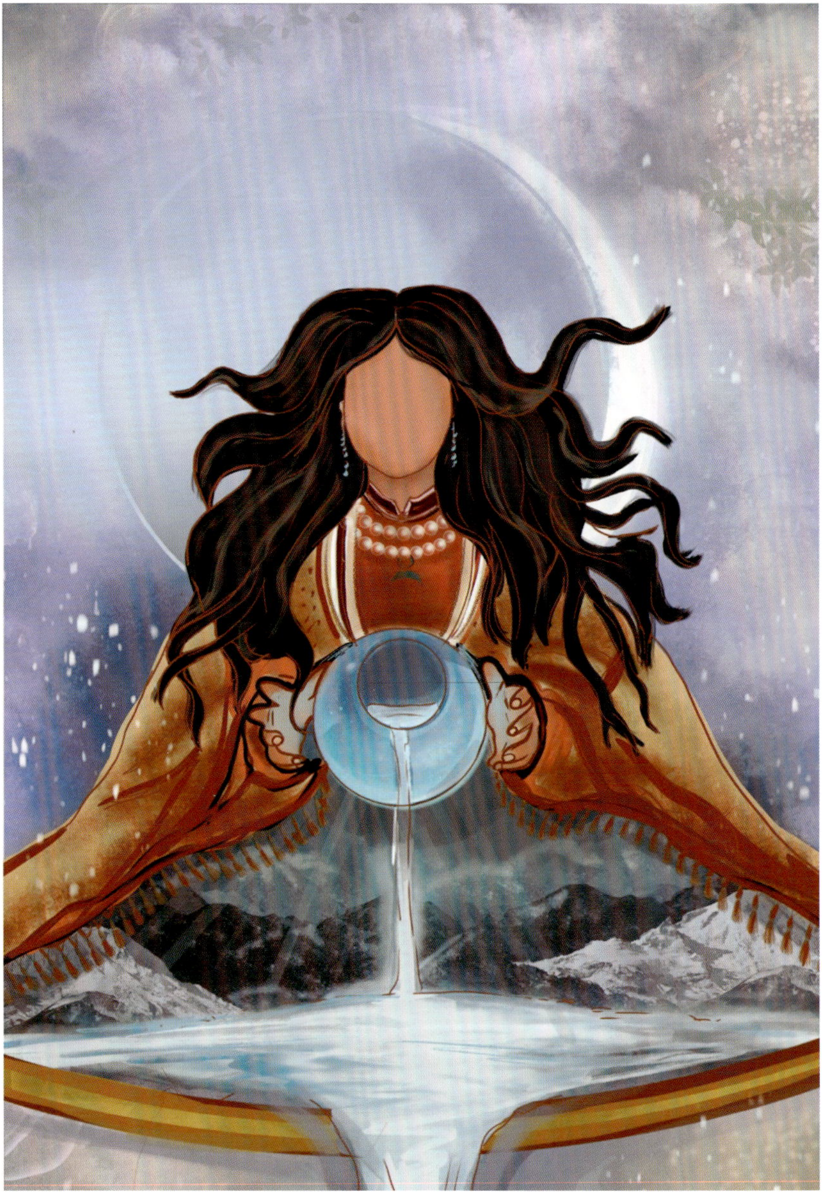

ARCANUM 2. THE SECRET

> Quietly and softly starting
> Like a stream in the high mountains,
> Syllable by syllable, Old man Mdovino
> Composes a new tale.
> Tell me a tale of truth, old man,
> What the winds have revealed to you
> From distant wild Dakota parts
> What news did they carry?
> Of rough river rapids,
> Of waters deep and merciless,
> Of peyote that stupefies the mind
> Of mothers, fathers and wives.
> Do not be angry, soulless shaman,
> Will our children return
> The will of those who are faithful in heart to their fates.
> To our native land from the ends of the Earth?

ILLUSION – INTUITION – INFORMATION

Mature Souls. They have come to the earth in this incarnation to be the keepers and revealers of secrets. People with the Second Energy in their Destiny Code are not just endowed with intuition, they are also masterfully skilled at using it.

In the Tarot deck, the Second Major Arcanum card is the High Priestess — the servant of the cult. A woman who is dedicated to secret knowledge and who has the power to initiate others into this knowledge.

Second Energy People are drawn to all things secret (to the mystical and earthly in equal measure). They are fascinated by puzzles and riddles and love to solve them, they gravitate towards the search for truth, hidden meanings, intrigues, gossip and other people's secrets.

My practice has taught me that people endowed with the Second Energy in their Destiny Code are very mysterious people. Those around them and in their circle know and understand very little about their true thoughts, reasoning and motives. They are very secretive people who take enormous pleasure in unraveling others' secrets and take no less pleasure in creating their own. For them, life is an illusion — an image or a narrative that exists to facilitate their self-realization.

With Second Energy people nothing is as simple as it might first appear. This is not to say that the mysteries they possess are nothing more than the fruit of their over-developed imaginations. Quite the opposite! The thing is that the Second Arcanum leaves the people under its influence with no way of living otherwise. Perhaps this is because to reveal, keep and convey those things that are hidden and sacred, those things that have their own path and their own hour — is precisely one of their karmic tasks.

The Second Energy can only exist in the Portrait, Higher Essence and Material Karma zones of the Destiny Code Matrix. In terms of the contemporaries in our lifetimes, the only people that can possibly possess the Second Energy in the Material Karma zone are those who were born in the year 2000.

People with this energy in their Destiny Code Matrix are utterly different to everyone else. Their deep desire to absorb the unknown often makes Second Energy people appear to have frozen in space, time and reality. They appear to have no determinate age, no immediately obvious gender, a certain detachment from reality and to be wandering in the clouds.

The New Age philosophy is probably what best describes how Twos perceive the world. Knowledge is stronger than conventions, the spiritual is higher than the material.

Men with the Second Energy in the Portrait or the Higher Essence zones are endowed with a particularly pronounced softness of character. Outwardly, one might well be under the impression that they are completely detached from reality. They can talk at great length, philosophize, look for the causes and consequences of events, and in their picture of the world, everything is logical and comprehensible. But the more they "perceive truths" and immerse others into them, the greater the number of questions they ask themselves. In particular, those around them may seriously question the adequacy of their thinking. People endowed with the Second Energy have many of the following characteristics:

- Spirituality (a prioritization of the mental over the physical);
- Introversion (an immersion in their own personal world);

- A remoteness from reality (which might even manifest itself as a refusal to accept reality at all);
- Wisdom and depth of knowledge;
- Slowness (this can even manifest itself at the physical level;)
- Coldness (a certain detachment from emotions and expressing them).

WATCHWORDS

Second Energy People are philosophers to the core. Depending on their caste, their wisdom can take numerous manifestations. But one way or another, whether the situation in question concerns simple earthly issues or matters on a truly universal scale, the view held will be approximately the same.

It is important to understand that the key thing about Twos is that they are not just endowed with the opportunity to work with their impressive spiritual resources but to examine and test themselves in the context of the reality they find themselves in. After all, you have to remember that energies are very capricious things and can easily flick from a state of hyperminus to a state of hyperplus – like a pendulum swinging from one extreme to another. But the energy of the Second Arcanum is, first and foremost, an illusion and there is a danger that sometimes people under its influence do not understand the state they are in and how they should proceed further: towards a state of disbelief and closed diffidence or towards a leap of faith, searching for the truth and flying far away into parallel realities.

- Pinch me! And tell me this is really happening!
- Strength lies in the thirst for knowledge. Weakness lies in its concealment.
- The truth is somewhere nearby.
- All secrets will be revealed.
- Information is an opportunity and a resource.

FINANCES

Twos are extremely ambiguous when it comes to finances. For a more specific idea of their attitudes to money, you need to consider the links between a double-up or a triple-up of their energies in the Material Karma zone. But what can be said for sure about Second Arcanum people is that money and material values are not as important to them as information and the desire to possess it, which they can use to open and strengthen their Monetary energy.

Twos always find it hard to use the deep knowledge they possess in everyday life. They are not very practical when it comes to work of a systematic nature as they are not very down to earth and their thoughts start to stray towards higher things. Entrepreneurship is not their element, with the exception only of those cases where the goals are educational or, on the contrary, perceptive in nature. Every sphere of activity should contain an element of spiritual development and the desire to get to the nuts and bolts of a matter.

Second Arcanum people attract others who want to speak out about something or share a secret. They act like a magnet, drawing out of others what is often hidden from the majority of people, whether it is a personal secret, a confession or some hot gossip. In their turn, Twos put up no resistance to these advances because they themselves are fascinated by what the latest "artifact" of information they are about to receive might be.

Twos are consummate professionals when it comes to the business of investigation. They are often brilliant detectives, investigators, spies, lawyers and secret agents.

Given their innate craving for the truth, Twos are often drawn to professions such as historian, archaeologist, biologist, anthropologist, psychologist, psychoanalyst or psychiatrist. They are also happy working in the fields of science or education. Perhaps the desire to engage in a particular activity can arise in childhood after an individual has had a dream about it and later becomes precisely this sort of specialist when they became an adult.

HEALTH

The health problems that Second Arcanum people suffer from are largely related to their mental condition. They are more prone to psychological breakdowns, depression and nervous disorders than others. But it is always important to remember that a person's health directly depends on the state of their energy — whether it is in a state of positivity "+" or negativity "-".

Women endowed with the Second Energy often have problems with their menstrual cycle and conceiving and bearing children as well as problems with their gastrointestinal tract.

But apart from this, Second Energy people do not have karmic health programs. On the whole, most of them are likely to be in excellent physical health. However, there could well be problems regarding the state of their spirit (soul).

Twos have the ability to heal with the power of the spirit. These are precisely those rare cases when spiritual practices can completely heal physical diseases however complex they might be. But beware! I make a point of asking all the Twos that I see to use their common sense when it comes to their health and always insist that their first call should always be to a qualified health professional.

Very often, the underlying causes of illnesses in Twos are symptoms that affect a person over many years, gradually harming their bodies and health. Likewise, the presence of the Second Arcanum in the Health zone or in the Health Map indicates the presence of hidden, slowly developing diseases that do not betray any immediately obvious symptoms.

RELATIONSHIPS

When talking about emotions and the manifestation of feelings, it is important to understand that Twos see the World in a completely different way to others (regarding people, things, life and everything in general). But their system of perception is arranged in such a way that the "truth" for them is carefully concealed deep inside them and no one except them has access to it. Except for those rare exceptions, when they encounter a kindred Soul on their journey through life.

Second Energy people take a very close look at potential partners and the process can take a very long time. Very often, they won't allow others anywhere near them. But sometimes, when they find themselves in difficult situations, they can fall into promiscuous liaisons out of a sense of hopelessness. This behavior for them is a bit like a cry from the heart. An extreme form of behavior that is contrary to what is essentially true about them.

INDICATIONS THAT THIS ENERGY IS IN A –

- A constant struggle and search for balance.
- A sense of a lack of talent, inhibiting the desire to move forward.
- Vanity.

- A desire to seek popularity.
- A dependence on others' opinions.
- Hysterical behavior (sometimes inappropriately hysterical).
- Mistrustfulness.
- Substituting love for an unhealthy obsession.
- Manic behavior.
- Organizing their relationships to suit their own convenience, often trying to live at someone else's expense (in their marriage, with their parents or with their children).
- An unwillingness to work.
- A tendency to manipulate information.
- A desire to seek out intrigue and gossip.
- Being envious of other people's lives (especially the lives led by others on TV or social media).

INDICATIONS THAT THIS ENERGY IS IN A +

- A philosophical outlook on life.
- The ability to get to the bottom of things.
- The ability to draw valuable information out of others. The ability to look at things from an unusual angle.
- Critical thinking.
- A refusal to perceive life in linear terms.
- A subtle sense of the truth.
- The ability to listen to others.
- The ability to keep a secret for many years.
- The ability to remain loyal to an idea.
- Not overly scrupulous (this can be both a plus and a minus).
- A certain slowness in decision-making (mostly a plus).
- The ability to create an illusion.
- The ability to bring out sincerity (the truth) in other people.
- The ability to heal the body and soul.

KARMIC TASKS

- To prevent the transmission of false information;
- To learn to keep the secrets of others;
- To develop intuition;
- To learn to sense the energies of other people;

- To collect and transfer useful and necessary knowledge;
- To accept reality.

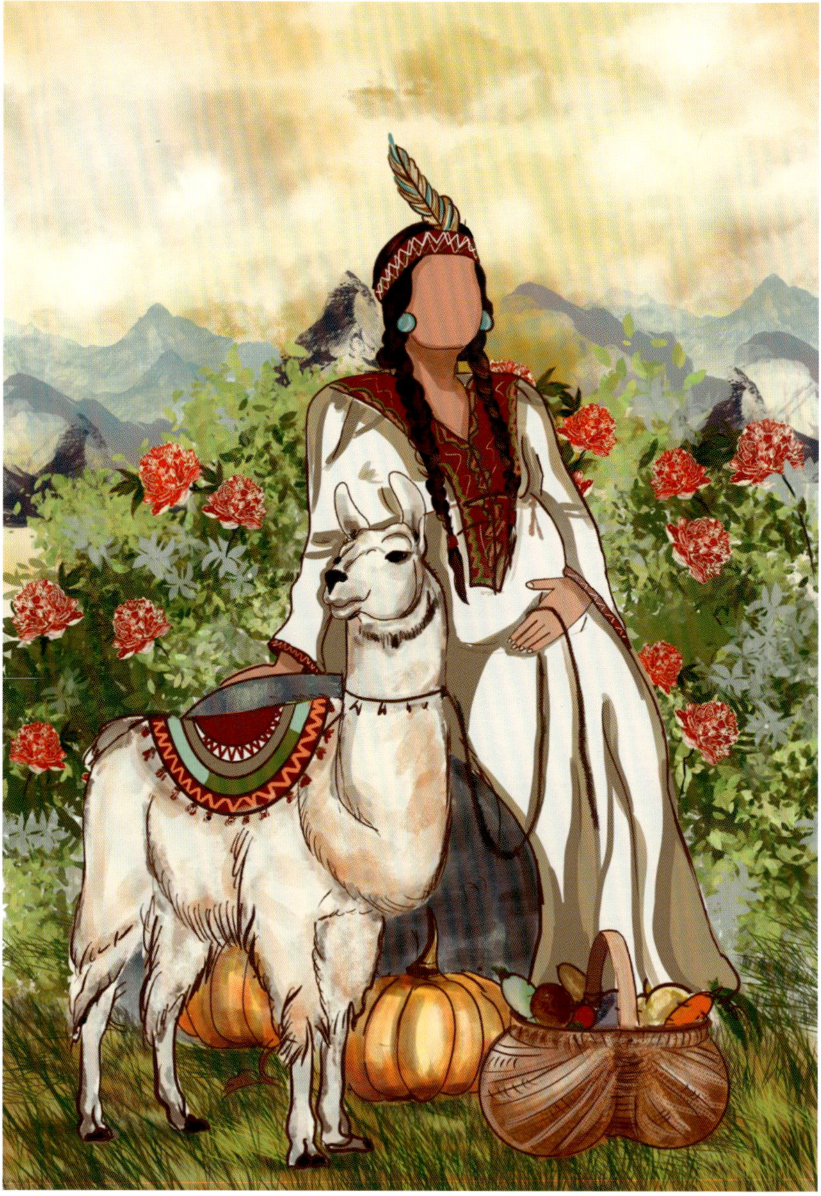

ARCANUM 3. FEMININITY

> We thank you mother earth
> For the fertile meadows and wild forests,
> For the fish that you send up the river estuaries,
> For the prairie with its astonishing beauty.
> We thank you for the sunshine
> For warmth, humility and generosity,
> For the fact that over hundreds and thousands of years
> We have been so generously warmed by your care.

TENDERNESS — FERTILITY — BEAUTY

The energy of Femininity is the manifestation of all that is feminine, beautiful, delicate and finely arranged. The energy of fertility, nurturing and creation.

In the Tarot deck, the Third Arcanum is the Empress. The mother and mistress. The woman who gives care and warmth.

The presence of the Third Energy in the Destiny Code Matrix indicates an unbreakable bond between an individual and their mother and the feminine in their family in general (including grandmothers, great-grandmothers, aunts, sisters and all the womenfolk in their family group). It is important throughout life to have a good and stable relationship with your mother and if there are problems in this respect, then the energy of the Third Arcanum can lead an individual into a negative state throughout their life in general. This can affect women when "coming to terms with and accepting their femininity" and lead to a weakness of character in men.

Having children is more important for Third Energy people than others. Caring for their children is on a different level for them than just being a parent. Their mission to raise and get their children standing on their own two feet is something they need to work out as a part of a personal karmic task set by the Third Arcanum. It is very important for these individuals to "nurture" something and a child is the ideal option for this purpose. Providing care and protection, tenderness and motherhood (or fatherhood, if we are talking about a man), enveloping the object of your care with your own energy are the most pronounced characteristics of this energy of Femininity. In general, people with the Third Energy in the major Zones of their Destiny Code matrix are best advised to have a lot of children and not stop — the more they have, the better!

Everyone who possesses the Third Arcanum is subject to female energy. If the subject is a woman, then it is important that they accept the woman within and use all the advantages that being a member of the fair sex provides in everyday life. It is important for Third Arcanum women to take good care of themselves, to be beautiful and well-groomed, and to choose feminine-looking and feminine-shaped clothes. They need to develop talents related to those things that are delicate and beautiful (for example, to be able to professionally apply make-up, to understand art, to play musical instruments).

Men with the Third Arcanum in their Destiny Code Matrix very often have feminine character traits. They are flexible, wise and sometimes cunning people. Often the softness and subtlety of their characters are seen as weakness and a lack of clarity about their position in life. But this is not the case. Third Energy men make great parents and loving and caring partners. Their strength lies in the fact that they put their interests to one side for later, leaving other significant elements in life as a priority (for example, children, a family, a partner, or an important business to which they can devote themselves, raising it like a "child").

There are also men among them who prefer to live off the backs of women. They have no scruples about shifting the responsibility for the maintenance of the family to their partners.

Some Third Energy men choose to stay at home, managing the household and taking care of the domestic side of the family's welfare, or even choosing to take paternity leave and devote themselves entirely to raising their children. They can live with their parents for a long time, or look for easy ways to live off government benefits, for example, or look for some similar arrangement where they can make themselves feel secure without having to make an effort.

If the Third Energy is located in the second half of their Overall Destiny, then this could indicate a high probability of having children late (children born to parents over the age of 30).

If the Third Arcanum is located in the Karmic Tail, then in accordance with the theory of reincarnation, this suggests that this person was a woman in their previous incarnation. In order to analyze the negative (complex) aspects that might affect this person's current incarnation, it is also important to take a good look at what other energies are located in the Triple-up of energies in the Karmic Tail.

When the Third Energy is in the Higher Essence, this means that a person will inspire and be inspired by beautiful things, looking after themselves and socializing with women. These people often possess a very subtle sense of perception. For example, people with a Three in the Highest Essence are often able to distinguish subtle smells, see subtle shades, and detect subtle changes in the moods of others. Men with this female energy in the Highest Essence know how to make women happy: by giving them a beautiful bouquet of flowers, decorating the house with rose petals or surprising them with an unexpected night out.

WATCHWORDS
- My children are my most precious resource.
- Beauty is a terrifying force.
- Caring and acceptance are the key to well-being.

FINANCES

Since the Third Arcanum is aligned with female energies, then its influence on an individual's financial situation should correspond with all the female qualities and features in the Three's professional activities.

The most favorable activities for these people will be those related to working in a team largely made up of women, or working with and for women. Professional fields related to beauty, beautiful things, aesthetics, as well as everything related to children and the relationship between parents and children. This could be work in the state and public sphere, where issues of guardianship and the care of children are involved.

Professional activities related to organizing children and women's entertainment are also propitious for those with female energy in their Destiny Code Matrix. The creation and promotion of goods and services where the target audience is women and children (children's toys, clothes, cosmetics). Creating works of art, tailoring and creating fashion and jewelry and even simply being creative are all promising fields that can provide Threes with a good income.

Any activity related to the cultivation and breeding of animals and plants will also be a successful venture if undertaken by Threes.

In addition, the presence of the Third Arcanum in the Destiny Code Matrix may indicate that this person is in receipt of a passive income from their children or parents and even that they are able to live off it.

HEALTH

The energy of the Third Arcanum is an indicator of inherited diseases through the female line. Naturally, if the energies are in a negative state, then there is a high probability that there will be problems with childbearing and a higher risk of conditions that affect women. If a Three is suffering from health problems, it is important to work out their relationships in the female line of the family.

If the Third Energy is located in an individual's Svadhisthana, they often find themselves prone to headaches and migraines. They also suffer a high risk of experiencing nervous breakdowns, mental disorders and hysteria. In other words, Threes need to pay close attention to and take great care of their nerves, because, as the latest scientific research shows, the human body does not restore and replenish its nerve cells.

RELATIONSHIPS

FOR WOMEN:

If you are a person with the Third Energy in their Relationship zone, first and foremost, you need a partner with a finely tuned level of mental and spiritual organization. You need a man who wants children and is committed to taking care of you and the family, which he wants to have. Your partner will be on good terms with his mother (maybe even to a slightly scary degree), but he will also build a secure relationship with your mother.

Your ideal partner will not be a workaholic or a 'go-getter'. More likely, he will be a reliable family man who is calm and faithful.

Women with the Third Energy in their Prosperity Line should be advised to be careful when choosing a partner, as there is a chance of succumbing to temptation and falling into the arms of a philandering male sponger. This is especially common with women who have a Major Ninth Energy in their Destiny Code Matrix.

If a woman has the Third and Fifteenth energies in their Prosperity Line and Karmic Tail, there is a high degree of probability that they might become pregnant after a fleeting one-night stand in their early sexual life or pregnant after rape.

FOR MEN:

The ideal partner for a Third Energy man will be the embodiment of feminine perfection and the partners that they will choose are often extremely beautiful and feminine. An important criterion when choosing a spouse is that they should have a good relationship with the mother of their potential partner. Or sometimes, it is even possible that the couple might meet through the good offices of the mother.

INDICATIONS THAT THIS ENERGY IS IN A −

- They feel upset and insulted by their mother.
- They reject the woman within themselves (if a woman).
- They fall ill and get rid of their pets and let their house plants die.
- They become less attractive.
- They become indifferent to all manifestations of beauty.
- They exhibit a lack of desire to have children.
- An unhealthy obsession with everyday chores (cleaning, washing, cooking).

INDICATIONS THAT THIS ENERGY IS IN A +

- Femininity (for women).
- Sensitivity and attentiveness towards others.
- The desire to nurture or create something (a child, a project, a garden, a business).
- Strong bonds with their mother or other women in the family.

KARMIC TASKS:

- To bring beauty and sensitivity into the world;
- To learn to adapt;
- To create beautiful material things;
- To correct the family karma along the female line;
- To accept their relationship with their partner as it is, maintaining the union;
- To value and appreciate the connection with the mother;
- To continue the family and strengthen it (to have many children).

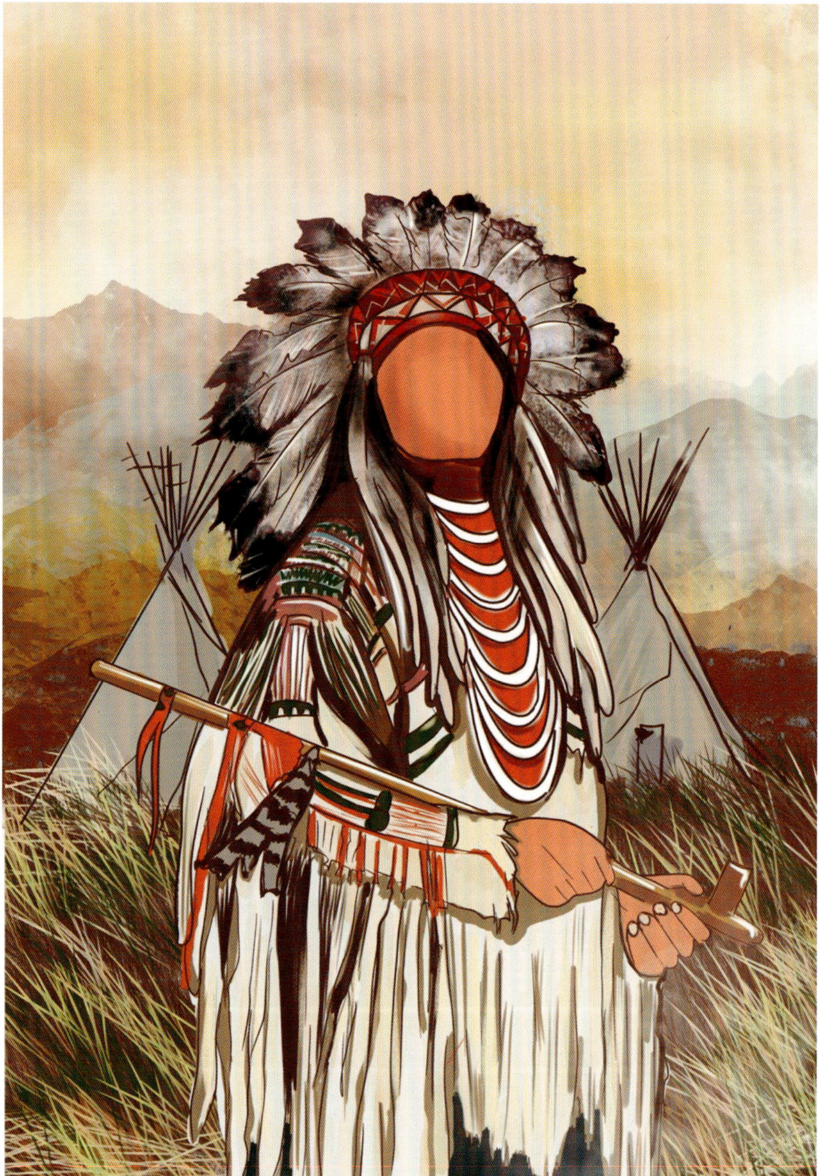

ARCANUM 4. MASCULINITY

> You are the bear — the master of the forest —
> the guardian of the sons of the Cherokee.
> Our brave warrior, our Sequoia,
> Our explorer and protector,
> The chronicler of our days.
> As wise and great as an oak,
> Standing among the aspens, birches and firs
> A great Chief leading
> His people on the Road of Tears.

LEADER — FATHER — HEAD OF THE HOUSE

In the Tarot deck, the Fourth Arcanum is the Emperor. The Arcanum of male energy, self-sufficient people who need (and this is important!) to take everything into their own hands. They are leaders in life, striving for power and able to defend their position and standing in life. They are the embodiment of true male power externally, physically and spiritually.

Individuals with the Fourth energy in the Major Zones of their Destiny Code Matrix are guided primarily by a sense of duty. They are leaders and protectors. More than any other type, it is very important for them to have everything under strict control, which, incidentally, can often lead to them breaching and violating other people's boundaries and interests. But in this instance, by taking such actions, the person in possession of this male energy instead of bringing negativity into his karma does quite the opposite. By exercising and strengthening the energy inherent in the Fourth Arcanum, individuals in possession of this energy will, in turn, strengthen their personalities and open up new opportunities for their self-actualization.

Fourth Energy people are often quite dispassionate and unemotional. But they will never abandon their own in a fight and will always take responsibility when difficult situations arise. Whatever the case, they need clarity, pragmatism and an understanding of the reality going around them without any concealed meanings or contexts as well as the need to unravel complex situations and narrative strands.

Fourth Energy people are very often used to a high degree of independence since early childhood. It's a very good thing if at a young age they are allowed to understand the values of life, the need to defend their interests and to learn the skills needed to care for and protect others. If a young boy with Fourth Arcanum energy is raised by a man from childhood, teaching him about responsibility, survival skills and how to make money, this will form a basis which will provide this child with the opportunity to achieve great success in the future. If the situation is the opposite, then a young Four might find himself unable to learn how to actualize himself from childhood, his energy might turn negative, and subsequently, it will be difficult to return it to a positive state. This is because male energy by its very nature is unusually strong. It is like a locomotive train or an icebreaking ship — extremely powerful and heavy. It is difficult to set it in motion but once it is, it is almost impossible to stop or reverse it, or it will at least take a great deal of effort and time to do so.

From early childhood, Fours need to be brought up as leaders and not subordinates. Regardless of whether they are a girl or a boy. A child with male energy needs to be told from the earliest age that: "You are the most important", "You are the head of the family", "You will achieve all your goals thanks to your strength and 'can-do' attitudes."

There are several karmic features that need to be taken in to consideration with Fours. Remember! Fourth Arcanum people are very bad at accepting help (especially material support) from their mother and other women (from early childhood, a mother should not just give their child money or gifts — these are things that they need to feel are deserved or have been earned), living together with their mother or at the expense of another woman can have an extremely negative impact on their lives (in this instance, Fourth Arcanum men's energy can become negative, which in my experience will seek an outlet in the form of aggression, addiction and domestic violence), it is also important for them to maintain close relations with their father (or sons). It is important for a child with the Fourth Energy in their matrix to have an extremely positive image of their father (grandfather, great-grandfather), as this is their karmic program for their male energy — the strengthening and protection of their Family line. Accordingly, it is important for adults to devote a large share of their attention to bringing up their sons.

Once again, it is worth mentioning that the main thing we're talking about here is leadership. A person with the Fourth Energy is first and foremost a leader in everything they do and everywhere they are. He has to be in charge of his activities, in charge of his family, an authority for others, in charge of his life, in which he needs to make every decision and take every step himself. If Fours find themselves in a supporting position (as a subordinate, or without being able to demonstrate their independence and responsibility), their energy does not allow them to achieve their possible potential and can lead to a polar opposite state of personality and specifically — despotic behavior, aggressiveness and a lack of success in and satisfaction with their lives. When a Four's energy is in a negative state, it can eat them from the inside, as a rule, venting itself in negativity and violence on those in their immediate surroundings who are weaker than them such as junior colleagues, women, children and animals).

In order to nurture the Fourth Energy, it is very important that the person in possession of it is in charge of their home. That they are the protector and guardian of the family. That there are sufficient funds, cleanliness and order in the house (food on the table, no leaks anywhere and bills paid). It is very important for them to feel that they are responsible and not shifting this responsibility onto others. They need to be on good terms with their father and involved in bringing up their sons (or a male successor).

If the male energy is present in a woman's Character zone, then they need to be able to determine the balance between all the major energies located in their Destiny Code Matrix. It is important for them not to be forced into taking on the role of the "man" of the house. This energy should provide them with a resource to unlock their potential but not be a source of harm to the person in possession of it. It often happens that female Fours "unman" the men in their immediate circle — not allowing them to get close, they crush them with the strength of their character or authority, which automatically brings this energy into a negative state. A woman with the Fourth Arcanum needs to be in charge of her life, to be a leader and a strong personality in life but this energy needs to be used in the right way. For example, they need to demonstrate their ability to protect or take on responsibility for their partner but not demand more from their men than they are able to give.

All of the above can be attributed to men with the Fourth Arcanum in their matrix. A very active male energy can crush those in its immediate environment, which likewise blocks their resources. Their high demands on the world are often only that — demands and not a stimulus to action.

Fourth Energy men and women need to be active but not critical or too demanding of action from others in return.

WATCHWORDS

- You are the master of your life.
- Power is not given, you have to take it for yourself.
- Strength is not asserting your superiority over others. Strength is about your responsibility for others.
- You are responsible for those around you.
- Your father is your past. Your son is your future.

FINANCES

Perhaps the most important point when trying to understand how the Fourth Energy affects an individual's financial matters and their level of material wealth is that Fours must always be responsible for everything and conscientiously answer for every action they take.

The fourth Arcanum strives for power and prosperity, therefore, the needs of life and material desires are inherently critical for people endowed with its energy. They desire a lot of money, a good house, expensive things and high status, as this strengthens their authority. And, incidentally, it not only strengthens their standing in the eyes of their circle and wider society (as a natural indicator of their success), but also for a Four these feelings provide them with nourishment, a stimulus to develop further and, of course, a feeling of confidence in the rectitude of their actions.

Fours can achieve great heights and establish a stable material income. Success will depend solely on the amount of responsibility and the weight of the burden they take upon their shoulders.

If the Fourth Arcanum arises in the Finance zone, this is a direct indication that this individual can successfully create his or her own business, opening a business is a clear pointer to their path to power. Fours are unambiguous leaders (bosses, managers), therefore, if they find themselves in a position where they are unable to prove themselves, this subordinate standing will negatively affect their energy balance and block their potential opportunities for development.

For Fours, it is always important to be busy. The more actively these people prove themselves in their actions and behavior, the more independent they will be when taking on complex tasks and the more effective the result achieved.

It's also worth noting that loans and debts have an adverse effect on Fours. If they do not have enough funds, they need to consider how they should go about increasing their capital, but under no circumstances should they set themselves any restrictions or money-saving austerity measures.

HEALTH

Fours have outwardly masculine traits. They are strong, stocky people with angular faces, large hands and thick-set bodies. They are physically well-developed and hardy, with high levels of muscle mass. They are excellent athletes and sports people — often heavyweights, wrestlers and weightlifters.

When it comes to their health, they need to carefully monitor the balance of the trace elements in their bodies. It is important that they strengthen their bones and develop their musculature. Weight gain and problems with bones and teeth are signs that their energy is becoming negative.

RELATIONSHIPS

When the Fourth Energy is located on the Prosperity Line in the Relationship zone, it is a sign that the individual in question needs a partner in a position of leadership who has all the main features and characteristics of male energy. Even if a man has the Fourth Arcanum in the matrix in the Relationship zone, it means that he needs a strong woman with masculine character traits, able to be active and show leadership in relationships while taking responsibility for solving important issues when necessary.

If there is a Four in the Relationship zone, then this person will subconsciously begin to look for a partner-leader with a conspicuous standing in life, who has power and influence. Their evaluation criteria when selecting a partner will be: a strong character, a willingness to take on responsibility, wealth and the potential ability to take parental responsibility and protect. Their partners must take an active role in expressing their feelings and do so precisely without unnecessary flannelling and understatement. Everything in their relationships needs to be clear, comprehensible, honest and open.

INDICATIONS THAT THIS ENERGY IS IN A −

- Living with their mother (parents) or at someone else's expense.
- Borrowing money.
- Telling others "how to live" and not following up their words with actions (saying that you need to have two cars, but not having one of their own).
- Avoiding responsibility (for themselves and their family members).
- Avoiding difficulties (sitting on the sidelines).
- Refusing to exercise their power in situations where they need to make a show of masculine strength.
- Using their strength and being aggressive towards those who are weaker than them.

INDICATIONS THAT THIS ENERGY IS IN A +

- Taking an active position in their lives.
- Taking on responsibility and obligations.
- Showing care and concern for their loved ones.
- Taking positions of leadership.
- Controlling their aggression and physical strength.
- Being grateful to their father and having a close relationship with him.
- Raising a son (successor) and bestowing all their attention, strength and experience on him.
- Being in charge of their lives, their households and what is going on in their heads.
- Being independent of the influence of others (being in a position of power, not a subordinate).

KARMIC TASKS:

- The ability to take responsibility
- Fighting against selfishness;
- Showing enthusiasm and strength in their actions;
- Eradicating emotional immaturity;

- Learning to defend their opinions;
- Not being dependent on others' opinions;
- Being in charge of their lives;
- Processing and working out insults taken and grudges held against men.

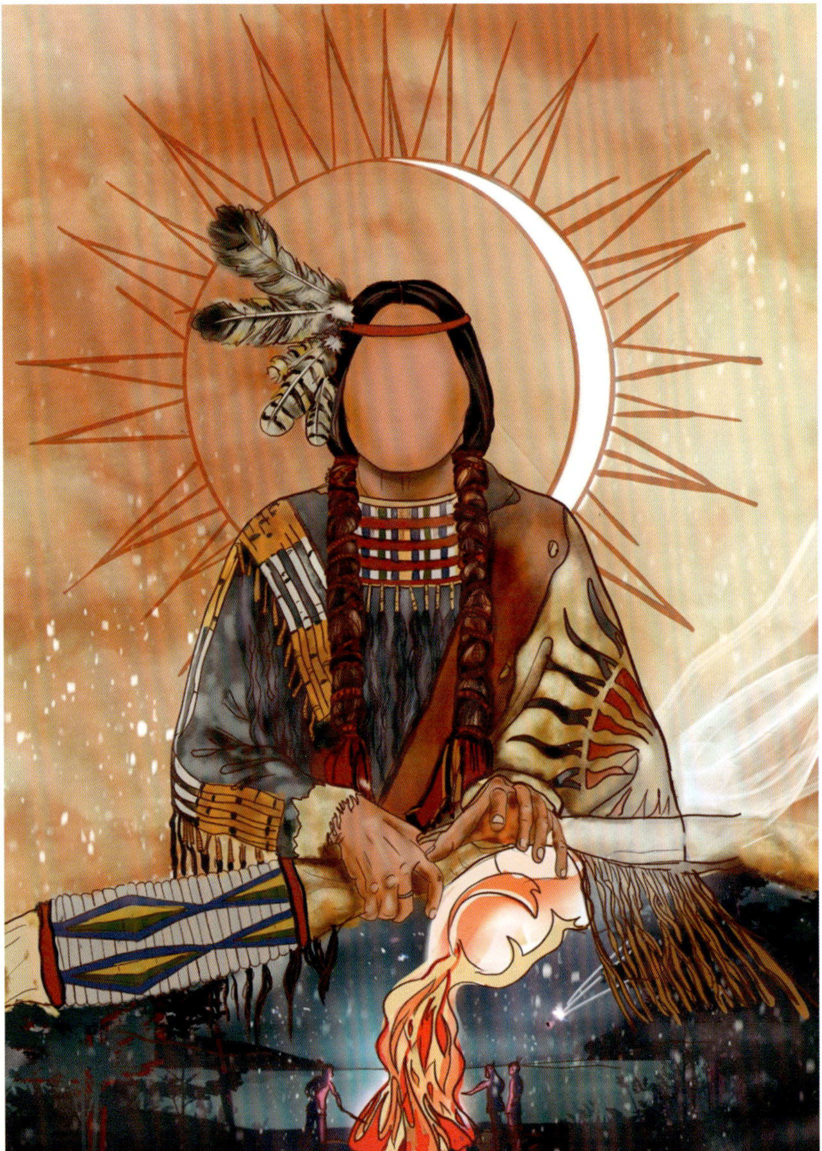

ARCANUM 5. KNOWLEDGE

> Sing this song loudly, Heya-Hey
> Let the old and young know
> That the Spirit is here today
> And he is joyful to be with us.
> Tabeku will feed him,
> Having received the gifts of the ancestors,
> To teach the children of the plains
> And to command them to honor their memory.

LEARNING – FAITH – TRADITIONS

The Energy of Knowledge is one of the most important and powerful energies in this world. People endowed with the power of the Fifth Arcanum are the most important distributors of the most priceless knowledge and traditions. People with the Fifth energy in their Destiny Code Matrix are those souls who observe the preservation, multiplication and dissemination of all the possible types of knowledge ever received by mankind. They are like the Chief Librarians of the universal bank of information. They are Guardians.

The Fifth Arcanum in the Tarot deck is the High Priest (the Hierophant). This is the force that prompts people to satisfy their irrepressible need to strive to understand Higher things. To develop and obtain Faith. Faith in God, the Universal Powers, in truth and falsehood and, most importantly, faith in themselves.

People with the Fifth Energy are drawn to knowledge by an irrepressible force. Like sponges, they can absorb terabytes of information, process it and broadcast it to those who have not yet had time to receive this knowledge. And sometimes to transmit to people what, in their opinion, they need to know, even by force if necessary. These are the "teachers of life" in the literal and figurative sense.

People with the Energy of Knowledge in their Destiny Code Matrix must always be learning something. It's like a self-preservation instinct for them – if they feel there is a small piece of information missing from their knowledge set or that they are not 100% informed, they are afraid that they will be left on the sidelines and of no use to anyone in this world.

And being "of use" and "service to society" are some of the most important requirements that the Fifth Energy makes of its possessors.

It's likely that some Fifth Energy people might disagree with the above, but if you give me a second, I think you'll understand everything I'm saying.

It often happens that people with the Fifth Energy in the Major zones of the matrix don't have a great liking for people in general and those in their immediate circle in particular. They often get irritated by superficial opinions and judgements as well as outright stupidity and, most importantly, a lack of education. This factor can be an irritant but at the same time a stimulus for their further development. It is a signal to action for them, a challenge — to teach!

It is important to remember that for Fives — increasing their level of knowledge and disseminating it to others is vital. In order to maintain and achieve a balance, it is very important that they share their knowledge. If they have completed a training course, read a book, or listened to some educational content — then they feel obliged to transmit the experience they have gained, to talk about the information received and share it.

A Fifth Energy person is exactly the sort of person who, after reading a book or a popular science article, would be able to create their own course, master class or even write a book on the topic. And the knowledge imparted will be in great demand and quite likely become even better known and more widespread than the original source. This is because Fives have a unique ability to process information and prune it into the correct and necessary form for it to be best perceived, understood and easily digested by the majority of people.

In addition to the missions of "learning" and "teaching", there is another important task that they like to undertake, which is to lead others to find Faith. But I think we should talk about Faith as a secondary consideration — this is not in any way to reduce the significance of this aspect in the lives of Fifth Energy people. It's just that sometimes people have problems with the notion of Faith but do not have any with the notion of obtaining knowledge. Therefore, it is very important to examine and consider things in the context of the specific individual, within the framework of their specific Destiny Code Matrix and from the point of view of the totality of the interaction of all the specific Arcana contained in it.

For the Fifth Arcanum energy, Faith is the acquisition of meaning. It is through their Faith in something that a Five finds him or herself. By believing in God, in the Power of the Sidhas, or in the energies of Nature, it doesn't matter which; it is important that a person thus finds "his or her place" in life.

For those endowed with the Fifth energy in their matrix, it is very important to have traditions and a set of rules and dogmas that need to be followed. Following certain actions and perfecting the ritual process gives them a sense of the "correctness" of their actions. By observing rules and traditions, they are leading themselves towards their ideal. And in this instance, this works brilliantly for these people's karma. The pinnacle of excellence for them would be not only to observe (for example) their family or religious traditions and reveal them to others but actually create their own. Creating a set of dogmas and rules and algorithms of behavior, actions and rituals allows them to process their Fifth Energy effectively and this is especially the case for those who are too dependent on the influence of other sources. In other words, if a person is overly religious or dependent on another source that is having a negative impact on them, if a person feels that their life force is depleted, the surest way to restore the energy of the Fifth Arcanum is to create for him or herself a personal rule, a ritual or a certain set of actions, which, when performed, will allow this person to replenish their reserves of strength and rid him or herself of this dependency.

As a rule, Fives have a tendency to allow themselves to be influenced by religious and spiritual trends. If there are any pathologies in their chakras, they will often become "victims" of religions: members of sects, religious fanatics or go crazy on religious grounds. It is very important to try to prevent this sort of "unhealthy behavior" because Fives have many of the prerequisites that can make them very prone to this sort of thing.

Faith is undoubtedly very important. Everyone, regardless of their personal energies in their Destiny Code Matrix and the personal goals and objectives they have determined for themselves, is stepping out on the path towards the acquisition of Faith. It is important for everyone to find themselves and know the truth. Everyone is set the task of finding "their place" in life and to be of use to the Universe. But the degree of their readiness to plunge head first into this task will naturally differ from person to person despite the importance of the matter.

Fifth Energy people always need to be in a sound state of mind and remember that sometimes the paths that people seek to gain the benefits of purity and well-being can be very radical, and the consequences and sacrifices that they end up making can be very sad. Faith is a good thing, it is light and purity. But you should always be sure to see the precise source of the light and what is behind it.

There is no person or thing that is truly and genuinely the primary source of truth. If you find yourself in the presence of someone who claims to know exactly what needs to be done — think to yourself, who this person really is and where he or she acquired this infallible knowledge. Perhaps they are wrong, after all, do you have the complete answer?

Fives are some of the smartest people on Earth. This is a fact. But people with the Ninth Energy are smarter yet. Fifth Arcanum people can process large amounts of information and effectively extract from it the most useful elements that can be applied in the here and now — effectiveness and productivity are the aims of this process. People with the Ninth Energy, on the other hand, set themselves the task of "getting to the truth at the bottom of a question" and often the practical issue of how to go about it doesn't even occur to them.

Fives lack the ability to delve deeply into a question (as Ninth Arcanum people can). If a Five were to begin to dig deeply into researching each question they confront, looking for causal relationships and analyzing all the information that he or she is so desperate to get hold of, he or she would simply not have enough time in one human lifespan let alone the capacity in his or her head to make such a huge universal task a reality. But fortunately, this is not what the universe requires of Fives. Their main task when it comes to Knowledge is to follow the algorithm: collect, process, transmit.

When the Fifteenth Arcanum is located in the Destiny Code Matrix in addition to the Fifth, this individual finds themselves torn between good and evil, light and darkness and God and the Devil. The Fifteenth Arcanum does not allow a person to blindly throw themselves into something or surrender and submit to a cause without a trace. This person will be inclined to doubt what he or she has encountered and will want to play "the Devil's advocate". The Fifth Energy in this individual, in turn, will restrain his or her obsession with the Devil and help this individual always strive towards the Light, to find the right path thus protecting him or her from temptation and the Dark Side. A big plus for such an individual with the 5th and 15th energies in terms of their implementation of their karmic tasks in life would be the acceptance of both sides of the Truth, the awareness of the presence of Good and Evil in all things.

Blindly following someone else's path is a great temptation for people with the Energy of Knowledge. And this is the wrong way. Surely the best way is to analyze the route others have taken and then draw your own conclusions without making their mistakes. To collect information from different sources like a puzzle. To create your own unique recipe, follow your personal plan, even if other people are walking by your side on the path to the same goal as you.

Fives are also moralists. This is especially the case if the Karmic Tail is in a 15-5-8 matrix. The unbridled desire to teach others about life and to punish wrongdoing almost borders on insanity. My advice to such people is that they should remember that they are not a judge and do not have the right to make decisions for others. But to be honest, even threats won't work against these sorts of "moralists" and they still won't listen. If a Five is determined to "teach" — others will have to learn.

WATCHWORDS

- Knowledge is Power, provides Opportunity and is the Truth.
- Faith is like the air that we breathe and life is impossible without it.
- Believe, but verify.
- There is my opinion and there is the wrong one.
- It's never too late to learn.

FINANCES

First and foremost, I would like to say here that people with a Major Fifth energy in their Destiny Code Matrix are without a doubt primarily God-given teachers (by birth and by nature). And this is undoubtedly so. They are born educators, mentors and teachers. Find out the date of birth of your favorite teacher at school or university, or your child's best teachers and then take a look at his or her Destiny Code Matrix. I can guarantee you that the Fifth Energy will feature strongly somewhere.

Likewise, Fifth Arcanum people are often drawn to medicine. Passing on the knowledge they have acquired through service is an ideal mission for these people. And for Fives their mission is more important to them than it is for other people. Therefore, teachers and doctors, and all those who are associated with professions where service and knowledge predominantly feature are not only very good people in their own right but they are also following the right path when it comes to their Destiny.

Material well-being matters to Fives, of course, but it is not as important as it is for people endowed with other Arcanum energies. Fives blossom and develop depending on the amount of experience and knowledge they have accumulated and thanks to this they are able to earn much more than they desire.

Fives are generally happy to do charity work and do it simply out of the goodness of their hearts and their sense of duty often when they could have been well paid or rewarded for it.

Although, of course, improving their finances allows Fives to increase their knowledge levels. If a person is determined to reach a new level of knowledge, then he or she should simply set out to learn more. The more information a person receives, the more he or she will be able to pass it on to others and, accordingly, receive a greater reward for this.

Of course, it would be foolish to suggest that teaching and medicine are the only professions that Fives go in for. Nothing could be further from the case. They can be engaged in almost any professional activity. Nevertheless, whatever profession they do take up, a Five will always strive to learn, teach and carry on their mission of advancing knowledge. Therefore, it is important that they direct their natural gifts in the most productive direction so that their desire and striving for "what is right" and consequent criticism and moralizing come from a position of a teacher and master who knows more than others and is ready to share this knowledge with them.

One of the main things that can cause a Five to lose the energy endowed to them is when their professional activities lack a mission. The three main touchstones for the Five's personality in general and the healthy development of their financial and material lives are: Firstly, Faith. They need to believe in what they are doing, that it is the right thing to do, in the necessity of doing it and the need for this activity. Secondly, the mission. It is important to have good goals and good reasons for following this path, and a Five needs to be aware of these. And thirdly, there needs to be a structure, a set of dogmas, rules and conditions that a person needs to fulfil impeccably and irreproachably.

It would be simply impossible (for a person with a Five on their Prosperity Line) to hide and embezzle income, to take part in the fraudulent activities of some religious organizations, to violate the rules or "ethics" of any company or business they might work for, to allow chaos and disorder reign in any endeavor they are engaged in (be it in their workplace or in their heads) or to perceive that the activities they are engaged in are a punishment or something they are doing against their will. You need to remember that a Five's profession and the field of activity in which they have decided to throw themselves into as their life mission and life work is of prime importance to them. Otherwise, their work will suck their energy out of them rather than increase it.

HEALTH

As a rule, Fives do not have any particular idiosyncrasies as far as their health is concerned. However, there are several factors that are worthy of attention and a potential source of envy for many who haven't been endowed with this energy. Fives have a wonderful sense of humor. And this has a certain relevance, no matter how strange it may sound, in the context of a person's health. If Fives can look at themselves and the situation they find themselves in from the sidelines, if they can see the signs of their fate that have come into play and draw their own conclusions about how and why everything has turned out as it has and then laugh at it, then everything will be fine, they will have passed through this experience and learned their karmic lesson from it. To put it another way, they will have understood the Universe's (God's) joke.

It's important to take this on board because Fives often find themselves in situations in life when their physical condition suffers in order to benefit their spiritual condition. A good example is when Fives find themselves in too much of a hurry (to get to a meeting, to work or just somewhere in general) and it's just not worth rushing to get there. It is often in these situations that the Universe is switched into our lives and is clearly trying to let us know that we need to wait! To stop! Otherwise, out of the blue, the person who is in a rush can slip or fall badly, thus hurting themselves or breaking something. These sorts of situations are highly characteristic of Fifth Energy people. And it is important for them to listen to these internal warning signs, and stop and reassess the situation.

People with the energy of Knowledge subordinate everything to their convictions. It is important for them to understand the validity of this or that fact. They try very hard to provide themselves with the "correct" sort of nutrition and their approach to sex is much the same, they are prone to forcibly limit and restrain themselves in all spheres of life.

For the most part, Fives have a tendency to choose very specific diets. They are drawn to vegetarianism, raw food and various types of diets in general and the observance of religious fasts and fasting. But, in most instances, these lifestyle choices are completely unsuitable for them. And, as a result, a similar picture to the one that I described above emerges — after tormenting their body in some way or another, individuals with a minus in their matrix are able to look at themselves from the sidelines and, as a result, "appreciate" the Universe's sense of humor and return themselves to a state of harmony and normality as far as their diet and nutrition is concerned and no longer allow themselves to overeat, which led them to take up these diets and apply these restrictions in the first place.

In general, people with the Fifth Energy in the Destiny Code matrix are prone to overeating, being overweight, and being addicted to alcohol, sweets and starchy foods with a resulting loss of self-control. But this can all be reversed and returned to a state of normality, even when an individual is at the point of no return. Even when they are on the very "edge", Fives are able to analyze their behavior and draw the relevant conclusions.

People endowed with the Fifth Energy (especially when it is located in one of the Major Zones of the matrix) can have two polar states of attitude towards their own health: they are either deeply indifferent, resulting in them taking no physical care of their body at all, or overly anxious about it, in which case the slightest sneeze can end up with a visit to the doctor.

Fives' health can be very negatively affected by other people's advice, especially when it comes to harmful diets and observing strictly controlled and restrictive ("correct") eating regimes. Unfortunately, Fives very often suffer as a result of a doctor's incorrect diagnosis.

RELATIONSHIPS

When considering Fives' relationships, it is vital that you remember their main touchstones: Faith, tradition, mission and knowledge. These are their pillars and foundations.

If a person has a Five in their Relationship zone, this indicates that his partner will be pious and religious, and their relationship will involve a large element of mutual education (when one partner teaches the other and vice versa). For them, in a relationship with a partner, it is important to always understand the mission and to believe in it. Any lack of faith or belief will lead relationships in the opposite direction — a state of total distrust and jealousy.

The Fifth Energy carries a yearning for reliability: stability and well-being through the observance and adherence to fundamental rules and traditions. Often Fives will meet their partners in a place of worship or on the basis of common religious ties.

Fives take marriage seriously and very responsibly. There would need to be very serious reasons why a Five would decide to sue for a divorce. Conventionality and piety and the observance of traditions and principles are more important to a Five, than feelings and passion.

The extent and power of their knowledge can put Fives' relationships under a lot of pressure with their tendency to criticize, teach and judge their partners. This destructive behavior very often leads to the Five's own self-destruction. But it also leads them to come to the appropriate conclusions and allow themselves to reach the level of "accepting knowledge" and not just being a "teacher of life".

In general, being in a relationship with a Five makes for a strong alliance, which adds up to much more than just passion and feelings. People who have their energies in balance are able to help each other develop, go through life lessons together, have common interests and believe in the same things together (in God, in the Cosmos, in the Forces of Nature). All of the above serve to unite and strengthen relationships.

People with the Fifth Arcanum in their matrix need to understand that the "right" partner (the one they really need to be with) will only appear when they have brought their energy into a plus state of positivity. Up to this point, each partner that appears on the horizon will bring their own life lesson with them, which on each occasion will become increasingly difficult for the Five to negotiate if the individual in question has entered into a state of negativity. The best advice for anyone with a five in their Major Arcana is to "learn to learn".

INDICATIONS THAT THIS ENERGY IS IN A −

- A refusal to accept new knowledge.
- Constantly teaching and criticizing others.
- Imposing their principles and life positions on others.
- Disorder (either in their house, in their head or behavior).
- No longer observing traditions (family, religious, or those that are generally accepted in their circle or wider society).
- Pointless attempts to learn and grasp everything immediately and at once (not wanting to apply their knowledge to life).
- Propagating dogma and all sorts of teachings as propaganda.
- Blind faith.
- Not transmitting the knowledge they have accumulated.
- Being very conservative.
- Limiting themselves to stereotypes or other people's opinions.

INDICATIONS THAT THIS ENERGY IS IN A +

- Learning from and teaching others.
- Disseminating information and being a source from which others will seek knowledge.
- Faith (in God, in a theory, in an idea).
- Respecting order and tradition.
- Having a set of rules in life, a mission.
- Creating new customs and traditions.
- Providing structure for everything everywhere.
- Making plans and strictly following them.
- Being truly religious and being involved in a greater and wider universal process.
- Having the moral courage to follow their own fundamental principles.
- Enjoying public approval.
- Having a following or audience (students, followers).

- Maintaining order and cleanliness in the home, in the workplace and their immediate vicinity.
- Accepting alternative opinions.
- Being tolerant.
- Accepting others as they are.

KARMIC TASKS:

- Learning to distinguish good from evil and truth from lies;
- Applying the knowledge they have acquired to their lives (not just accumulating it and putting it to no good use);
- Creating values and traditions;
- Acquiring Faith;
- Learning not only to teach but also to receive knowledge from others;
- To avoid fanaticism in their deeds and judgements;
- To help everyone who asks for it — to be a source of hope.

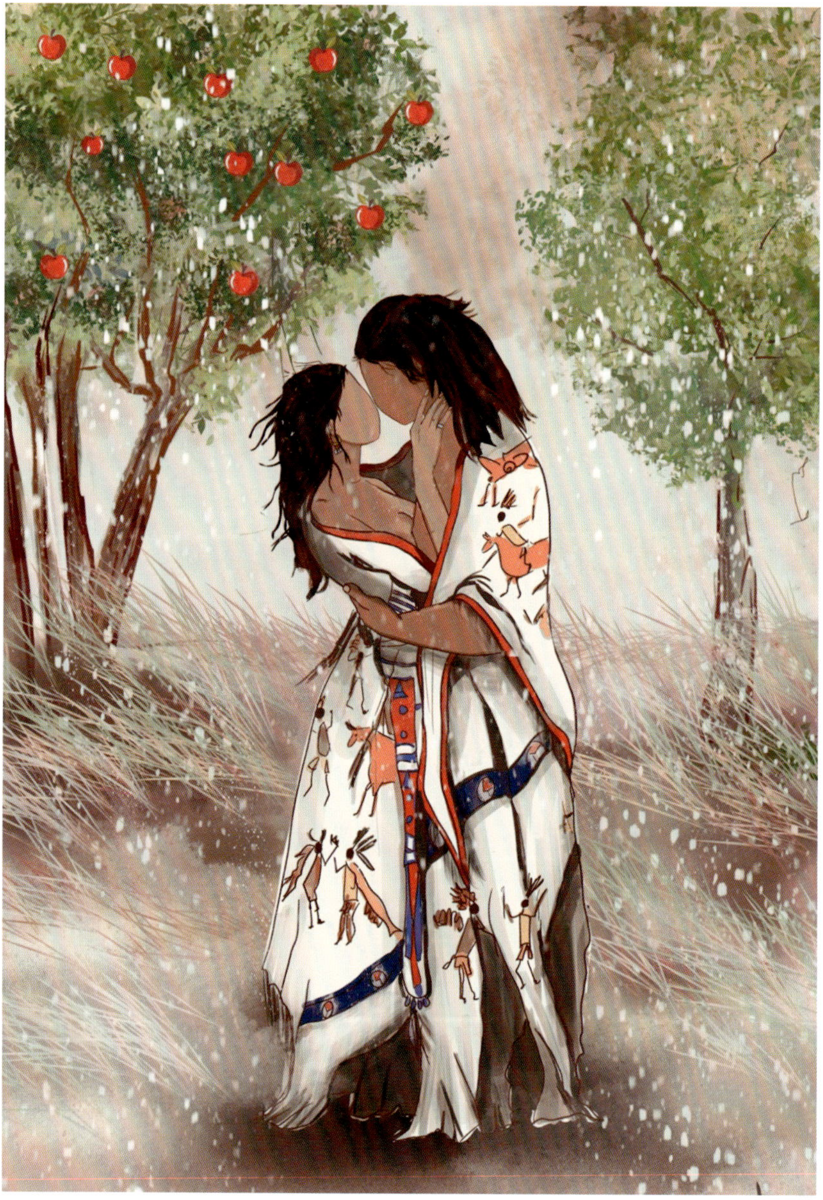

ARCANUM 6. LOVE

> Beyond the alder bushes on the waters of Lake Seneca
> Among the wild water lilies, as naked as children,
> Two youthful bodies splashed, unembarrassed by the presence of the old willow,
> Contrary to the teachings of the wise, avoiding the gaze of others.
> There, on the cusp of sunset, like a light birch leaf
> Their hearts fluttered as they touched skin to skin.
> And there between the trees at the ford, the sleeping canoe
> Hid these lovers' secret
> Under the cover of the dark night.

COMMUNICATION – BEAUTY – CHOICE

The sixth Arcanum is the energy of Love, the desire to love and be loved. In the Tarot deck, the Sixth Arcanum is represented by the Lovers. This is the Arcanum of communication and the vital choices in life. This is one of the most frequently encountered Energies in the Destiny Code Matrix.

The Energy of Love is the most complex to deal with. And this is because people with a Six in their matrix "hoover up" love. Their need for energy is much higher than that they themselves are able to produce, so the Sixth Arcanum is primarily about how to learn to love themselves for themselves.

The complexity of the lives of a person endowed with this energy will depend on how 'major' the Six is in their matrix (in which zone it is located). Accordingly, the more major the Six features in the individual's matrix, the greater their need will be to pay attention to themselves and the more widely this energy will influence all aspects of their life.

People with the Sixth Arcanum in the Character and Portrait zones are the embodiment of beauty, grace and refined taste, outwardly they possess great charm and are very attractive to others. They love and highly prize socializing and communication; it could be said that "connections" and "contacts" are one of the main skills in the Six's toolkit, it is the "trump card that they have hidden up their sleeve", their secret weapon.

Love Energy people spend a lot of time and place a lot of emphasis on socializing and making connections. They get on with others very easily and they have many acquaintances and friends. Sixes are very affable, courteous and open when communicating and socializing. They are always striving to impress and win others over, trying to smooth out any prickly moments in any conversation and act as a peacemaker should they suddenly find themselves in a conflict between two other parties. If their energy is in a state of negativity or their chakras have pathologies, all of the above qualities will appear exaggerated and excessive. Their openness and friendliness will turn into bombast and hypocrisy and falsehood and farce that will appear obvious to others. In this instance, a Six with their energy in a state of minus will be perceived as an outcast and will repel people. Sixes have an obsessive need to "be loved" by others and this often causes a personality breakdown, driving them into a deep depression.

In a situation where there is a risk that a person's energy can destroy them, it is important to realize this in time. So that the Six, like the Phoenix, will be able to be reborn by accepting the Love within him or herself. Then he or she will be able to receive the vital flow of energy they need, without any complications or difficulties. What they need to do is simply open themselves up and accept their reality. For people with the Sixth Arcanum, the most important thing is to learn to love themselves, and by accepting themselves as they are, to open up to others.

The Sixth Arcanum requires that Sixes be honest and pure in soul, thought and action. A state of self-deception is a highly typical characteristic of those endowed with the energy of Love. The illusions and wishful thinking they suffer are often just an attempt to satisfy their appetites and lack of energy. For example, if a person is lonely and they do not have a close friend or society does not accept them as openly as they would like. Then he or she comes up with a delusion in which he or she has a friend, there is acceptance, and he or she feels that he or she is valuable and in demand. This person then shares their "story" with others, elaborates it, incorporates it into the story of their life and adapts their way of life so that this delusion and reality become intertwined. Then one fine day, this individual ceases to be able to distinguish where the truth and falsehood lie and the entire story becomes a reality for his or her circle and, most importantly, for him or herself. Even though this can happen at the subconscious level and most likely would not be obvious to the individual, this behavior would nevertheless not go unnoticed by the

Universe and it will begin to send tests and set new tasks and lessons for this individual and having passed them he or she will eventually find the truth and him or herself in the process.

The Sixth Arcanum always sets choices for those who are endowed with it. In one way or another, everyone is faced with making decisions and choices and defining priorities for themselves. But people with a major Sixth Energy in their matrix have great difficulties with this.

It is as if people with the Energy of Love are destined to a fate of always having to make choices and decide on one step or another. Often it is precisely for this reason that Sixes lack energy and end up 'freezing' in indecision. This happens both in the global sense (throughout their lives) and at the small ordinary and everyday level. For example, a Six might want to buy some shoes (or some other thing). And then they end up in a quandary about "which color", "exactly which size" they need and indeed whether they "need anything new at all". Eventually, the poor Six will end up spending many days, a lot of time and, of course, a lot of energy on this decision. A person who is "frozen" in this way when making a choice is in danger of turning their energy negative.

People with the Sixth Arcanum in their Destiny Code Matrix are attracted to all things bright, beautiful and elegant. Sixes are connoisseurs of the arts, often gourmets when it comes to food and understand all the intricacies and idiosyncrasies of fashion, design, architecture and just about everything else that is an object of beauty.

Outwardly, these are people who like to attract attention to themselves. They may not be so beautiful by nature, but their charm, charisma and ability to present themselves to others always prompt a reaction from those around them and Sixes will almost always get the attention they deserve.

Sixes tend to surround themselves with beautiful objects, they prefer fashionable and stylish clothes and are always up to date with the latest trends. They surround themselves with interesting people and collect acquaintances, so to speak, where the value of the exhibit collected will depend on the potential opportunities that may open up when communicating with them.

It is absolutely vital to every person with a Major Six in their Destiny Code Matrix what other people think of them, what others say about them, how they look in the eyes of others and what impression they make.

Aristocrats by nature, Sixes want to enjoy life and bask in the energy of love and adoration.

The Energy of Love provides its owner with a unique gift — the most wonderful and powerful ability to love and be loved! It is the power that holds everything in its sway. If a person is honest with others and him or herself, the power of Love will provide them with everything they want, open all the doors they need and lead them along the right path. The main thing for them is to accept love and be as truthful as possible.

WATCHWORDS

- Love and Beauty will save the world.
- Every choice completed is the right one!
- Love yourself and the world will love you back.
- Everything can be resolved depending on who you know.

FINANCES

When the Sixth Energy is in the Finance zone, this person should be encouraged to work in alliances, partnerships and cooperation with others. Their connections and contacts resolve all issues, open the right doors and provide great opportunities.

The energy of Love also attracts the opposite sex. In other words, if the Six is a man, then women will be their most favorable audience for communication purposes and vice versa for a woman. Flirting and coquetry, play and sexuality are very successful tools used by Sixes in the Finance zone to get the best results.

People with the Sixth Arcanum are very creative and appreciate grace and beauty. It is very important for them to be in love with their work, to burn with passion for what they do. Otherwise, if there is no fire, there will be no final result. As soon as work becomes a chore and fails to create positive emotions, Sixes can become disappointed and disenchanted, thus reducing their motivation, activity and efficiency to zero.

Accordingly, their spheres of interest tend to lie in those areas that are associated with beauty, luxury, fashion and style, along with art and culture, or at least publicity.

It does not matter in what professional field a Six develops — the important thing is how much attention they garner. A clear indicator of success for them is the number of phone numbers in their address books and the frequency that they are mentioned by people of authority.

Regardless of whether Sixes work for themselves or someone else, their place of work will always be the most prestigious, their company the largest and their office the most fashionably appointed. Of course, this is all in their ideal world! But believe me, Sixes will strive with all their might to make it a reality.

Their finances improve when they are in partnership with somebody: a common business, a joint project or a collaboration. Their team's universal recognition and love will provide them with the nourishment and incentives to develop further.

Sixes are excellent salespeople, real estate agents, headhunters, PR people, marketers and advertisers, fashion brand representatives, museum workers (who are involved in promoting art to the masses), TV and radio hosts. And basically, many other professions that involve the need to capture other people's attention and bring beauty and love into the world.

Without exception, all Sixes are very sociable but the more major a Six features in the Destiny Code Matrix, the stronger this characteristic becomes. They have the contact details of just about every imaginable specialist in their address book. If you ever suddenly need someone's phone number, then look for the nearest Six in your circle and they will definitely have it.

HEALTH

Sixes' health depends entirely on what is going on in their heads. People with the energy of Love can come up with all sorts of hypochondriac illnesses to attract attention to themselves and will be so successful in convincing themselves and those around them that, as a result, they really will get sick.

Sixes suffer from psychosomatic illnesses more often than others. They can recover from the most complex illnesses only thanks to the support and love that others give them (by absorbing the global energy flows given off by their loved ones). And vice versa, out of the blue, they can convince themselves they are in a state of complete exhaustion and end up developing real health problems.

According to the metaphorical meaning of the Sixth Arcanum, the Energy of Love completely and utterly permeates the person endowed with it and every cell, every drop of their blood carries the fire and passion of the "Lovers". Therefore, their most vulnerable organs often turn out to be the heart, brain and blood. If their love for themselves is strong, then everything will be in perfect order, but if their energy suddenly becomes negative, it is the aforementioned parts of the human organism that will suffer first.

An insufficient supply of love quickly depletes the Six's body and it can rapidly age. Whereas an abundance of this energy can keep a Six looking fresh and youthful for a very long time.

RELATIONSHIPS

The energy of Love permeates and fills Sixes' entire lives. Love is everywhere and in everything. It can manifest itself as romance and strong feelings or beautiful and memorable stories. Their lovers can elicit the most extraordinary emotions in a person with a Six in their Destiny Code Matrix. Because they can provide the most exceptional gift — to love and be loved.

For people with a Six in their Destiny Code Matrix (especially if there is more than one), it is vital that they do not overwhelm their partner and suck all their energy out of them. As I mentioned above, Sixes must, first of all, learn to love themselves and accept a partner through their inner love.

The ways that they manifest their love can vary dramatically. It is very important for them to radiate love, to receive love and to be able to love themselves, so that later they can endow these feelings to their partner and be able to receive the degree of love that their partner can give in return.

When Sixes are able to love themselves, it means that their Love Energy reserves are full. Sixes need to become the sort of person who knows how to give without demanding anything in return.

It is important to remember that the Sixth Arcanum always presents the person endowed with it with choices. So, in their relationships, Sixes will always find themselves having to make choices. Whether it's a choice of partner, a choice of priorities or the choice between love or prosperity — they are always confronted with a choice.

When a Six is located in the Relationship zone, this is a sign that this individual's love life will be particularly bright and romantic. When a Six is in the Character zone, these individuals are, on the whole, very amorous and can easily get carried away by even the most unpromising relationships, which will nevertheless cause them to burn out without a trace. The presence of a Six and Fifteen in the matrix is a dangerous mixture that can spur these individuals to take unnecessary risks in their eternal search for adventure in matters of love.

An important aspect to bear in mind is the fact that the holders of the Sixth Energy should never reject or push away a partner that they really want to be with. If a Six cheats on their partner, then they are not only depleting their own resources but also those of their partner who, sooner or later, will end up leaving and taking what belongs to them. For example, if a couple get to a stage where it's time to divorce, then the Six will lose everything: their property, their livelihood and sometimes their children and friends will take their partner's side. When a Six fails to fulfill their partner's need for love, that partner will go where he or she can get the attention they need.

The power of the Sixth Arcanum makes it abundantly clear that the ability to attract attention is a powerful weapon when placed in the hands of those endowed with it. People with the Sixth Energy know precisely how to get what they want by manifesting their love. For example, by preparing a delicious dinner, you can easily get that new handbag from your spouse, and in return for exceptional lovemaking you can create the ideal mood to suggest that vacation or a new car. Sixes are very powerful manipulators in matters of love and relationships, so those endowed with other energies should be on the alert when dealing with them.

INDICATIONS THAT THIS ENERGY IS IN A –

- Vulnerability, resentment, mistrust.
- Showing signs of being a "know-all" and a superiority complex.
- Flattery and hypocrisy when socializing with others.
- Delusional perceptions of reality.
- A refusal to consider the opinions of others.
- Egotism and self-absorption.
- Becoming 'frozen' when making a decision.
- Betrayal and deception of a partner (a rejection of being a united whole with another).
- Trying to be "all things to all men" (for the sake of personal gain).

- Dependence on the opinions of others.
- Putting people on pedestals (delusive perceptions of others) and being subsequently disappointed.
- Judging people by appearances and not who they are.
- Demanding excessive attention from their circle.
- Difficult relationships with children.
- Financial dependence.

INDICATIONS THAT THIS ENERGY IS IN A +

- The ability to love oneself (to accept yourself for what you are).
- The ability to appreciate life and whatever it has to offer for what it is.
- Being able to make choices (immediately without any procrastination or postponement).
- The ability to share with others (everyone).
- Honesty in dealing with others.
- A highly developed sense of wonder.
- Being physically and spiritually beautiful.
- Being surrounded by order and comfort.
- A willingness to open oneself up for the good of others (to help others at a difficult time, to warm others with one's own warmth).
- Emotional maturity (the ability to both laugh and cry).
- Loyalty to and unity with their partner.
- Manifesting one's love and kindness in everything.

KARMIC TASKS:

- To learn to love yourself and not demand love in return;
- To learn to make choices and accept them without regretting the consequences;
- To accept people for who they are;
- To accept your place in life without creating illusions or having delusions about your own significance;
- To learn to give and demand in return;

- To develop a sense of beauty in oneself and create and organize harmony and beauty all around (for oneself and others);
- To learn to be happy.

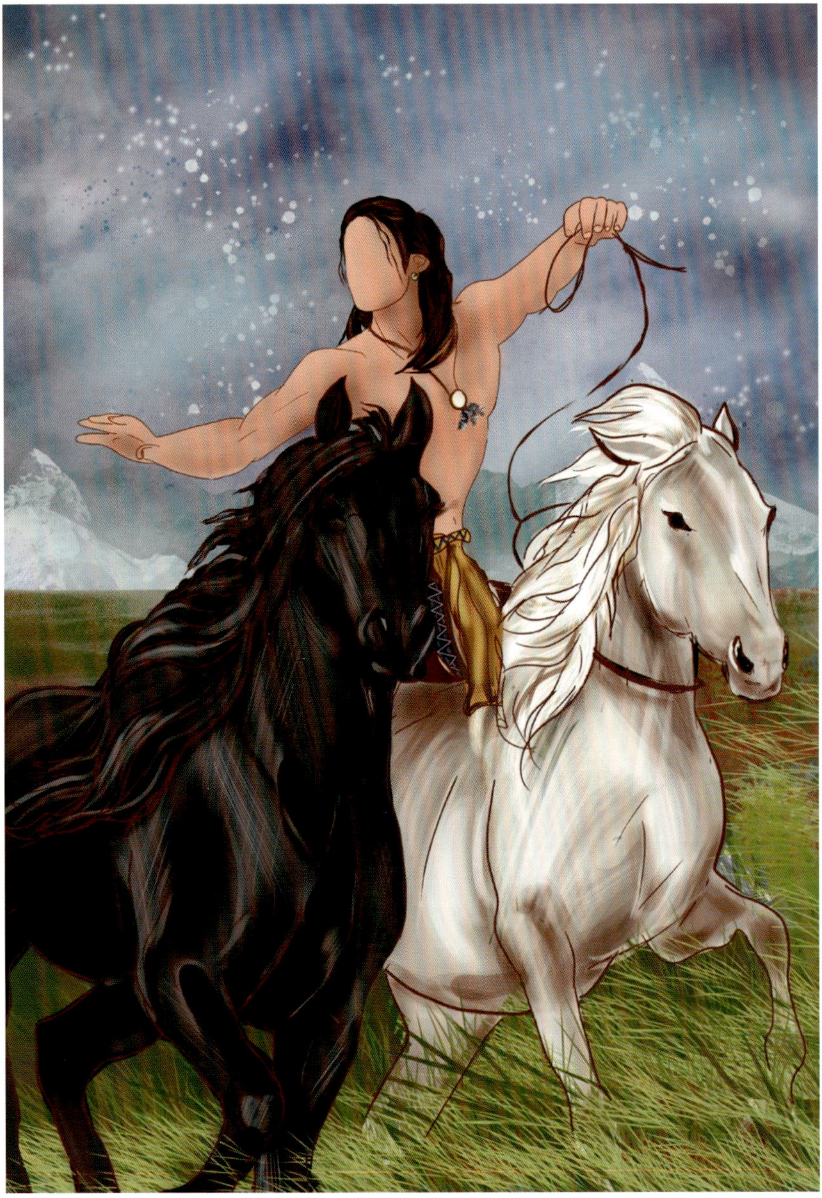

ARCANUM 7. MOVEMENT

According to ancient lore, a wise man said
That in the middle of the prairie in the lands of the wind, among the high mighty mountains,
At the summit of the furthest peak sits the Warrior of Light,
The ancestor of our ancestors and father of the plains.
Thunderer and Lord, Chief of Chiefs, the Great Eagle.
So, Young Brave Kenokeh,
keep to your way down below, downwind in the distant West,
Stretch your supple bow, loose your arrow
And run swifter than the doe, swifter than your arrow,
To the Center of the Universe.

GOAL — ACHIEVEMENT — SPEED

Seventh Energy people are "achievers", the people of the arrow, ten steps ahead of others and swifter than all others. If their arrow is fired in the right direction, along a clearly defined route, then Sevens will always achieve their goal, hitting their bull's-eye. They will achieve their goal whatever the cost and do so faster than anyone else.

The Seventh Arcanum in the Tarot deck is the Chariot. It is the Energy of movement and speed. Feeling the wind in their hair and the anticipation of victory are key drivers for those endowed with the Energy of Speed.

The slowness of their circle and society as a whole is a source of great irritation and suffering for the people of the Seventh Energy. They constantly feel the need to accelerate and speed up, otherwise, they will fail to get where they need to be on time and simply be left behind. Sevens need to understand that it is they who are "fast" and "swift" and it is not the world that is being obtuse and slowing them down and that their circle and the wider world are running at a healthy rhythm — in other words, Sevens are too active, they need to stop, look around and take stock for a moment.

The Seventh Arcanum in the Destiny Code Matrix provides those endowed with it the ability to think quickly, absorb information instantly and act immediately. This is a feature that can manifest itself both positively and negatively. It is a unique ability that can endow a person with incredible strength and energy, giving them the necessary resources for self-realization and to achieve goals that others could only ever dream of. This unique trait is the Spirit of Competition.

The stronger the Seventh Energy is in an individual's matrix, the more pronounced the spirit of rivalry in their lives. When this energy is positive, a person can set their goals high and fly towards them, overcoming any obstacles in the way.

People with a Major Seventh Energy in their matrix take life by the scruff of its neck. They are absolutely certain that whatever the goal they are trying to achieve they need to fight for it and defend their position at all costs and, if need be, they must fight to the death. Sometimes stubbornly and blindly sticking to an idea can cloud their minds and prevent Sevens from properly and sensibly assessing the situation. Often, when they are rushing along "full steam ahead", they simply do not have the time to realize what they are doing and the sort of mayhem and madness they are careering towards. Sometimes, they literally do not hear and do not see those around them, they are so busy defending their position and trying to achieve what they want.

The Seventh Arcanum provides drive. People with a Seven in their Destiny Code matrix have great physical and mental stamina. They can undergo and overcome great difficulties for the sake of their goals. But there must be a goal in the first place! An aimless existence can be devastating for Sevens causing them to activate an internal whirlwind. Then they will be blown in all sorts of directions, rushing from one extreme to another, doing one thing then another, running first in one direction and then the opposite. The key to controlling themselves and curbing this energy is, first and foremost, to try to create for themselves at least some kind of goal and set some kind of task for themselves, or at least determine a point B (the position in which they want to see themselves in). Then, having decided on a course, their incredible drive will kick in and they will rush forward.

Sevens are the engines of any process. In a team, it is they who get everyone up from their seats, inspire momentum and dash forward, bringing everyone else along with them.

Sevens rarely think about tomorrow or yesterday. They operate in a space beyond the bounds of time because mentally they are already somewhere far away from here and close to their goal. In everyday life, this can often cause difficulties especially when communicating with loved ones. The constant commotion, haste and sometimes chaos in their actions are very difficult to endure on an ongoing basis in everyday life. But this is something you're going to have to get used to if there is a Seven in your life.

The Seventh Arcanum endows its owner with free will. The ability to put up with stress and go forward, no matter what, are the strongest features of people with the energy of Speed. But sometimes, these characteristics become hypertrophied. And the very thing that can be a great tool in achieving a goal becomes a trap and a limiting factor that holds back the individual's ability to realize themselves. When pride captures people and they no longer pay sufficient attention to nuances, when people are blinded by their power and overestimate their capabilities, when, underestimating their opponent, Sevens flounder on ahead contrary to all common sense (and often exposing themselves to physical danger), when their free will deprives them of their reason, blurring the boundaries between what is permitted and what is not, Sevens simply blunder off the path, finding themselves completely off course with no way of getting back on track. It is important at this stage to maintain a balance of expectations and opportunities. To curb one's free will within the bounds of what is permitted, to find softer solutions to problems, without losing one's clarity of purpose. It is important to always remember what you are aiming for and what price you are willing to pay for it.

People with the Seventh Energy are very fond of all forms of transportation. They love speed. They are fascinated by movement in all its manifestations. Whether it's running, dancing, sports or fairground rides. However, when this energy is in a negative state it will, on the contrary, repel a person from all of the above activities, he or she will become afraid of them and avoid them. Often, this negative energy can give rise to phobias about such things as flying, driving and all types of extreme sports.

However, extreme sports are like fuel for Sevens both in terms of entertainment and in other areas of their lives. They love activities that require you to achieve, to set high standards and climb high to reach them, to take risks and test your nerves — these are motivations that spur Sevens ever onwards to achieve the goals they have conceived.

WATCHWORDS

- The only way is onwards — towards your goal!
- Go get what you want no matter the cost.
- Life is movement.
- Ideas are the engines of progress.
- Be the Captain "at the helm" but also be in control of the wheel.

FINANCES

Momentum, movement and motion in all things and in all settings is a fundamental concept for Sevens in their lives as a whole and in professional matters and likewise in spiritual and material matters.

But financial rewards and opportunities will always come Sevens' way on the condition that they are able to formulate a clear goal and a strategy to achieve it, without fear of any obstacles preventing them from moving forwards. Financial rewards for Sevens can be facilitated by the simplest of things. First of all, they need to define a wish list, next they need to find out the price they need to pay for what they want, and then prepare themselves mentally to rush into battle and achieve the results they need, no matter what.

The Seventh Arcanum endows its owners with leadership skills and encourages them to take on the role of the engine in any process in which they participate. Sevens will not be able to stick at being a subordinate for long if there is no prospect of growth and furthering themselves. If a Seven is happy to go to work from nine to five and performs routine activities, then this is a distinct sign that their energy is in a very negative state, or perhaps that he or she is not a Seven at all!

The Energy of Speed goads people to climb over others to achieve their goals. This is a unique and highly valuable ability. There is nothing negative in this because if you want to reach great heights, you need to be ready to sacrifice everything, including friends and their interests. Admittedly, at any given moment Sevens need to maintain a balance of energy and keep their free will under control. Yes, Sevens are able to forge ahead, and in most cases, this is totally justified. But sometimes Sevens themselves, without adequately assessing the situation, are blinded by the overall end task they have set themselves and fall under the wheels of their own locomotives.

Management, prioritization and targeting are areas where Sevens can shine in all their glory. Because Sevens are able to perceive and apprehend the world very quickly, they are quickly able to come up with something that others have not yet had time to think of. Often, Sevens are extremely good at coming up with bright ideas or innovative solutions. However, they are often unable to actualize it themselves. Sevens need to be able to delegate responsibilities, build a plan and strategy and then pass on their implementation to other people while moving on themselves without getting bogged down in the routine processes of making it happen.

Sevens are great motivators. It is important that they have a team which they can inspire with their ideas. Setting the necessary pace, getting things started and drawing up ideas — are all areas where Sevens are well ahead of others.

As mentioned above, the Seventh Arcanum endows individuals with a spirit of rivalry. Therefore, competition in business is a very promising area of development for them. Sevens love competition, they love the recognition that comes from winning various titles, prizes and ratings. They are precisely the sort of people who measure themselves in terms of their success, the sort of people who will only be satisfied if they are in first place on top of the podium. If someone wants to encourage a Seven to do something, they just need to activate their spirit of competition (just be sure that you are happy coming in second place in all probability).

The Seventh Arcanum encourages a person to seek high earnings and luxurious things and to improve their level of prosperity. It's all about being constantly on the move and constantly raising the bar.

Bearing in mind the meaning of the Seventh Arcanum in the context of the Tarot deck, it is important to transfer these characteristics to those areas of activity that Sevens are drawn to. First and foremost, it is, of course, about travel and transport. Everything that might be connected with trips, adventures and travel, activities that keep you constantly on the move — all these have a positive influence on a Seven's life and end with a good outcome. Logistics and any other activity related to transport, correspondingly, stimulates the Seventh energy and helps Sevens attain high earnings.

Sevens are excellent athletes, especially when it comes to high-speed sports and competitions. They are natural strategists and good at team sports. The higher the speed involved, the more productive a Seven becomes.

HEALTH

Sevens are constantly in motion, they always need to be doing something. When a Seven is at rest and seems happy about it, this is a warning sign that something is wrong and that their energy has turned negative.

Sevens are perhaps the people at the highest risk of getting an injury in the Destiny Code Matrix. Injuries can happen completely out of the blue, a Seven might get seriously injured slipping down the stairs or tripping over a carpet. Bearing in mind their passion for extreme sports and speed, it is worth taking into account the risks that Sevens take so lightly.

First and foremost, Sevens need to make sure they have all the right safety equipment in place, have undergone all the necessary training, and carefully and responsibly weighed up all the risks involved.

It is no coincidence that Sevens have the most car accidents or fall and break limbs and suffer all the consequences and side effects of their love of speed and testing the law of gravity.

People endowed with the energy of Speed quickly recover from their injuries and get better from illnesses. They are very hardy and able to overcome all sorts of difficulties, even when it comes to fighting complex diseases.

Sevens can teach themselves to walk again despite the prognoses of doctors to the contrary, they are the sort of people who try to resist disease and illness with all their might.

It is important for people with the Seventh energy to remember that speed can be an enemy as well as a friend. Speed gives them certain advantages (on the road, in life, in achieving their goals), but it is also able to instantly knock them off balance and throw them to the wayside, rendering them immobile and depriving them of the ability to travel further down the road.

RELATIONSHIPS

People with the Energy of Speed are warriors and conquerors, they measure the strength of their feelings by the difficulty of the challenge of winning over their potential partner. The more unattainable the object of desire, the brighter their emotions and the stronger their passion.

When the Seventh Arcanum is in the Relationship zone, this indicates that relations with a partner will develop very rapidly. This might involve moving a partner to their house. This might involve having joint goals and a single plan to organize their life together. These are those cases when a common goal unites a relationship, and when its absence breaks and destroys the union.

Being a Seven means wanting to be in a position of leadership in all things, including relationships. People endowed with the Energy of Speed are always in a rush blinded by passion and therefore dive in head first, seeing only the goal ahead of them. It often turns out that having won the heart of the person they have chosen (having attained their goal), they lose interest, and the relationship loses its relevance and significance.

With a Seven for a partner, it is important to always have a strategy and think through each of your actions a few steps ahead, not so much to win them over but more to understand them and see the relationship from their side. It is worth taking this valuable advice on board because Sevens are always on the move, and if their partner isn't able to keep up with them, their Seven will soon have a new goal in sight and be rushing off to attain it without a backwards glance. Sevens' blindness can manifest itself in another, fairly common scenario. Having achieved their goal and melted and tamed their partner's heart, once they are finally able to appreciate their "prize", Sevens often realize that the person they have 'won over' isn't quite what corresponded to their original ideal. When 'conquering' their partners, Sevens are not always able to evaluate them realistically and sensibly and having 'won' their hearts, they don't always see in them what they were hoping for. This is a question of "expectation" over "reality".

When the Seventh Arcanum stands in the major zones of the matrix (especially in the Character and Higher Essence zones), a partner of this type will always need to be inspired to act — to add fuel to the relationship. This is not the same as the Sixth Energy, which requires attention and strength. The Seven needs gasoline — to pour oil on the fire — something that will ignite and spur their feelings.

When the Seventh Arcanum is in the Relationship zone, and its energy has turned negative, there is a likelihood that this individual might meet the sort of partner who will burst into their life like a hurricane, turning everything upside down, initially caring for them, promising a 'happy ever after' but, at the vital moment, disappearing just as quickly as they arrived, leaving the former "love of their life" somewhere on the side of the road that was meant to lead them onto a new goal and a fabulous future.

When the Seventh energy turns negative in the Relationships zone you can be sure there are going to be scandals and showdowns. These involve leaving home, hysterics and eternal rivalries with their partners.

The Seventh Arcanum can indicate the importance of the coincidence of life rhythms in partners. Sevens need partners who will be their equals enjoying a similar way of life with the same principles and aspirations. Sevens make great lovers. They have more passion than Sixes. They are great lovers of experimentation and extreme sports in everything they do and the bedroom is no exception.

When people with a Seven in their Relationship zone feel that they are falling out with their partner, it's a good idea to recommend they go on a trip or travel together in order to determine a common goal and so that they can find themselves in 'extreme' (although, of course, not life-threatening) situations.

An interesting fact about people with a Major Seventh Energy in their Destiny Code matrix is that they are often obsessed with the manic idea of eliminating their partner. Eliminating and destroying them — in the literal sense. An analysis of the matrices of prisoners convicted of the murder of their spouse (or business partner) reveals that a large percentage of them are Sevens.

INDICATIONS THAT THIS ENERGY IS IN A –

- A state of stasis, immobility and complete rest.
- A lack of goals and objectives.
- Constantly late and a sense that they never have enough time.
- A restlessness and chaos about their actions.
- Busy doing a million things at the same time.
- Reassessing their strengths.
- Megalomania (a sense of superiority over others).
- Underestimating others.
- Hasty assessment and conclusions.
- Revenge, envy, pettiness.
- A propensity to bear grudges.
- Unaccommodating and quarrelsome with their colleagues and team.
- Pathos and pride.
- Blinded by an idea.
- Leaving the agreed route halfway.

- Being stuck in one place (not moving house or traveling).
- A certain passivity about life.
- Suspiciousness in their relations with others (the habit of seeing an opponent and competitor in everyone they meet).

INDICATIONS THAT THIS ENERGY IS IN A +

- Purposefulness and a specific list of thought-out tasks to be completed.
- A habit of working out a route or a plan of action.
- The desire to achieve the goal, no matter what.
- Concentration and clarity of action.
- Taking information on board quickly and the ability to make instant decisions.
- Composure and the ability to control their confidence in their own personal impunity.
- Personal growth and progress (which can be assessed and measured).
- A thirst for self-realization.
- Trips, travel and house moves.
- Inspiring and motivating others
- Sports and active physical activities.
- An interest in various forms of transport (as a hobby, for pleasure and for work).
- High status and power.

KARMIC TASKS:

- To always have goals and to achieve them;
- To avoid criticizing others and expecting more from them than they are able to achieve;
- To give their thoughts expression and their actions agency — charging others with energy;
- To delegate tasks — to learn to trust others and their actions;
- To always be on the move — to fight and eradicate laziness and stagnation;
- To inspire others to action;
- To be one ste
- p ahead

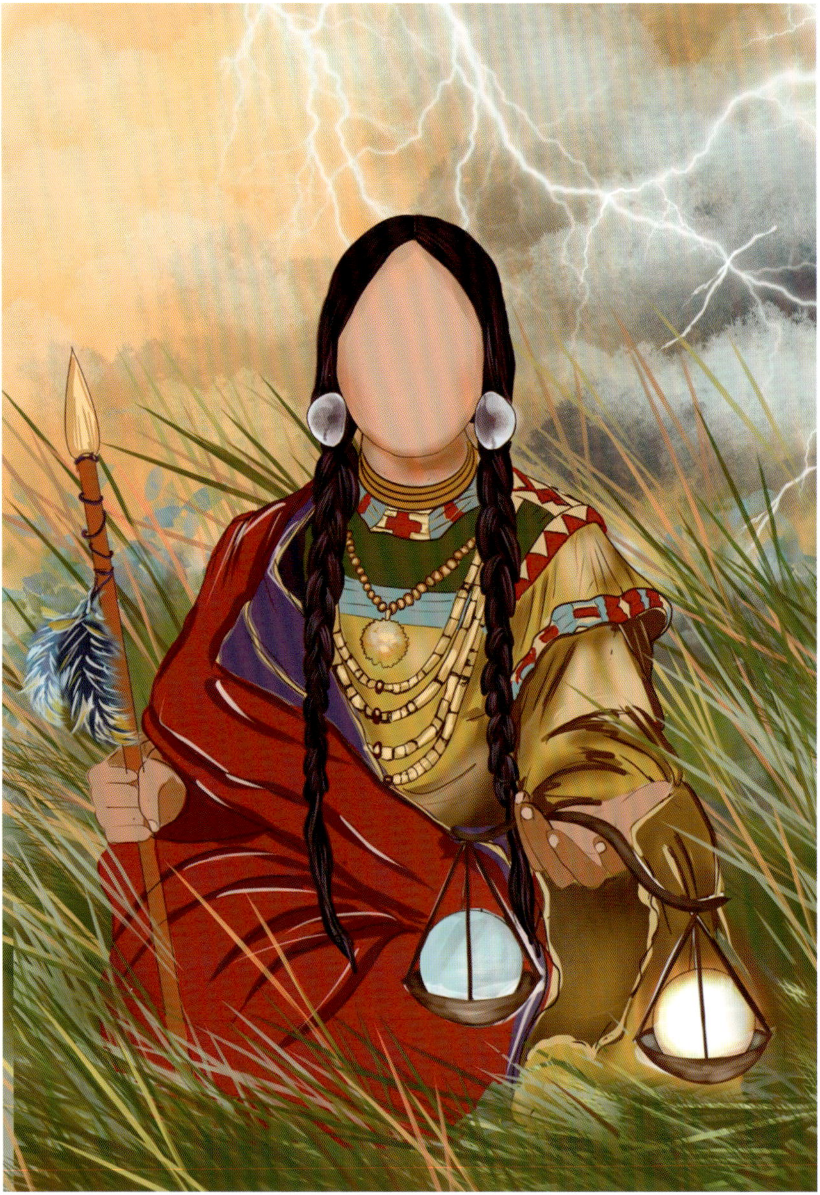

ARCANUM 8. JUSTICE

Beat your tambourine, shaman! Call the Spirits to the powwow.
Let the court and rulings be fair.
Let he who has committed the misdemeanor, answer for the deed,
And let he who is innocent, know no fear.
Beat your tambourine, shaman! The holy herbs have been scattered!
Circle around the fire, call upon the Heavenly Father.
He who sees everything from above, He who is just and wise,
Let him pronounce the verdict, maintaining the full weight of the Law.

RESPONSIBILITY — LAW — KARMA

In the Tarot deck, the Eighth Arcanum stands for Justice, the energy of law and order, the energy of karma.

An individual with the Major Eighth Arcana in their Destiny Code matrix is also known as the bearer of the "Karmic Scales". Everything is changeable, unpredictable and unstable and a person with an innate thirst for justice needs to accept this because they are the sort of people whose personal energy is precisely that Justice. It is sometimes difficult to differentiate between good and bad, and here it is worth recognizing that by concentrating too much on one element in one's life, it is very easy to upset one's balance and go astray.

The Energy of Justice endows its owner with the ability to see the causes and consequences of actions. Each step needs to be considered and weighed — otherwise there is a danger of not being where you should be on the course that has been laid out for you. More than anyone else, individuals endowed with the Energy of Justice, are characterized by their strict adherence to their principles. These people's internal code of honor limits their range of opportunities in life, but at the same time improves the quality of their lives. It is difficult for Eights to go with the "flow" and to find a role in life, which coincides with their clear and precise requirements. If everything works out and they do not experience any internal contradictions, success is guaranteed.

People with the Arcanum of Justice tend to be attracted to all things "official". And the Universe karmically justifies and even recommends this path for them. If we are talking about work, then it needs to be clearly defined by a contract or agreement, the salary should be set out on a legal footing and any action taken should be confirmed and fully notarized. That last bit, of course, is a slight exaggeration, but not without a certain grain of truth to it.

Every word spoken by someone with the Eighth Energy in their Destiny Code matrix is perceived by those around them as if it has come from an official source and is the gospel truth. This characteristic draws many people to consult Eights for advice. An Eight will generally advise the following: if you have thought something — then don't say it out loud, if you have said something — don't put it down in writing, if you have put something in writing — don't sign it, and, if you've signed it — well, you'll just have to fulfil your obligations no matter the cost. Otherwise, failure to do so will be costly, and your karmic comeuppance will be swift.

Individuals with a Sixteen and Major Eight in the Destiny Code matrix are better off not promising anything out loud in front of other people because the Sixteenth Arcanum will destroy even the best-laid plans. In this situation, a person with a combination of Eight and Sixteen must simply perform or not perform the action required without any further ado. This also applies to their personal plans — anything they have written down should not be read aloud or shared with others.

People with the Energy of Justice are very responsible individuals. Perhaps of all the 22 energies, there is no other that can match it for its power of self-control. But this energy, like all the others, has two polarities. When it is in a positive state, an individual can be demanding and responsible: they are remarkable for their precision, organization and honest approach to everything they do, as well as their one hundred percent dedication to any process. When they are in a minus state, these individuals strive to keep their actions simple and systematic — the vital thing for them is that they have correctly completed the requirements of the algorithm they are serving, and that's it.

Eights' strengths: their ability to work extremely hard, their responsibility, their strict adherence to their principles and their sense of justice — can be positive qualities (when in a state of balance) and negative (when in a state of hyperactivity). When these qualities become over-pronounced and disharmonious in an individual, then it is worth paying attention to the state of their Eighth Energy and identifying those factors that are causing this hyperactivity. For example, the apparent opposites of being irresponsible or hyper-responsible can both be symptoms of a negative manifestation of the Eighth Energy and, accordingly, may have the negative side effect of interfering with an individual's path in life and creating additional difficulties for them.

WATCHWORDS

Perhaps, the first and most important point in an Eight's code of honor is diligence.
- You said you'd do it — so do it! You made a promise — so keep it!
- A man of his word is a man of honor.
- Every action taken — carries a consequence.

FINANCES

People endowed with the Energy of Justice are workaholics and do not shy away from any type of work, regardless of whether it is physical or mental. Eights have the unique ability to be able to engage in any business and do it well.

But there is one caveat, which has already been mentioned above. The Eighth Arcanum is very demanding, a person with a Major Eight sets themselves very high standards and has a list of precise criteria, that he or she inexorably and stubbornly adheres to. At first glance, it may appear that this excessive adherence to their principles, might prevent them from expanding their horizons but this is not the case for Eights. Because their innate pedantry means that they possess qualities such as perseverance, patience and the desire to see things through to the end, whatever business Eights decide to devote themselves to will in due time guarantee their success. The main thing for them is to define what step needs to be taken and to do so in a timely manner.

Karma is something that Eights always needs to bear in mind. Karma keeps particularly close tabs on the Eights of this world. It is highly recommended that any Eight engaged in business or public service should strictly follow any official agreements they enter into. There can be no "borderline" business schemes, "cash in hand" payments or creative accounting as far as Eights are concerned. Any activity they are engaged in must be carried out in strict accordance with procedure and the law. Any Eight involved in a business or activity, which by its very nature is criminal or requires an "alternative" approach, will have to adapt their code of behavior to allow them to adhere to the "laws" of the environment in which this business or activity is carried out. Otherwise, you can almost guarantee that it will be the Eight who will find themselves carrying the can, or losing much more than they initially invested.

The Energy of Justice provides good opportunities for those endowed with it to improve their financial standing. The main prerequisite ensuring their success will depend on how "official" the status of the particular activity they are engaged in is. The personal qualities mentioned above are an excellent complement to the strategic mindset that Eights are endowed with. Therefore, a persistent, step-by-step career path is their best approach to achieving success, authority and wealth.

As a rule, Eights are the sort of people who work their way up from the very "bottom" and achieve great success as a result of their perseverance and aspiration. The strong backbone and character endowed by the energy of Justice provide those that possess it with stamina, endurance and diligence, which will sooner or later bring great results. After all, karma not only gives people a "slap on the wrist" but also provides them with rewards.

People with the Energy of Justice love money and know how to handle it. Individuals endowed with the Eighth Energy have a more developed sense of responsibility and rationality than other people. Therefore, once an Eight becomes rich, he or she will never lack for money for the rest of his or her life.

HEALTH

Responsibility is a quality that is inherent to Eights and they honestly take responsibility for whatever activity they are engaged in. However, when it comes to their own health, Eights lack any sense of responsibility whatsoever.

People with the energy of Justice highly value productivity and, therefore, work very hard. Workaholism and overwork are the main causes of a large number of the illnesses and diseases they experience.

A strong backbone and character are also among their special personal characteristics. But this moral stamina often manifests itself at the physical level in a certain "ossification" of the body and a complete lack of flexibility and plasticity. Outwardly, they might look sporty, fit and slim, but they will not be flexible at all. This "resistance" can harm the development of the joints and the musculoskeletal system, therefore, it is highly recommended that Eights concentrate on developing their flexibility through regular stretching. Regardless of their profession, Eights are prone to wear and tear by allowing their bodies to get exhausted and dehydrated. And, of course, overwork can lead to burnout, both on a physical and emotional level.

Eights' predilection for a systematic approach to everything can manifest itself in chronic diseases that require regularly following defined and detailed instructions. For example, taking a long course of drugs prescribed over a long period, or using complicated medical devices to maintain their health at the required level.

It is worth adding that water often works as an excellent treatment for ailing Eights. It might be a simple bath to relieve their fatigue after a hard day's work, a glass of water taken regularly, or a vacation near a large body of water when they are physically and emotionally exhausted. Of course, when you encounter someone with a serious illness, they should always immediately seek professional medical advice.

RELATIONSHIPS

Individuals endowed with the energy of Justice are very straightforward and honest with themselves and their partners. Whenever an Eight enters into a relationship, it is initially weighed up and regulated in advance. The Eighth Arcanum requires precision and clarity, and accordingly, if Eights decide to invest in a relationship with someone, they will be honest, straightforward and clear.

People with the energy of Justice are faithful and reliable spouses. They are people of honor and dignity and therefore require the same of their partners. For them, as in all other areas of life, matters of love work very much in accordance with the Law of Karma. Marriages should be officially declared, your house should be your own, as should your slippers, your own personal mug, and even more importantly (almost obsessively) your own toothbrush. Initially, each stage of a relationship and every anticipated event should be discussed and agreed upon in advance. And if any clause of any agreement is violated, Eights find it very difficult to disguise their displeasure.

Eights have a fairly limited emotional range. They do not know how to show their feelings and talk about them. As a rule, they express their feelings for their partners through their actions. Respect and trust are the main foundations on which their partnerships are built. Don't expect dazzling courtships, vivid emotional experiences and crazy adventures from Eights. At times, you might be excused for thinking that they are as cold as ice, but this is not the case at all. Other people's excessive displays of emotion and endless chatter often confuse them. But the fact that they will always stand by their partners speaks far more eloquently about them than the strongest emotional outburst or a thousand sweet nothings.

Eights are just as demanding of their business partners and friends as they are of their sexual partners. They will never mention it out loud, but they will always take note of anything they consider to be important. Any person allowed into an Eight's inner circle has to meet certain very strict selection criteria. If a potential partner or friend does not come through this casting process, then they are likely to be cast off forever.

Eights are endowed with excellent communication skills and can attract the attention of large audiences, however, this is not something they necessarily need or crave. They might have just one friend or partner, or they might not have any at all. In this regard, Eights unambiguously prize quality over quantity.

INDICATIONS THAT THIS ENERGY IS IN A –
- An inflexibility and rigidity of character.
- Coldness and a lack of emotion.
- An inability to pick up on tones and nuances (things are either black or white, and people are either friends or foes).
- Bullheadedness (a lack of flexibility).
- Stinginess (in all its manifestations).
- To fail to fight and seek justice.
- Being excessively principled.
- A crippling sense of responsibility.
- Links with the criminal and illegal.
- The desire to break or circumvent the systems governing life and official state, commercial or personal relationships).
- An uncompromising personality.

INDICATIONS THAT THIS ENERGY IS IN A +
- Nobility of character.
- Stamina and backbone.
- An internal code of honor.
- A consistency in their judgements and actions.
- Responsibility and impartiality.

- Objectivity.
- The desire to see things through to the end.
- A love of hard work and constant striving for productivity.

KARMIC TASKS:
- to pay their way, holding themselves to their every word;
- to look for causes and determine their consequences;
- to act in accordance with the law (state, moral or personal);
- to be honest with themselves and others;
- to seek justice;
- to create a system for everything in their lives, be it their opinions, lifestyle, meanings or values;
- to learn to discover their true feelings;

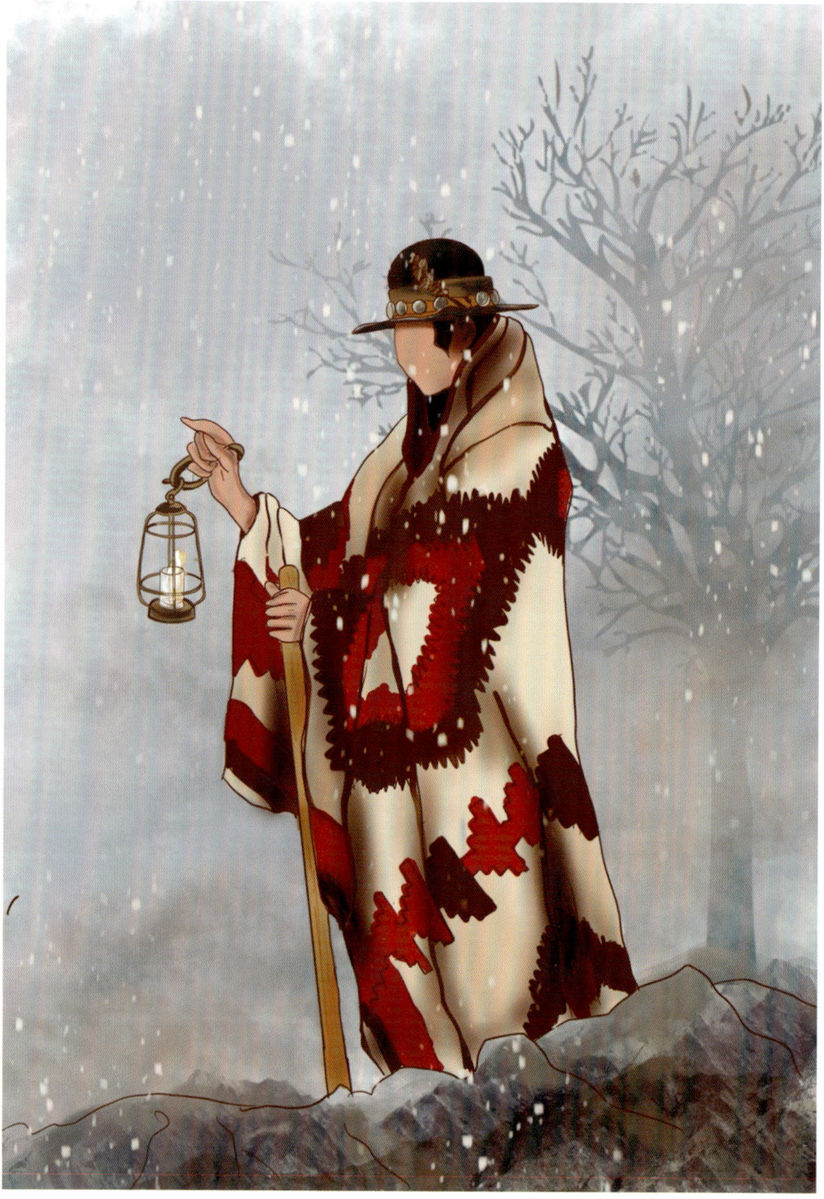

ARCANUM 9. THE HERMIT

> What are your thoughts, my friend?
> What is this sadness, this burden that lies on your heart?
> Why do you depart, leaving others only with sadness?
> Without your words, their lives will be empty.
> Let's smoke a pipe for the road,
> The tobacco will judge us like a wise old chief.
> And maybe, remembering our years of friendship,
> You won't set off to the ends of the earth.

SELF-SUFFICIENCY — WISDOM — DEPTH

Nines are wise, deep and self-sufficient. They always strive to get to the bottom of the truth. As a rule, they are rather diffident when it comes to communication as, for the most part, they prefer solitude.

In the Tarot deck, the Ninth Arcanum is the Hermit. This card is cold and deep and if you end up with it in your hand it will reveal many meanings. The hermit will always open a person's eyes to the truth and the essence of the matter at hand.

One of the specific characteristics of a Nine is their need to search for depth and meaning. They can also be attributed to the strengths of the personality, considering these qualities as a kind of "secret weapon". The hermit is always looking for the original source of information, the whole picture and meaning is important to him. Nines search for meaning everywhere and in everything, and every stage of their search is thoroughly and carefully evaluated.

Nines seek meaning in every area of their lives. After all, everything that happens is done for some reason and in the name of something. Why are interpersonal relationships built, why do people need to prove themselves, why do other people appear on our journey in life, why does the Day, the Sun, the Light, the Universe exist?

People with the Energy of the Ninth Arcanum sometimes have an unhealthy sense of pride. Often Nines are disappointed and irritated by the "naivety and ignorance" of those around them and believe that no one but they are able to understand the true meaning of things. They consider themselves superior to others and, as a rule, this can create difficulties for them in life. Being by nature diffident and uncommunicative people who rarely reach out to others, they complicate their lives and miss many opportunities to realize the karmic programs that have been set for them.

The Energy of the Hermit and the Energy of Knowledge share many similarities. Being based on the desire to acquire knowledge, they perform an important function with the Universal Supertask of accumulating and conserving information. However, there are some basic differences between them, which are fundamental to these two energies. Both Arcana (9 and 5) endow their owner with intellect, a high level of intelligence and, of course, the desire to learn and transmit new knowledge.

Over a long period, by dint of their hard work Nines collect knowledge piece by piece and share it with the world in the form of a written book, where every word is carefully weighed and makes sense, and every fact is painstakingly checked. A Five does not have the ability to spend a lot of time collecting information and putting it down in a huge "tome" due to the lack of perseverance and patience in their nature. The Five studies the book written by the Nine, and, having gathered its meaning, creates their own training session or master class, becoming a conduit for the knowledge they have received from the Nine.

A person with the Energy of the Hermit prefers to share his or her teachings with a narrow circle of elect students, believing that only a few are able to perceive the truth and take on board their ideas. A person with the energy of the Fifth Arcanum, on the contrary, strives to disseminate knowledge to the masses and believes that the more people have it, the more productive this knowledge will be for society. Nines try to delve deeper into the systematic nature of processes and pay a great deal of attention to the complexity of constructing their text, whereas Fives simplify the content, preserving the most important and valuable thoughts, which, accordingly, makes the information more accessible to the wider public.

The common purpose and differences of approach unite the energies of these Arcana in the implementation of the vital process of transmitting and preserving knowledge. Both ways of doing things are important, and as a result, they guarantee the transfer, maintenance and availability of knowledge at all stages of its distribution.

Among other idiosyncrasies, Nines do not like to put their names to their achievements and are often not fully recognized by society as a whole. Fives, on the contrary, strive to have their names associated with their achievements and do their utmost to be recognized as an integral part of them.

One of the main qualities of people with the Ninth Energy in the Character zone is their self-sufficiency. Nines are so independent of the outside world that they are able to look after themselves and self-actualize regardless of external factors.

Hermits' "maturity" will always make them stand out from the crowd and their peers. It's as if Nines exist beyond the realms of time, reality for them has a completely different, other worldly decelerated rhythm. This becomes very obvious when you observe how they live their lives. Nines ponder their decisions and actions for a long time and take even longer to come to them. By delving deeply into themselves and any given situation and by resolving and determining truths, Nines are quite capable of losing track of time. They have a tendency to forget how old they are because this is not something they particularly perceive. Nines have a very specific idiosyncratic taste in clothes. Nines are often dressed in old-fashioned clothes that seem out of date for the times they live in.

Their ability to dig deep within themselves is perhaps the Nine's most complex character trait. They spend their entire lives investigating their inner worlds, analyzing themselves and studying the depth of their personalities. And at times, they find it difficult to re-emerge from their inner "I" without some outside help. The demands that Nines place on themselves to push boundaries and get to the source of knowledge can create difficulties for them when it comes to realizing themselves in the outside world. In other words, the deeper and more complex the personality, the more difficult it is for it to exist in and adapt to the generally accepted way that life is organized.

A person with the Ninth Arcanum in their Destiny Code Matrix will always strive for self-sufficiency and independence in everything they do and sometimes they can become lonely. But this is perfectly normal.

It is a very useful thing for people with the energy of the Hermit not to have to depend on external factors. When an individual has a Nine in their Financial or Relationship Zones or on one of the points of their Ancestral Square, this indicates that these individuals will be at their most productive having separated themselves from the factors that characterize these zones. If the Ninth Arcanum is located in the Overall Destiny section of an individual's Destiny Code, then the main task in their life will be to learn to be self-sufficient and accept themselves as a complete and separate world in their own right, who require nothing more than that which they can provide for themselves. They are in and of themselves the Truth and Meaning of their own lives.

When the Ninth Arcanum is located in the Health Map and Material Karma and Relationships Zone, this indicates that potentially difficult situations will arise in their lives. Situations where this individual will have to face loss and deprivation. Being a Nine indicates the end, departure, loss, the final outcome.

WATCHWORDS

Nines are very complex people. They are multi-layered, and it is very difficult to establish the motives and reasons for their behavior. They are guided by a principle that is inflexible and stubborn. Therefore, they are often left only with their principles and miss the opportunity to gain possession of something or make it happen.

- You're better off with nothing than the first thing that lands in your lap.
- Solitude is a way of life.
- There is only one point of view and only that one is the correct one.

FINANCES

The Ninth Energy is very heavy and powerful, and accordingly, it is not a fast-flowing one. And this can clearly be seen in people who possess the Ninth Arcanum in their Character Zone.

Their slow pace, the depths that they go to when engaging in any process, the length of their reflection and the desire to study any issue from every angle can stretch out any activity that a Nine is engaged in for days, months and years. As a rule, they themselves do not notice their slowness and perceive the protracted time they take to do anything from the point of view that the longer something takes then the better the result will be.

Nines work at a strictly intellectual level. They make brilliant teachers, scientists, writers, intelligent technology engineers, professors of complex sciences, and researchers and are among the most advanced minds in society. It can be unequivocally argued that the goal of any activity to which Nines devote themselves is to achieve something of global significance for humanity, and the material in life does not mean very much to people of this sort.

The Energy of the Hermit is definitely not about money. Material values for people endowed with the Ninth Arcanum are, if not the least important priority, then at least the second least important. Material well-being, wealth, luxury and excess are alien concepts to them and not of paramount importance.

If the Ninth Arcanum is located in the Finance zone, then this would suggest that any activity this individual undertakes should be of a self-reliant and independent nature. Working in a team, a large company or in conditions that require a large number of people is not going to suit Nines. Likewise, they are not going to be engaged in the sort of work that requires travel, business trips and a strict schedule.

The Ninth Energy is all about freedom. Freedom from control, management, dependence on other people and outside factors and freedom, above all, from time constraints.

Hermits' strength lies in their intellect, physical labor tires them out and forces them to go deeper into themselves. Nines should be advised to choose intellectual over physical employment.

Nines are the most valuable people in society. Their karmic task is, first and foremost, to discover and find uses for new knowledge, to recover lost knowledge, to clear the truth of all pollution and falsehood and transmit all of the above to other people to be used for the benefit of humanity.

People with the Ninth Arcanum in their Character, Portrait and Higher Essence Zones are endowed with the ability to use alternative sources of information. Cosmic communication channels, extrasensory perception, the whisperings of our ancestors — you can call it whatever you like. By diving deep down into themselves and removing themselves from the surrounding reality, Nines are able to hear more than others. And these sources are also able to provide them with material opportunities in the form of outside support, sponsorship and various kinds of passive sources of income.

HEALTH

Hermits are drawn to asceticism. Their lifestyle is arranged around the principles of simplicity and accessibility. A passion for simple cuisine and easily digested foods is the key to their good health and healthy bodies. Nines often choose restrictive diets and get into vegetarianism, raw food, or any number of other proscriptive diets.

People with the Ninth Energy can go without food and water for long periods, they are hardy in uncomfortable situations and can travel long distances.

When engaged in a prolonged bout of self-discovery, Nines often drive themselves into a timetable and framework that can cause psychological breakdown. Nines are more prone than anyone else, (perhaps only on a par with the 18th energy) to serious psychological trauma and mental illness. Their mental health is their most vulnerable weakness and requires paramount attention on their part.

RELATIONSHIPS

When the Ninth Energy is in the Relationship zone, it can indicate a high probability that there will be a large age difference between these individuals and their partners. Nines are faithful, wise and deep people who will allow their partners to have their own personal space and will not be high maintenance.

Respect for their personal boundaries should be taken very seriously. Any partner will have to understand that Nines are self-sufficient and need their own personal space and time for themselves in life.

Sometimes, the life of a Hermit can seem like a frozen lake. If you want to swim or fish in it, you will need to wait until it gets warm and thaws. You will need to wait for the right time and fill your expectations with meaning. You should not break the ice by force — after all, it's not all that pleasant swimming in cold water and the fish are asleep at the bottom anyway.

When the Ninth Energy is located in the Relationships Zone, (regardless of which Arcanum governs the Character zone) then a guest marriage or relationship where there is the option of living separately and independently is recommended. Living in different cities and countries, or going on long business trips or travels are often convenient arrangements for a relationship with a Nine.

Most people with a Major Nine in their Destiny Code Matrix find it difficult to open up their bodies to others. It takes a long time for Nines to enter into physical contact with another person and they are very careful about doing so. Initially underestimating and disliking their physical looks, Nines often consider themselves a bit of an "ugly duckling" and sincerely believe that everyone around them sees them in the same light.

As a rule, this sort of self-negation can cause a person's energy to enter into a minus state, and it is important to work on this when working out karmic programs for their Character and Overall Destiny energies.

Nines can take a long time searching for "the one" and remain single for years on end. Nines are monogamous more often than not and value deep attachments and strong feelings. Love, for the Hermit, is about finding someone who can provide them with a reflection of themselves: someone with the same thoughts, of the same time and of the same essence. They place no emphasis on physical attraction or their partner's external qualities. Nines are looking for a bonding of souls and not bodies.

If they fail to meet the right person in their lives, or if for some reason their partner passes away, then a Nine can quite sincerely and happily enter into a life of voluntary solitude. Nines are quite satisfied with the feelings they experience in such a 'unilateral' relationship. When it comes to love, for a Nine the very presence of Love is what is most important and not the number of its sources that it radiates from.

INDICATIONS THAT THIS ENERGY IS IN A −
- Closing themselves off from the outside world.
- Refusing to share the knowledge they have acquired.
- Suppression of their innate desire to develop their intellectual abilities.
- A fear of and withdrawal from society.
- Remaining in a state of deep disappointment.

INDICATIONS THAT THIS ENERGY IS IN A +
- The realization of the potential of their minds, intellect and abilities.
- The desire to share and disseminate valuable knowledge.

KARMIC TASKS:
- to comprehend and collect knowledge;
- to transmit knowledge to followers, students, descendants;
- to find answers and reveal truths to others;
- to be self-sufficient — accept yourself as a complete unit;
- to learn to be independent (from people, circumstances, things, morals, values);

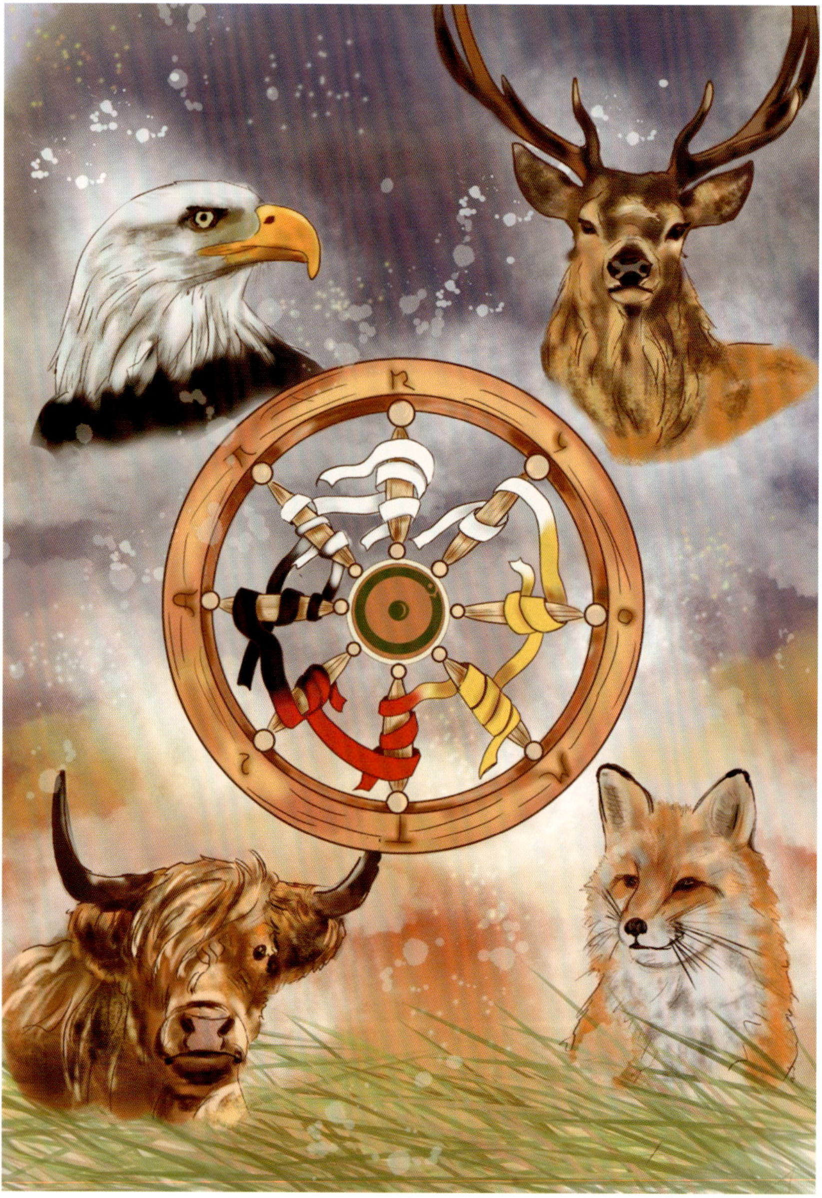

ARCANUM 10. THE WHEEL OF DESTINY

*The Great Eagle Spirit circles over the buffalo herd.
He watches from the blue skies so that life flows peacefully below.
And under the cover of darkness, as soon as the moon rises,
A new beast cunningly takes dominion.
By the light of the sun's rays at dawn, and then the brilliance of the stars
So, the cycle of our days continues in accordance with the Wheel of Life.
And He who looks down on us from above during the day,
Becomes powerless and broken during the night.*

CYCLE — LUCK — FATE

The Wheel of Fortune is the Tenth Arcanum in the Tarot deck. It is the Energy of Flow and Destiny. It is a light energy, weightless in its essence, but sometimes a complex one to bear when passing through human life.

The main task of a person with the Tenth energy in their Destiny Code Matrix is not to stress too much. What is important is to "go with the flow", relax and not resist its currents. The seemingly simple resolution of this task is precisely that — seemingly simple. For the most part, the majority of people are incapable of relaxing and trusting in the seemingly chaotic flow of their lives. Everyone wants to control their lives, make plans and make choices. But with Tens, things are different. Possibly as a result of their upbringing or the influence of other external factors, some still retain a craving to control the course of their lives, but the essence of the Energy of the Flow will somehow make sure that they are in the right place at the right time and remind them that life is subordinate to Fortune.

The Arcanum of Flow is a very positive energy and encourages those endowed with it to enjoy life's pleasures, find the good in it, create positive vibrations and share them with others. The more relaxed and ready a Ten is for good fortune to come knocking on their door, the less resistance and insurmountable difficulties he or she will encounter in his or her life.

You just need to let things happen and submit to the inevitable. It is important as early as possible to accept that a person is powerless before

Fate. It makes no sense to resist the Flow and run against the wind. People with the Tenth Arcanum in their Destiny Codes are the lucky ones who are destined to go with the flow without a single chance of their course being sabotaged.

The universe evidently pays particularly close attention to Tens, showering them with bonuses and good luck to pass through life luckier and happier than others. Tens can lie on the couch for days on end without the slightest twinge of conscience waiting for a miracle, inspiration or a fantastic opportunity to fall into their laps. And the most interesting thing is, no matter how paradoxical it may sound, this really is what happens to them.

Tens are people governed by inspiration. It doesn't matter if they're an engineer, a plumber, an artist or a civil servant. If they do not feel inspired, if the "light bulb" does not light up in their heads, they will not budge an inch.

The energy of the Flow works very much in the same way as the wheel. If today, a person finds himself at the top, tomorrow he will be at the very bottom. The cyclical nature of life is an integral part of the karmic program for Tens.

The chronicle of a person's life with a Ten in their matrix could be represented like a zebra's black and white stripes. After a difficult period of life, a happy one will surely follow, which in all likelihood will probably be followed by new trials... This is the nature of fate. You just have to accept it, learn to appreciate the joyful moments and discover valuable meanings and ideas in every lesson that life puts in your way. It's a good thing for Tens to work out as early as possible whether the zebra they are personally dealing with is one with white and black stripes or, on the contrary, one with black and white ones.

The Tenth Arcanum has some very particular combinations of triple-ups, which require very close attention in the context of an individual's Destiny Code Matrix. They are very important! When an individual has a personal energy of 10 in their Character zone and likewise a double up of 10-15 in their matrix, this indicates "an unhappy fate" and a high risk of life and death accidents or death as a result of their own negligence, as well as the risk of ending up completely down and out having lost everything with no chance of getting themselves back up again. The incidence of the triple up 10-16-22 indicates a high probability of being imprisoned due to their taking part in criminal activities, scams and fraud.

WATCHWORDS

What happens to you is all a question of fate. Joy, fun, happiness, success, silence, searching, emptiness, exit. Life is full of ebbs and flows, one always follows the other. People with the Energy of the Flow have to learn to accept that all things pass and that something new will come along, but that sooner or later this will also pass, giving way to what follows next.

- Fate gives and fate takes away.
- Resistance is futile, so you're much better off relaxing and enjoying the ride.
- The most important thing in life is to be in the right place at the right time.

One of the important moments in the lives of Tens is when they learn to perceive what it is that they "want". Tens do not need to bother with "being able" or "having to", it's enough for Tens simply to "want to", to "allow themselves to" and this is sufficient for the Universe to pick up their signal and inevitably react and respond. Tens are living evidence that in 100% of cases various kinds of affirmations and "wish lists" can work.

FINANCE

Tens find it difficult to fit into any kind of generally accepted regime. Activities that require adherence to a clear schedule and work plan are completely unsuitable for Tens since their productivity depends solely on their "inspiration".

"The state of resourcefulness" is a term that 100% relates to people with the Tenth energy. If they are not feeling resourceful, then there will be no getting any productivity out of them. No amount of pressurizing their sense of responsibility, duty, obligation or anything else of that sort will have any effect on a Ten and will not induce them to even lift a pinky to help. But as soon as the necessary cogs click in their heads, as soon as their energy is activated, they are capable of achieving the impossible, moving mountains and launching themselves into space.

Tens love money and money comes easily to them. But in accordance with the laws of life, their money runs out quickly, and Tens again have to wait for the next "manna from heaven" to drop into their laps. And sure enough, in due course this is exactly what happens — a happy coincidence provides them with a new lucky opportunity.

Tens are incapable of saving money for a rainy day. Tens who try to do this and go against the natural flow of their nature end up depriving themselves of their next lucrative opportunity from the Universe by keeping money in the bank.

When their energy is in a minus state, Tens can end up pointlessly running like a hamster on an exercise wheel. They then fall behind schedule, miss their deadlines, are late for everything and are incapable of getting anything done on time. And so on, day after day. People with the Tenth Energy are quite capable of becoming very rich several times over in their lives, but then they immediately lose their fortune and again sink back to the bottom. The Energy of Destiny throws Tens from one extreme to the other, and the swing of their pendulum of fate increases until it reaches its maximum. Having received a lot of money (it doesn't matter whether it has been hard-earned or won in a casino), a Ten can easily lose it all, but it is equally likely that they will be to get it all back again — this is just another manifestation of the "wheel" effect.

People with the Tenth energy in the Finance Zone typically change their jobs frequently and therefore work periodically. Tens can turn their hands to any sort of work as long they are not required to stick to a tight schedule because they can only live at their own pace. They often confuse day with night, productive periods with those when most people are resting. The important thing for them is to enjoy following their path and complete what fate has "by chance" led them to do while maintaining their own rhythms and adhering to them.

Fortune loves money, so any activity related to money, but not involving being paid a salary for their work, will be extremely attractive to individuals with the Tenth energy in their Finance Zone. And they are also much luckier than others when it comes to gambling, often winning big in casinos and lotteries.

HEALTH

On the whole, Tens are lucky with their health. They are very quick to react to everything and this includes responding quickly when their body is trying to tell them something.

A certain vulnerability to seasonal illnesses, colds, allergies and migraines reflects the cyclical nature of their lives, which plays such a big role in their fates.

Tens need to beware of falling into cycles of remissions and relapses after falling ill, which can be very likely. They should also not be surprised if illnesses or diseases recur even if this is not typical behavior for this malady at all. Likewise, female Tens can find that their menstrual cycles can be quite painful.

The periods of dawn and dusk do not sit well with Tens and it is not recommended that they go to bed or wake up at these times. These periods of the day are best avoided by Tens to help conserve their strength and energy.

People who are endowed with the Seventeenth Energy in their Destiny Code Matrix as well as the Tenth, need to concentrate on developing their flexibility with gymnastics or yoga. Especially yoga. People endowed with the Seventeenth Arcanum have the ability to develop the vibrations of their bodies and unleash the potential of all seven of their chakras. Meditation and exercises aimed at developing the mind and body can be a great help to them when faced with depression and feelings of emptiness.

People with Flow Energy are prone to extreme mood swings. In an instant, they can change from being cheerful and full of the joys of life to being sad or depressed. Hysteria and extremes of emotion are an integral part of everyday life for Tens.

RELATIONSHIPS

Wild mood swings are a typical characteristic of Tens and this applies to their relationships as well. In addition, Tens are very changeable when it comes to love and they can also be very capricious. Sometimes, it is very difficult to negotiate with them, make up with them or calm them down. But the very next day, everything can be absolutely fine as if nothing had ever happened. An individual with an active Tenth Energy loves being emotional. Passion, showdowns, quarrels, tears, laughter and misdemeanors are things that are important to Tens.

When it comes to love, Tens cannot bear monotony, and if they are forced into a relationship with a permanent partner, then their life turns into a romantic soap opera filled with all the above plot twists and entertainment.

People with the Tenth Arcanum in their Character or Portrait Zone very often change their partners, leave them, split up with them and then pair up with them again. This is because Tens find it difficult to adapt to others — this state of affairs contradicts their essence. Their idiosyncratic rhythms and way of life along with their unstable characters can take their toll on their relationships with others. Tens would rather choose their interests over their partners and will give up everything they have without any regrets. After all, Tens know that by closing one door, they increase the chances of a new one opening up.

Therefore, for those who have partners who are Tens, it is important for them not to put their Ten under too much pressure, as in life so with their relationships — they just need to surrender and go with the flow. They should not make too many plans and build up their expectations because everything can turn out completely different from how they expected. There should be a light touch to everything in a relationship with a Ten, and if it doesn't work out, then that's just the nature of Fate.

INDICATIONS THAT THIS ENERGY IS IN A −
- Moving against the flow and trying to resist it.
- Static life flow (no events — no life).
- The desire to comply with generally accepted frameworks and requirements.
- A state of unhappiness.
- Not living "their own lives".

INDICATIONS THAT THIS ENERGY IS IN A +
- Life is in constant flow and the ability to enjoy everything that life gives.
- Adventurism and willingness to take risks.
- A busy life and an active and rapid succession of events.
- Positive and open perception of everything and everyone.
- Constant change of place, change of activity, change of environment.
- Accepting Destiny with gratitude and an open heart.

KARMIC TASKS:
- to develop intuition and trust it;
- to accept life and circumstances as they are as the only true way in life — to try not to avoid your Fate;

- to learn to live life following the flow and feeling the flow of the wind;
- to live for today, knowing that tomorrow everything will be completely different;
- to believe in your luck;
- to boldly take risks;
- to trust the signs that fate sends your way.

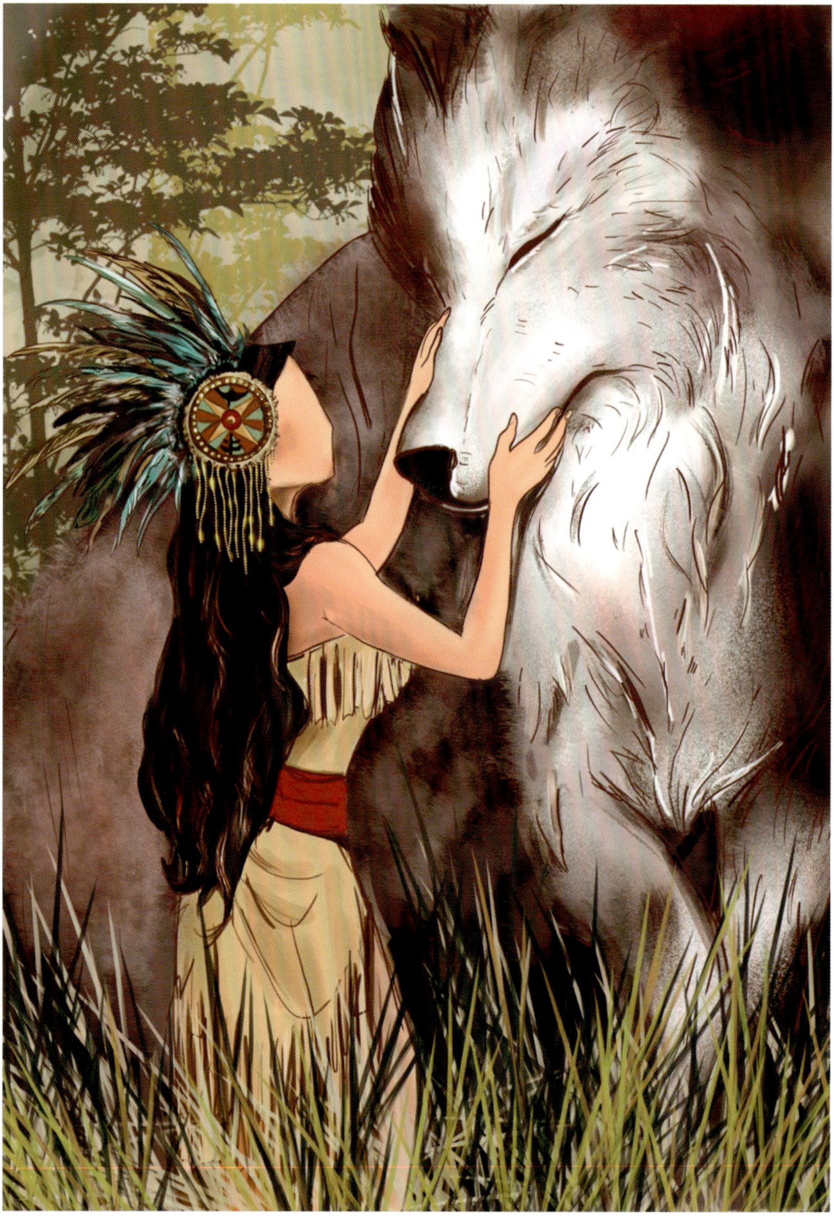

ARCANUM 11. STRENGTH

> The sun has gone out, concealing the whole earth,
> Neither the North nor the South can be seen.
> The Thunderbird, with a flick of its wing
> Has whisked the eternal lamp from the sky.
> The hurricane of the sandstorm,
>
> The rumble of the thunder, the sparks of menacing lightning...
> O Spirits of the rocks and Mother Earth,
> Give me the strength to overthrow this bird,
> So that the wonderful silence of the prairie
> May be returned to us as it was before.

LABOR — ENERGY — EFFORT

The Eleventh Arcanum in the Tarot deck is Strength. It is the energy of power and colossal potential. Elevens are endowed with huge reserves of energy. This is simultaneously their strength and weakness.

The Arcanum of Strength is the most powerful and potent energy, providing the person endowed with it with unlimited possibilities to realize what they want. People with the Strength Energy are capable of anything. For them, there is nothing that cannot be achieved, obtained or completed. Their physical and moral strength combined makes Elevens genuine titans, but only on the condition that they are ready to accept, curb and control this Energy.

People with Strength Energy in the Character zone have one of the most complex karmic programs. The gift that they have received from the Universe provides them with huge potential for self-realization, but at the same time complicates the conditions dictated by life itself. People with the Eleventh Energy have to work hard, in fact, ten times harder than others. The tasks set for those endowed with other energies, although not easy, are still relatively simple compared with those set for Elevens, which are definitely much more complex.

The Energy of the Eleventh Arcanum is so powerful that a single person's life will require several alternative outlets for it to be fully implemented and realized. Any unused Strength will end up making itself felt by erupting and overflowing in all sorts of directions. If this Strength is not implemented and directed in the right way, it will create difficulties for its possessor in their everyday life. Unrealized Eleventh Energy can manifest itself in heightened aggression, the desire for violence (the physical manifestation of strength) or tyranny in relation to those around them. Elevens need to channel this Strength in several directions and implement it in various different areas by learning to relax its flow and control its behavior.

When the Eleventh Energy is located in an individual's Higher Essence Zone, this indicates that this person is likely to be inspired when confronted with difficult situations. The more difficult the challenge, the more attractive the goal. If an Eleven's Energy is in a positive state, then they will deliberately set out to find difficult paths or complicate relatively simple processes. When viewed from the sidelines, this may seem like a pointless exercise in choosing to do things the difficult way when an easier path is available — and this might make sense for other people but not for individuals with the Eleventh Arcanum in their Higher Essence Zone. In addition, the Strength Energy in this zone contains a secret bonus that provides the answer to the important questions of how best to get what you want and how to achieve any goal. Although the answer is relatively simple — through huge effort and hard work.

When the Eleventh Arcanum is located on any of the points of the Material Karma and, likewise the Character and Portrait Zones, this indicates that this individual has a liking for prosperity and a high standard of living and will strive for them. As a rule, people with the Eleventh Energy surround themselves with luxurious accessories, designer dresses, and love expensive cars and houses. Of course, this manifestation of the Energy of Strength is multi-layered and is expressed to different degrees. But what remains constant is the fact that any person with the Eleventh Arcanum in the above zones loves to talk about and show off their treasures. When an Eleven rejects this desire and striving for prosperity, their energy will automatically enter into a minus state.

The Energy of Strength is large-scale and it endows its owner with the same power and scale. Elevens are people who are destined to do extraordinary things in life, make history and lead humanity to do things that others simply would never dare to do. The Energy of Strength erases all restrictions and everything becomes possible for an individual endowed with it. This, of course, is provided that this Strength can be controlled and directed towards the productive realization of that which is good, and not towards self-destruction and chaos.

Since people with the Eleventh Arcanum in the Destiny Code Matrix have more energy power than others, they require more space. Their powerful biofield subconsciously aspires to exist in vast spaces. Elevens choose houses with large rooms and high ceilings, and they like to cram a large number of possessions into them. Likewise, in everyday life, Elevens have a tendency to appreciate size and scale in all things — in architecture, the size of objects, the size of the portions served in restaurants. They have a natural tendency towards gigantomania, which dictates that everything should be on a large scale.

Another important factor is the constant perceived presence of an "Internal Enemy". They are plagued with a feeling of constant rivalry and the desire to keep their defenses up, sometimes leading to a permanent state of mental anxiety, persecution mania, distrust of those around them, and sometimes even more serious mental conditions. To avoid the negative manifestations of this tendency, Elevens need to identify what their "Internal Enemy" is and learn to make a timely truce with it, or at least to keep it under control.

Unfortunately, Elevens are prone to manifest their strength in a negative manner — both emotionally and physically. When their energy flow is not controlled, distributed and directed in a healthy way, they fall into a state of blind aggression and physically manifest their strength, taking everything out on those around them, as well as morally oppressing and humiliating them by casting them in a bad light. Based on my practical experience, I can say that nearly all cases of domestic violence, crimes, robberies, and reckless homicide are committed by people whose Eleventh Energy is in a negative state. And the same is true for maniacs who commit sex crimes or serial murders. One of the many channels that the Eleventh Energy is directed towards is sexual realization. Elevens are extremely sexually active. More often than not, in order to expend their considerable supply of sexual energy, Elevens tend to have several partners on the go at the same time. When their sexual potential is not realized, this energy can be passed back into the physical body and manifests itself accordingly in inappropriate sexual behavior and a dysfunction of their reproductive systems. This is particularly pronounced in men.

When an Eleven expends less than the required amount of energy and resources, this can also manifest itself on the physical level in the form of extra pounds deposited in the body. When Elevens fail to reach their potential and evade the responsibility of using their Strength, when instead of leading armies, being an engine of progress and governing the masses, they end up in a small-time job in a small office on the outskirts of a small city, then their strength and energy is transformed into a form of morose obesity that settles in the internal organs and body. In esoteric practise, it is believed that if a Master is overweight, then he or she has blockages in his or her energy flows that need to be removed if he or she is to fully realize his or her abilities. Both of these facts are considered signs of a Master's professional unsuitability.

A person with the Eleventh Energy in their Destiny Code Matrix cannot be soft or weak-willed. The huge potential of power they possess must be supported by a strong inner core and steadfast confidence in their true natures in order to keep this Strength under control. The individual must be able to "endure" the strength of the energy that flows within them. The thinner the walls of the vessel, the more likely it is to break and spill its contents.

WATCHWORDS

For the most part the saying: "Where there is strength — there is little need for wit," is quite fitting when it comes to Elevens. With the caveat that it needs to be rephrased a little bit: "The potential is all there — and little beyond that is required." This is because when their energy is implemented it will lead them to achieve the goals to which they aspire in any case, but knowing how to do it without the ability to achieve it will merely leave that person only with the ability to talk about that goal.

- Any action will lead to a result, no matter what.
- Strength lies in having the strength to do something and the ability to apply it.

FINANCES

Elevens are strong motivators. They can get any mechanism going, stimulate any thinking process and get any person moving. This can manifest itself both in relation to themselves and other people depending on whom the overall end result depends. In this respect, the Eleventh and Seventh energy have a certain similarity — they both have a powerful influence on large groups of people. Only unlike the Sevens, who, having motivated those around them, go on their way and carry on with their own business, Elevens seek to immerse themselves in the process in question and, like an ox, carry the main burden of the process on themselves by sticking around and bearing the responsibility for everything.

One of the most important factors that have a negative effect on the development of Elevens is their soft-heartedness and nobility of character. It is important for Elevens to initially prioritize their actions, otherwise, the activities they are engaged in might not end up being productive.

A lack of determination and inner strength are signs that the Eleventh Energy is in a negative state. In this situation, an Eleven might hide behind circumstances and excuses, which make them weak and cowardly and prevent them from realizing their true potential.

This situation often arises when an Eleven voluntarily refuses to realize their potential, when they are trying to juggle and balance several different areas of their lives, afraid that an action taken in one of them might end up harming one of the others. It is in the karmic nature of the Arcanum of Strength that the individual wielding it will have to work and determine where and how they want to realize their immense potency and power. Most often, the choices they have to make fall between two opposing demands — family (relationships) or career (work, activities). It is difficult to imagine how hard it is for Elevens to have to make this choice. Only a person with an Eleven in their Destiny Code Matrix can truly understand the full meaning of the words, pain and burden.

People with the Energy of Strength have a liking for money and the means that allow them to lead a luxurious lifestyle. As soon as the energy within them allows it, they try to make it clear to everyone around them that they are very hard workers and that everyone should value and respect them for this. There's no denying the fact that Elevens do have a tendency to be boastful but it's easy to understand why. The thing is, it's just about the only way they can relax. Elevens perceive the world through the physical body (at a tactile level through their sensations and objects). Therefore, having expensive high-quality clothes, a good car, and the ability to pay a big bill in a restaurant is the only way they can evaluate their productivity and fulfilment. Quite often, Elevens will pay everyone's bill at a restaurant, or get a large group of friends together and take them on vacation at their own expense.

Any field of activity that involves managing people, the use of power, manipulation skills and controlling the masses such as politics, lobbying, the development and launch of powerful processes and mechanisms, physical labor and physical activity are all areas that are ideal for people with the Eleventh Arcanum in their Finance zone.

You can safely say that the most suitable professions for Elevens are politics, law enforcement and the military and businesses that involve large-scale processes such as engineering, metallurgy, oil and gas, forestry and agriculture. Elevens are quite capable of proving themselves in their chosen profession no matter at what level they enter it. By dint of their hard work, they regularly rise from the shop floor or a menial job in an office to managerial positions. Elevens need to remind themselves that in order to achieve the result they are striving for, they need to stretch themselves to the maximum and apply all their strength to achieve what they want. Their individual karmic program does not allow them to be careless workers and do anything by halves. The key to success for an Eleven is to work hard and then do it all again ten times over.

HEALTH

A failure to eat, sleep, rest or exercise properly, sexual inactivity and stress — are the main factors that have a detrimental effect on Elevens' health.

People endowed with the Eleventh Arcanum really do work hard and long hours. They often do the work of ten people without giving themselves a break. And this is where all the risks arise when it comes to their health problems.

But in addition to physical and emotional exhaustion, there is another area of their health that Elevens need to keep a constant eye on and that is their sexual health.

It is very important that the Eleventh Energy is afforded an outlet. When their energy is allowed to accumulate, one way or another it will need to be released. Failure to release this excess energy can lead to the accumulation of excess weight on the body or sometimes unstable mood swings and aggression in the mind, and other times it can provoke a failure of the body's internal systems and end up with illnesses that can end up destroying the brain's cells and neural connections.

The best way for Elevens to restore and strengthen their health is to engage in physical activity. Sports, physical labor, sex and just about any activity or movement can restore and get them back on their feet without any unnecessary medicines.

RELATIONSHIPS

Elevens make for passionate, loving, sexually active and jealous partners. They share a lot of similarities with Sevens in this respect because it is very important for Elevens to win their partner over by dint of their strength and effort. If the target of their attentions is too easily accessible, it won't hold and enchant their attention for long. Elevens are very fond of attention – both in terms of giving it and receiving it. Sometimes, even when they have a permanent partner, they show an interest in flirting with others. When they are doing it, they do not attach a great deal of importance to these sorts of antics, but they would never tolerate such behavior from their own partner.

The Energy of Strength endows its owner with the ability to be extremely expressive and emotional. Although it would be wrong to say that these people are emotional about everything, as they are used to restraining their considerable energy flows and controlling their behavior. Nevertheless, in exceptional situations, when their energy gets out of control, Elevens can become extremely dangerous. As has been mentioned above, Elevens are endowed with colossal strength, and in a quarrel or showdown, their partner can be extremely badly hurt either emotionally or physically.

Elevens set their partners extremely very high standards. Different Elevens may have different ideas about what makes for an ideal partner, but they all set a very high bar and make constant demands that it be raised.

If a partnership with an Eleven is to remain strong and endure, then it is very important that an element of tension is maintained between the partners. The regular and sometimes deliberate addition of "little tasks and complications" will keep Elevens on their toes and remind them that their relationships, like everything else in their lives, require their work and attention.

INDICATIONS THAT THIS ENERGY IS IN A −

- Playing the "weakling" (deliberately concealing their potential abilities).
- Greed (insisting on having everything for themselves).
- Being aggressive towards those who are weaker and in awe of those who are stronger.
- The inability to show their strength of character or status when defending their opinions
- Being surrounded by small spaces that are devoid of things and possessions.
- The fear of taking risks and losing their reputation.
- Being excessively proud and boastful.
- Being envious and slanderous of others.
- An inclination to be cruel and physically violent.
- An inability to prioritize between family and work or duty and their personal desires.
- Weakness (both physical and moral).
- Cowardice and indecision.

INDICATIONS THAT THIS ENERGY IS IN A +

- A high capacity for work and strong potential.
- The ability to fully implement and realize the huge potential of their energy.
- The ability to decide and prioritize.
- Nobility and humanity.
- The ability to surround themselves with luxurious and "grand" things (big houses, big cars, everything should be on a grand scale).
- Dedication and sincerity.
- Constantly in search of difficult tasks and paths.

KARMIC TASKS:

- to curb their aggression and overcome weakness;
- to dedicate themselves totally to a cause;

- to accept the fact that in order to achieve the results they have set themselves, they need to do the work of ten others;
- to recognize that life can be unprincipled;
- to manage the masses;
- to influence by dint of physical and moral strength;
- to accept their strength and power and the price that they have to pay for possessing this gift.

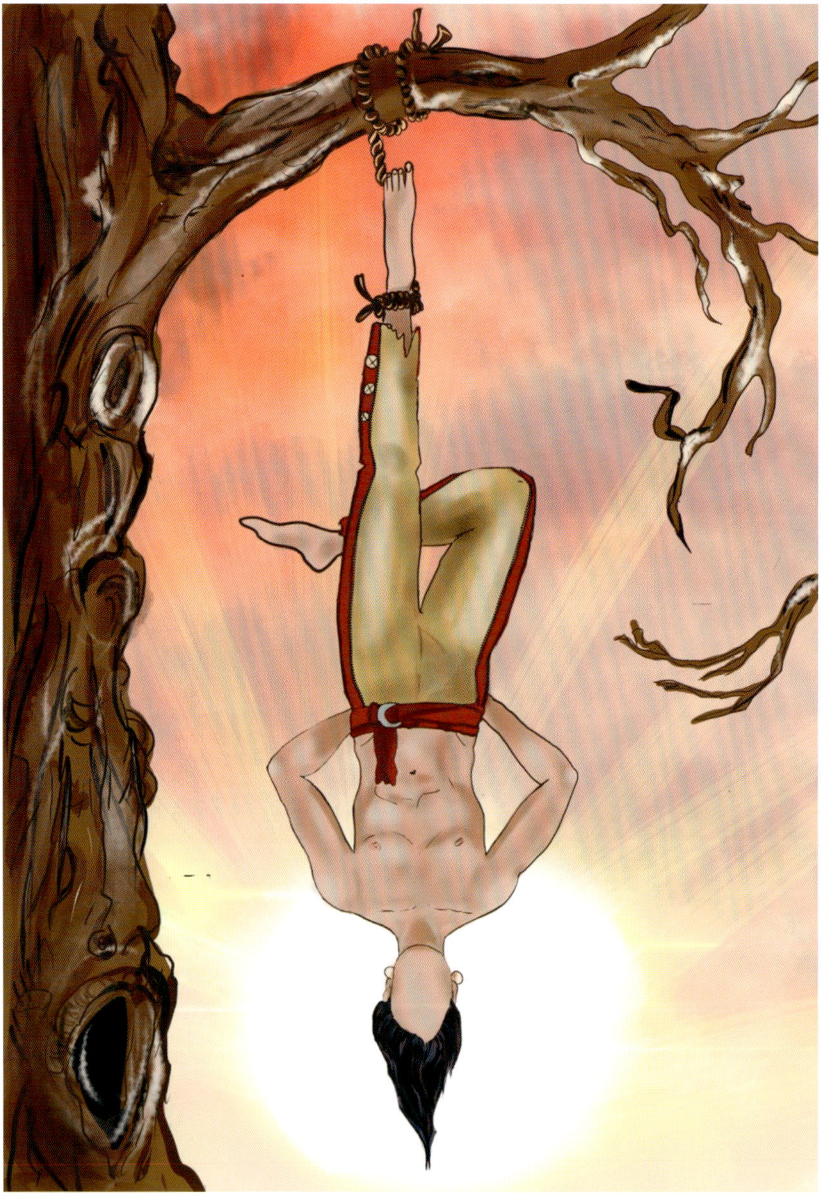

ARCANUM 12. SACRIFICE

> In the lands of North Dakota,
> Which rightfully belonged to the Sioux,
> On the third day of the Bloody Moon
> The white people came.
> The brothers did not keep the word
> That they gave to the Spirit of the Wind,
> Forgetting all the honor of their tribe
> The lands were given away.
> Only the time-tested Chief Hunkpapa,
> Warrior wise and stubborn,
> Faithful son of the Lakota tribes
> Did not leave the place of power.
> And remained like a stone
> Without betraying the covenant of the ancestors,
> Maintaining the honor and memory of the tribe —
> A sitting bull standing his ground.

SERVICE — ALTRUISM — CREATIVITY

Of all the 22 Energies of the Destiny Code, the Energy of Sacrifice is considered the most unstable. Like an hourglass, Sacrifice passes from one position to another, and so, a person transforms from one state into another, alternately trying on the wolf and then the sheep's "clothing". The bipolarity of the Twelfth Energy imposes serious complications on the lives of those endowed with it, which, on their own, they would not be able to cope with.

The symbol of the Twelfth Arcana in the Tarot deck is the Hanged Man. The energy of voluntary sacrifice, or sacrifice arising out of circumstances from which a person has no chance of being saved. The Twelfth Arcanum shows us that sometimes it is important to stop and take stock of a situation from a different angle, evaluate circumstances from a different point of view and first and foremost examine yourself in a different way.

A person with the Twelfth Energy in their Destiny Code Matrix tends either to linger in the past or to stand hesitatingly on the threshold of the future, agonizing over what they have experienced or what is to come.

Twelves cannot live calmly in the present, since they need to know in advance whether they are the "victims" after the storm or those who provoke the catastrophe.

From early childhood, people with the Twelfth Arcanum in their Character Zone have a tendency to suffer for various reasons. Regardless of its severity and extent, the important thing to realize is that the Twelfth Arcanum accumulates energy and provides itself with its reserves of strength through suffering and internal torment. Without the experience gained by passing through an emotional meat grinder, Twelves do not see the point of what is going on and will take little interest in it.

Twelves deliberately choose to be "victims" because this endows them with such qualities as dedication, altruism, selflessness and, of course, self-sacrifice. These are the sort of people who devote themselves to volunteering, doing good for the benefit of others, travelling to Africa to save children from hunger and selling their property to raise funds to save tigers in the Siberian taiga. They are also the people who will always help others, providing shelter and food for strangers off the street, they are the people who will always help out a friend in difficulty and sacrifice their personal interests to help others.

For the sake of a good deed, a person with the Twelfth Arcanum in their Destiny Code Matrix would be prepared to give the last shirt off their back and give it to the homeless. This happens because people endowed with the Energy of Sacrifice experience the emotions of strangers as if they were their own, they immerse themselves in them and accordingly try to change the situation, even if at some stages their actions may damage their personal interests.

The Arcanum of Sacrifice endows its owners with an acute sense of pity and empathy. They always feel sorry for everyone and at times feel even more sorry for themselves. If the altruism in their nature is being expressed in a healthy and adequate way, and they are not donating their last penny to a good cause, then, as a rule, their feeling of pity is directed towards their own personal suffering. Everyone who comes into contact with a Twelve is only too aware of their sufferings. Suffering from the bright sun, high prices, their uncomfortable shoes, from being forced to do something or not being allowed to do something. Suffering and torment are a way of life for a person with the Twelfth Arcanum.

When the Twelfth Energy is located in the Higher Essence Zone, it indicates that this individual is inspired by being useful in life. If the activities this person is engaged in benefit society, regardless of their scale, then this person will sense the importance of their mission and their reserves will be filled with strength by making their own usefulness a reality. If a person does not see the usefulness and value of what they are doing for others, then they will fall into a state of apathy and urgently feel the need to do the next "useful thing". In order to stimulate the Twelfth Energy in the Higher Essence Zone, sometimes it is simply enough to take some old things to a thrift store, make a donation to a support fund, or just sort the garbage.

Twelves have very lofty goals and strive to change the World for the better. They are not motivated by self-realization, reward or personal recognition. Altruists by nature, Twelves strive with all their essence to do good and find every means to make it a reality. They have a very subtle sense of others and they are sweet, kind-hearted, sympathetic and have very kind pleasant voices. They are bright and vulnerable people.

However, the Energy of the Twelfth Arcanum can also take on a completely different nature. When the hourglass is turned on its head, the energy of virtue and altruism transforms the person endowed with it into a victim. Making them totally dependent on circumstances, selfish and self-pitying. When it comes to their attitudes to the world, Twelves have a tendency to direct their energy flows either towards enslavement or tyranny. When in this state, Twelves are convinced that everyone is in their debt and that their lives are plagued with failure due to a combination of the cruel circumstances and negative influences that surround them. They are incapable of seeing any reasons for this in themselves and they become the voluntary victims of their circumstances.

This inner state of "victimhood" attracts situations to Twelves that turn this conviction of victimhood into reality. Fraud, bad company, being bullied and in unhealthily dependent relationships are just a few examples. Among other things, the statistics demonstrate that Twelves are often the victims of domestic violence and sex crimes.

WATCHWORDS

The most important thing in life for Twelves is to be useful and act for the good. Any task they take on must have a mission, which when realized helps Twelves to work out their Karmic Task, by devoting themselves to a greater cause for the sake of gaining experience.

No less important is the emotional element contained in the notion of "service". If there is no emotion, then there is no meaning; Twelves adhere to the worldview that there is no meaning where there is no emotion.
- Be useful.
- Carry out the mission.
- You live your life through your feelings and emotions.
- Pain and suffering are a source of redemption and purification.

FINANCES

One of the features of the Twelfth Arcanum is the craving to be creative. Creativity not only serves as a way of realizing the Twelfth Energy but also as a way of determining the sphere of activity that needs to be undertaken and the way to approach a particular situation or activity. The ability to look at the world differently helps Twelves to sense the vibrations of those around them, interpret their needs and anticipate their expectations. Since Twelves have the ability to sense the future and anticipate expectations with their feelings, they are deftly and accurately able to determine its demands.

Any activity a person with the Twelfth Energy undertakes should entail an element of usefulness. If a mission does not come to fruition, Twelves can quickly lose interest and plunge into a state of victimhood (which is the most convenient for them). Once in this situation, external support is very important for them. Twelves demand admiration and praise more than anyone else. It is important to let them know how great and talented they are, and also how well they perform their tasks but, most importantly, how useful these acts are. With such small compliments as these, a Twelve can be easily motivated to throw themselves selflessly into whatever good deed they are involved in and work even more productively. However, empty flattery will not cut the mustard, the compliments and appreciation shown to them have to be genuine.

Altruists and volunteers are needed in every line of profession and in every business. People who are ready to fight with all their hearts for the common good of all are needed everywhere. Therefore, Twelves might be engaged in all sorts of different professions. But Twelves will be at their most productive when they are able to actualize themselves with work, which has the common good as its mission and goal. This is often in the fields of medicine, ecology, scientific research, lobbying and, of course, charity, unemployment, social work and psychology. And, of course, there must be an element of creativity involved as well.

HEALTH

Twelves are real panic merchants. Even a small scratch can lead them to panic and become seriously stressed. On the whole, they are extremely wary of any physical injury and can't stand the sight of blood. But they are very interested in studying these matters as long as they are not directly involved. Most Twelves from early childhood take a great interest in the anatomy and physiology of the human body and such details as what the brain looks like in cross-section and how much blood is contained in the human body. But when it comes to their own bodies and the need for medical intervention, their feelings of pity and fear for themselves become so acute that they sometimes begin to panic to an almost unhealthy degree.

Twelves and Sixes share certain similar specific qualities when it comes to their perception of their well-being. Sixes are quite capable of psychosomatically convincing their bodies that they have come down with a serious disease and sincerely convincing themselves and others that this is the case. Twelves, however, are more likely to be so afraid of getting a disease that sometimes, this fear has the side effect of causing a different one. The surest way to help a Twelve recover is to calm them psychologically and meditation and breathing exercises are particularly effective.

For Twelves, any panic attack and consequently any illness will start and develop rapidly and in accordance with the above scenario. Twelves recover quickly and return to a stable condition as soon as the panic and fear are relieved. When the threat goes away, then Twelves have no opportunity to worry about their health and suffer, which in turn means that they will need to find new and different sources of emotional experiences.

RELATIONSHIPS

Twelves require care and empathy. Twelves throw themselves into their relationships and worry and empathize over every little detail and at the very least require the same of their partners. Being in love is not enough, they need to talk about it, prove it and act on it to show their emotional worth to the maximum. Their excessive displays of emotion and inherent neediness will naturally provoke regular showdowns with their partners, but Twelves are sensitive enough to stop what they are doing, turn their hourglass over, and altruistically offer their partner their total attention.

Twelves are very touchy and quick-tempered, but they cool down as quickly and unpredictably as they light up. Their quickness to bear a grudge and subtle feelings towards their partners can sometimes create an incredible emotional cocktail that not everyone can cope with.

Speaking from my own personal experience, I have heard many recollections and stories recounted to me by Twelves regarding what their ideal relationship would be. Twelves are the sort of people who love after the event, and these feelings are often motivated more by painful experiences, separations and reconciliations than by love being a constant presence in their relationships as such. Twelves first and foremost, value their relationships in terms of the emotional experience but the depth of feelings felt is not so important to them.

The tendency to act as the victim at a subconscious level often affects them when in search of a partner. Twelves sometimes strive to build the sort of relationship where one of the partners will end up being the victim. Taking an overly passive or dominant position guarantees them a cycle of emotional experiences and this is their main source of energy. Of course, the degree that these positions are expressed in such relationships can vary. In one case, a partner might be completely absorbed in the life of the other and all their actions will be directed for the benefit and development of their beloved. In another situation, a Twelve will play the role of the victim, where their partner will be obliged to empathize with and satisfy all their needs and requirements. There is a third option, which one often encounters in life when the Twelve attracts an abusive partner and becomes a voluntary victim of psychological or physical violence. It is important to understand that these individuals often enter into these relationships voluntarily and consciously. This is a karmic program that needs to be borne in mind in a situation where a Twelve is seeking outside help. In these instances, it is important to work with these Twelves' "hourglasses" and turn their minds on their heads, letting them look at the roles they have chosen from the other side of the coin.

INDICATIONS THAT THIS ENERGY IS IN A −
- Suffering from low self-esteem and loudly advertising it.
- Extensive borrowing and debt.
- Constant claims and complaints about their circumstances.
- A refusal to do good.
- A lack of charity and generosity in their lives (sometimes it is important simply to give and not demand something in return).
- To "dance attendance upon" instead of truly serving.
- A fear of showing their worth.
- Self-pity.
- Blaming others for their problems ("It's not me, it's them").
- Living their lives in the past or the future.
- The inability to say "no" to others.
- Rejection of their personal interests in favor of others.
- Being easy to offend and a tendency to panic.
- Refusing to move on from an event (this can manifest itself in prolonged stagnation or a long bout of dejection).

INDICATIONS THAT THIS ENERGY IS IN A +
- Kindness and responsiveness.
- Having a mission and a super-task.
- When the emotional prevails over the material.
- The ability to look at the world and see it from different angles.
- Sensitivity and attentiveness to the needs of others.
- The ability to put yourself in the place of others, to understand and evaluate their intentions.
- A sense of self-worth and self-importance.

KARMIC TASKS:
- to learn to say "no";
- to find a way to serve other people;
- to stop being a victim;
- to value themselves, their work and their own importance;
- to break out of their state of self-imposed doom;
- to learn to accept the mistakes they themselves and others make;
- to allow common sense to prevail over their subjective perceptions.

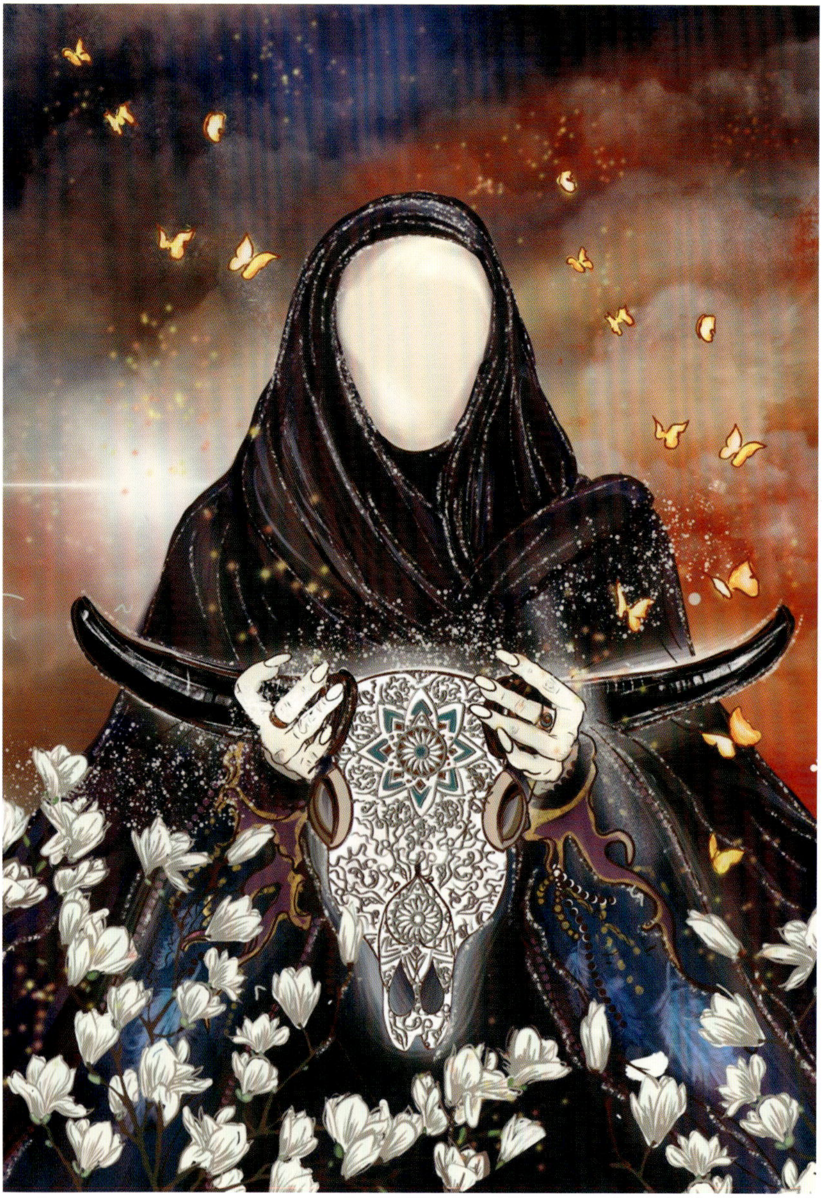

ARCANUM 13. DEATH

Somewhere out there in the depths of the forest, among the hundred-year-old giants
A brave warrior is resting — a deep-rooted and mighty oak.
He does not stretch his branches to the sky, he sleeps quietly, resting on the ground.
Defeated only yesterday in battle by an evil storm.
Many moons will pass and the great oak will turn black,
The Spirit of the Forests will cover his body with moss, concealing its child.
So that at the appointed hour with the moon and stars at night
He will turn back the stream — the fading years
Of decrepit Oseo, the son of the Stars of Love and Passion.
As if a cocooned caterpillar has been swallowed up by the hollow trunk of the tree
The body of the fallen old man will be endowed with the youth of the butterfly.

TRANSFORMATION — TO WIPE THE SLATE CLEAN — MINIMALISM

Death dissolves all things that are artificial, false and not genuine. By transforming and releasing energy from that which has outlived its purpose, it opens up new ways of realizing this energy. Death does not kill but resurrects, giving rise to the new. The death of the "chrysalis" marks the birth of the butterfly.

The symbol of the Thirteenth Arcana in the Tarot deck is Death. This is an arcanum that people are extremely wary of, causing them to tremble in fear. They fear to whisper its name out loud to avoid attracting its power and end up focusing on the direct meaning of card thirteen. But this is only a superficial perception of the Thirteenth Arcanum. Death is multifaceted, diverse in its manifestations, unique in terms of its capabilities and multi-layered in terms of its meaning. Death symbolizes the end of the old and the beginning of the new. "Death" equals "Life".

People with the Thirteenth energy are truly unique. There are not so many of them, which is quite understandable: The Thirteenth Energy is rarely encountered in the Destiny Code Matrix and is considered to be very special.

The main task in the Thirteenth Energy's Karmic program is the need to come to the understanding that in order to receive the new or to change yourself, you must first say goodbye to the old, find a way of purifying yourself and accept your new persona and become someone else. In order to realize themselves and be productive in life, Thirteens need to live through several roles in one incarnation of the soul, to pass through many paths of development, erasing their lives completely and each time starting everything from scratch.

The Energy of Death constantly pushes those endowed with it to never stand still. Those with a Major Thirteen in their Destiny Code Matrix are incapable of remaining on a single wavelength, doing the same thing throughout their lives or thinking the same way and socializing with the same people — they constantly feel the need for change and a change of circumstances. They need to start over, to become obsessed with something completely new, burn bridges and burn all their possessions. For Thirteens, this is all absolutely standard and a basic requirement in their lives. If Thirteens become too strongly attached to the past and cannot let go of it, their energy enters into a negative state and does not let them travel further down their required path of development. They need to let go of the past and likewise their former partners, lovers and enemies, they need to throw out all the old things and clothes in their houses that they are never destined to use or wear again. A complete reset of their Energy flows, transforms it into a positive state, opening up new horizons.

People with the Thirteenth Energy are pretty extraordinary, they differ from those around them not only in terms of their thinking and reasoning but also in their outward appearance. Because they are different Thirteens seem mysterious and attractive to others who want to get to know them and unravel the secret of their special attitude to life. However, Thirteens are "not everyone's cup of tea". Their easy charm and very specific energy make them an object of admiration and harsh criticism.

Every event in life has a meaning and carries a lesson that is important to take on board. However, the same events in parallel destinies will bear different meanings, depending on the energy that has been endowed to a particular human destiny in a particular incarnation. The lesson implicit in the karmic program of the Thirteenth Arcanum is that nothing belongs to a person in this life. When the conditions are created that force Thirteens to lose something in their lives, it prompts them to think that the time is right to acquire and take on something new because the old has already become depleted and there is no energy to be had from it. Consequently, Thirteens will remember and consider periods of loss as valuable and significant experiences for themselves in their lives. Passing the tests of destruction, failure, loss and feelings of powerlessness in some situations, gives Thirteens a sense of their own vitality, helps them determine the meaning of life and realize their desire to live in a new way.

The Arcanum of Death is a kind of escape from the comfort zone. People's fear of change blocks the prospective opportunities that can be obtained by rejecting what has already been experienced and is surplus to requirements. Thirteens need to learn not to cling on to anything material and to let go of the old in a timely manner on their way to obtaining that which is new and more valuable. Sometimes, Thirteens face thresholds that are extremely frightening to cross, but sooner or later they will have to do so and there is little point in them delaying the inevitable and giving themselves the chance to do more in their lives.

People with the Thirteenth Energy in the Destiny Code Matrix are transformers. By starting with themselves, they change those around them, scaling up the process each time they do so. By stimulating others to change and purify themselves, Thirteens become the "directors" of human destinies and this is where they often find their own true destiny.

Minimalism and purity are Thirteens' two main travelling companions. If Thirteens find themselves surrounded and mired by their old possessions, packed with memories and sentimental value — this is a sign that not all is well with their energy. Decluttering the old trash in your closets is one of the best ways for anyone to sort and clear out their lives, but for Thirteens this is an absolutely vital and fundamental process. For them, "clearing out" is not just a form of psychological training but an opportunity to save and resurrect themselves.

People endowed with the Energy of Death are very much afraid of death itself. Any mention of the inevitable end of life can send a Thirteen into a state of panic. Even references to death in music, films or any other art form can terrify them. This is because Thirteens fear the end of life and the unknown that lies beyond it. There is nothing more exhausting for Thirteens than the uncertainty of the unknown and the future. They are incapable of experiencing any sense of peace while anticipating the unanswered question that is the future. They find it much easier to draw a line under everything, pull up their roots and start a new process by declaring a new quest for the future. Their Impatience and the desire to resolve everything "right now" only serve to provoke Thirteens to burn their bridges, without giving others a chance to even explain or justify themselves.

WATCHWORDS

The metamorphosis inherent in life is the main thing that incentivises Thirteens. Any ending marks a new beginning, which is inevitably followed by a new ending and so beginnings metamorphose into endings... And so on without end. Each stage in life symbolizes growth, development and completion, telling us that the lesson has been learned and we should move on.

- If your horse is dead, it's time to get off it.
- Life is like the cycle of the "caterpillar-chrysalis-butterfly", each stage comes in its own good time and one cannot happen without the other.

FINANCES

The most striking peculiarity about Thirteens when realizing their true path in life is the speed and regularity that they change their profession. They cannot be doing the same thing for long, even if they are in with a good chance of advancement and development. If a Thirteen has been engaged in a repetitive and monotonous job for many years, their energy will enter into a negative state or become blocked altogether, which will have a very negative effect on their life as a whole. If they find themselves in this situation, they need to give their energy free rein, quit their job and go off and do something completely new and different. Their energy flow will shift, instantly allowing them to feel their life-changing and opening them up to opportunities for growth and development

Professions that require activities based around projects with a specific beginning and end suit Thirteens best. Even if the projects are kept within the bounds of one profession, it is possible for Thirteens to artificially divide these into stage posts and unleash their energy on reaching them.

Thirteens make excellent screenwriters, directors, writers and event organizers. They also do very well in architecture, design and construction. By creating life through their work, whether it is a script for their next movie or a design project for a new building, Thirteens pass through the Karmic Program of the Arcana of Death, by giving the world new life and creating something that is immortal.

People with the Thirteenth Energy love money, but do not have any sense of its value. They are more attracted to the emotional comfort it provides rather than its purely material value. But this very much depends on the individual, and it is important to look at the combinations of the energies present in each particular individual's Material Karma Zone.

Any activity related to life and death that entails transformations in all its many different manifestations will also be a good fit for a Thirteen. These include emergency room resuscitators, surgeons, criminologists, pathologists and archaeologists as well as any restoration work, photo editing, the transcription of old documents and restoration of archives, ritual services and work in crematoria and cemeteries.

Thirteens also tend to look beyond the limits of what is accessible and find themselves involved in esotericism. In particular, in necromancy, ritual magic and in working with artifacts. One way or another, at a certain period of their lives Thirteens are sooner or later drawn to esotericism. It does not matter whether it is something they become involved in professionally or simply something they show a curiosity in, they will nevertheless definitely be inclined to search for secret knowledge.

HEALTH

It has been statistically confirmed that Thirteens experience health problems from the outset of their lives. These might be tumors, amputations, the loss of an organ or complex diseases of the blood, brain, eyes and ears. General ill-health or a specific disease forces an individual to perceive and contemplate the concepts of "life and death" more acutely.

Sleep problems, the likelihood of coma and lethargy are more common among Thirteens than other people (even when it only occupies minor positions). Death makes its presence constantly felt and Thirteens should always appreciate the present moment, the "here and now", because tomorrow may never come.

RELATIONSHIPS

A person with the Thirteenth Energy in the Destiny Code Matrix is always on the lookout for something new. Like everything else in these people's lives, their relationships need to contain opportunities to move from one stage to another, to develop and reach a new level of significance on each new occasion. The Thirteenth Arcanum endows its owner with the desire to implement transformation, and this is what a Thirteen is looking for in their relationships with their partners. The opportunity to effect change and progress, to move away from old beliefs to new ones and move onto new cycles of development will be the key to their long-term partnerships. But if there is no transformation and the opportunity to start something anew, the relationship will fade away and come to its logical conclusion.

When the Thirteenth Energy is held in common in a couple's compatibility matrix, this indicates a situation where it will be quite normal for these partners to marry and divorce several times in their lifetimes. Thus, every time they pass through a certain stage, they will put an end to their relationship, but by transforming the experience gained, they will bring it to a new level and give it a new lease of life.

When it comes to relationships and love, novelty and the ability to change are elements that are particularly important for Thirteens. There can be many ways that one changes one's interests, environment, activities, work, image and lifestyle. But the main thing for Thirteeens is to move beyond the status quo.

INDICATIONS THAT THIS ENERGY IS IN A −

- A morbid fear of death (for oneself, loved ones and a fear of the concept of "death" in general).
- An attachment to material things.
- Living in the past (an inability to let go of past events, people and memories).
- A fear of change.
- Being cluttered with unnecessary things, thoughts and ideas.
- Remaining old-fashioned and refusing to accept the new (technology, opportunities, trends).
- Pessimism and a philosophy of hopelessness (that everything perishes, and there is no point in striving for anything).

INDICATIONS THAT THIS ENERGY IS IN A +

- Transformation and change.
- Inquisitiveness and intellectual curiosity (the desire to comprehend new things).
- The ability to influence those around them, to change the way others think and transform their lives.
- The ability to calmly burn bridges, jettison the extraneous, drop everything and start life from scratch.
- The ability to see things in a new way.
- The ability to accept death and not be afraid of it.
- To have no fear of a lack of stability and to easily move on from where they are.
- At all times and in all ways to be ready to travel light and carry no excess baggage.

KARMIC TASKS:

- to learn to jettison everything that is superfluous and excess;
- to let go of the past;
- to create that which is immortal;
- to accept change as a given;
- to systematically wipe the slate clean;
- to bring matters to completion;
- to move beyond the fear of death and the end;
- to not become too attached to people, things and events;

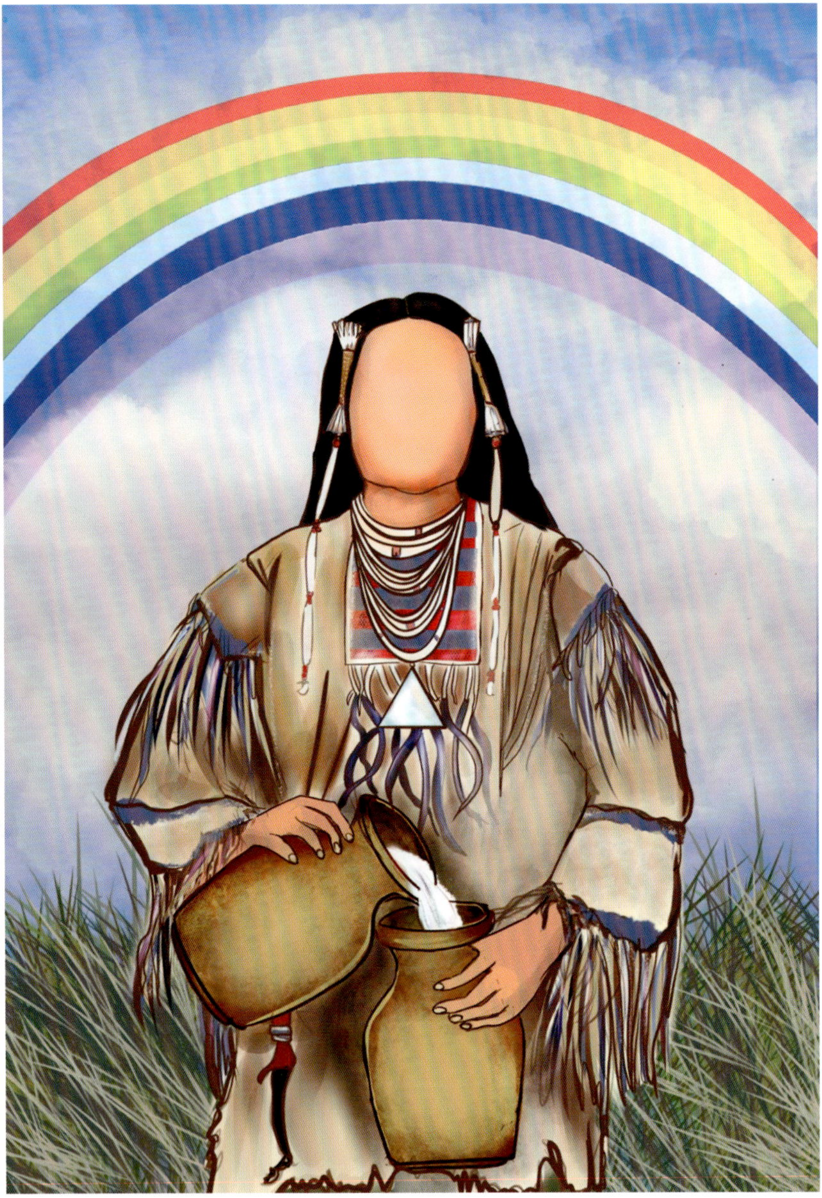

ARCANUM 14. MODERATION

How wonderful are the lands where the river's inlets run!
You can shelter in the shade
Where the water lilies bloom.
The soul of the Sachem rules here among the peaceful villages,
Honoring the union of the Earth and Sea.
When the time is right
The chief of the Pokanoket tribes will come in peace with furs, and food
To the pale-faced strangers
And smoke the pipe of peace
To protect the fate of the people
Who following him in his tracks
Will be grateful for that hour even to this day.

HARMONY — THE GOLDEN MEAN — COMPROMISE

Compared to the others, the Energy of Moderation is the calmest of all. The Fourteenth Arcanum is stable, balanced and tranquil in all its manifestations.

In the Tarot deck, the 14th Arcana is depicted as Moderation, a symbol of compromise and the golden mean. This card indicates the importance of finding balance and coming to a mutually beneficial solution to any issue. By switching off your emotions and assessing the situation sensibly, you can count on the objectivity of perception and eliminate the chances of committing erroneous actions. Stop, think, weigh up the pros and cons, identify the most important things and discard those that are secondary. The Fourteenth Arcanum is all about common sense and acting for the benefit of maintaining harmony and overall balance.

People with the Fourteenth Energy in their Destiny Code Matrix are cultured, polite, modest, tactful and subtle by nature. The main features of their characters are patience, endurance and the desire for harmony and peace. They have a deep sense of dignity and refined manners, outwardly similar to those of the aristocracy or the nobility. Their measured and unemotional manner is often interpreted by those they encounter as arrogance and condescension, but this perception is highly erroneous.

Fourteens keep their emotions under tight control and know precisely what they can allow themselves to do and what they can't.

Fourteens are well-grounded when it comes to material values. They can get by with very little, but on the condition that what they do have is comfortable and of high quality. Their wardrobe may contain only a few of the most necessary things, but they will be neat, elegant and expensive.

Throughout their lives, Fourteens are constantly having to look for compromises. The main karmic program governing this energy is the quest to find harmony and negotiate where the "golden mean" lies. It is important to learn to find a balance between what is possible and what is desired. When balance is found, the Energy of Moderation will reveal its trump cards and show the individual where the true values of his or her life lie. The eventfulness and rhythm of the life lived with the Fourteenth Energy is a slow one and, in this respect, there is a degree of similarity with the Ninth Energy of the Hermit. For Fourteens all processes are deliberately drawn out and require patience and calmness on their part.

Of course, calmness and inner harmony are indicators that this energy is in a positive state. When a Fourteen becomes hot-tempered, refuses to wait or take other people's interests into account and refuses to find a mutually beneficial solution, this indicates that there is work to be done on the energy they have been endowed with. Being argumentative and irritable can close many opportunities when an individual lacks balance and moderation. The more unstable the Fourteenth Arcanum, the more drawn out the processes that the individual needs to go through in their lives will be.

The Energy of Moderation challenges the individual to think, to build logical labyrinths in their mind's eye about how a situation might vary and, as a result, to find a balanced solution. Fourteens need to switch off the emotional component of any situation and keep their behavior neutral. Endurance and patience will show them the right way to find the solution — acting in the interests of your ego and insisting on having your own way will end up blocking all possible routes to achieving a result.

It is destiny's intention that Fourteens should live a measured life without stress. They should not try to force or rush events, otherwise, their vital energy will fizzle out and its source dry up. Peace, harmony and stability and wise, measured behavior are what is required of a Fourteen and will strengthen their Energy and allow it to reveal its potential. It is important for them to learn to limit their impulses and desires, to weigh all the pros and cons and to overcome and fight all contradictions. This requires endurance and an ordered distribution of their strengths.

People with the Fourteenth Energy tend to play the long game. Any event in a Fourteen's life stays with them for the whole of their lives. Their connections, businesses, hobbies, memories and just about everything that they have ever had will haunt them for a long time. Fourteens need to be very careful to maintain their reputations because with their slow karmic program any black marks gained may take them a long time to remove and only with great difficulty.

When a Fourteen's Energy is in a negative state, their behavior will accordingly be in direct opposition to that described above. They will become impatient, unreliable, refuse to compromise, try to get what they have not yet earned the right to and be constantly subject to mood swings. This sort of instability and lack of harmony are clear indicators that not all is well with this individual's Energy of Moderation.

But even when their Energy is in a negative state, Fourteens nevertheless strive to achieve harmony, peace and moderation. Because at the subconscious level their Energy will try to use every possible resource at its disposal to put this individual back on the straight and narrow path of true development. An individual's resistance to their personal energy is like a serious disease — the most important thing is to identify and diagnose it in time and, by applying every effort, restore it to its natural healthy state.

WATCHWORDS

Perseverance and the ability to give their time to find and develop a solution are special characteristics typical of Fourteens. The ability to wait, take time to think things through, check the stability of the situation, not rush into things, leave their emotions to one side and carefully weigh everything up, comparing the pros and cons.
- The morning is wiser than the evening.
- There is a right time for everything.
- True wealth does not lie in the hands of he who has a lot, but he who has sufficient.

FINANCES

Perhaps the best way to describe the range of professions suitable for Fourteens in their quest for self-actualization would be those that involve determining the golden mean. Any activity that requires patience, perseverance, endurance, and most importantly, an objective and precise compliance with the task set (including the ability to strictly carry out prescribed measures and observe a sense of proportion) will facilitate a Fourteen's development.

It is important for people with the Fourteenth Energy in their Finance Zone to realize their natural leanings towards observing rules and maintaining a measured sense of proportion. Professions such as pharmacist, aromatherapist, homeopath, chemist, laboratory worker, healer, perfume creator and culinary specialist are highly suitable for Fourteens.

Fourteens are also suited to professions that involve spiritual practices. Their moderation and sincerity, as well as their desire to find a balance between body and mind, the quest for equilibrium and the ability to think wisely, perceive the world in multi-layered shades and precisely and tactfully conduct a dialogue on complex issues — are all a great help not only to themselves but also to others who need their strength. Fourteens make excellent spiritual mentors, counsellors, coaches and judges.

Provided that their energy is in a stable state, Fourteens can be quite content in holding middle-ranking positions and happy to be paid only what they need to get by in life. They have no pronounced craving for luxury and a high level of prosperity. Here, as in everything, they are dominated and guided by a sense of proportion. When their energy is in a negative state, Fourteens can be as capricious as a small child and demand more and more from their employers. But when confronted and asked why they need more, they will not be able to provide a reasonable answer and come back down to earth because in actual fact they have no genuine need of what they have been asking for. Although admittedly, if a Fourteen also has the Nineteenth Energy in their Destiny Code Matrix, then this indicates a large and stable income.

HEALTH

The body is the temple of the Soul. The stronger the connection an individual has with their spiritual essence, the more harmonious he or she will feel inside and the more stable his or her health will be.

On the whole, people with the Fourteenth Energy enjoy good health. Maintaining a sense of proportion and balance remains the main touchstone for Fourteens both in terms of their attitudes towards their lives and health also. They enjoy taking wine in moderation and avoid the siren excesses of puritanical asceticism and hedonistic gluttony. Harmony and the golden mean are key to their productivity, happiness and good physical and moral health.

Fourteens should take up moderate sports and light physical activity without overdoing things. Hiking and moderate types of Eastern physical exercise such as yoga which involves measured breathing practices are the best types of sporting activity for them.

A combination of major Fourteenth and Eleventh arcana in an individual's Destiny Code Matrix indicates that they may be susceptible to such chronic diseases as asthma and diabetes as well as problems with the eyes and respiratory system (ear, throat, nose) as well as the musculoskeletal system. They also suffer from incurable illnesses that require them to learn to live with them and find a balance between dealing with the disease and carrying out a normal functioning life. As a rule, the causes and roots of these diseases can be found in the individual's karmic programs, which can be analyzed on the basis of their individual combinations of energies in their matrix.

RELATIONSHIPS

Individuals endowed with the Energy of Moderation accept their partners for who they are, with all their positive and negative sides. Fourteens' patience and desire to create harmony everywhere means that they do not put their personal interests on an equal footing with the common interests that they share with their partners. The Fourteenth Arcanum teaches its owner to undergo and pass the tests of endurance and patience and to accept reality as a given, and as a result, rewards those who respond well with the ability to attract the most amazing and special people.

As a rule, Fourteens have the most unusual and extraordinary partners. An alliance with a seemingly incompatible partner enables Fourteens to find a reflection of their own crazy potential dreams in their partners. For example, a couple of this sort might consist of one partner who is calm, balanced, aloof and cold, while the second is like a fire, blazing bright and completely out of control. These unions of seemingly incompatible opposites are nevertheless harmonious in their unity.

Fourteens are reliable partners, they do not strive for overly colorful and emotional experiences, and sometimes their company might even be a little bit dull. But they are nevertheless sincere and wise people who will always be there for their partners with support at the difficult moments in their lives, they are also capable of listening without interrupting for hours on end and know exactly what to say and how to say it at the most opportune moment. A partner with the Energy of Moderation knows how to find a compromise solution to any situation, listens to and understands their interlocutor and accepts their point of view. Fourteens are so wise and patient that their qualities sometimes suffice for two.

Among other things, the energy of the Fourteenth Arcanum indicates a balance of opposite extremes. The male and female energies in their union can give rise to androgyny. If the Fourteenth Arcanum is located in an individual's Karmic Tail, Material Karma or Character Zone this can often symbolize the homosexuality and bisexuality of this person's essence. The Fourteenth Arcanum provides its owner with the skills to accept reality for what it is and to reconcile themselves to it. According to statistical analysis, many Fourteens end up perceiving and accepting their special gender identity (gender) but hide it from those around them for many years, sometimes keeping it a secret until the end of their lives. This can apply to both men and women.

INDICATIONS THAT THIS ENERGY IS IN A −

- Impatience.
- Unreliability and a tendency to swing to extremes.
- The desire to get everything they want at once, without wasting any time.
- A tendency to be mediocre and ordinary.
- A tendency to be argumentative and capricious.
- An insistence on working out who is right and who is wrong.
- Life imbalance.
- A spontaneity and thoughtlessness in their actions.

INDICATIONS THAT THIS ENERGY IS IN A +

- A deep sense of their self-worth.
- A calm poise and balance in their thoughts and actions.
- The implementation of their obligations
- Striving for harmony and balance.

- The ability to forgive and accept the life and actions of others as a given.
- To take only what they need without going to excess.
- To be capable of uniting the divided and bringing the disparate together as one.
- A high level of tolerance, broad horizons and a wide-ranging perception of the world.

KARMIC TASKS:

- to learn patience;
- to think out of the box;
- to achieve calmness and stability in their thoughts, deeds and affairs;
- to learn to appreciate what they have;
- to be grateful to destiny;
- to not take more than is needed;
- to find a balance between what they want and what is possible.

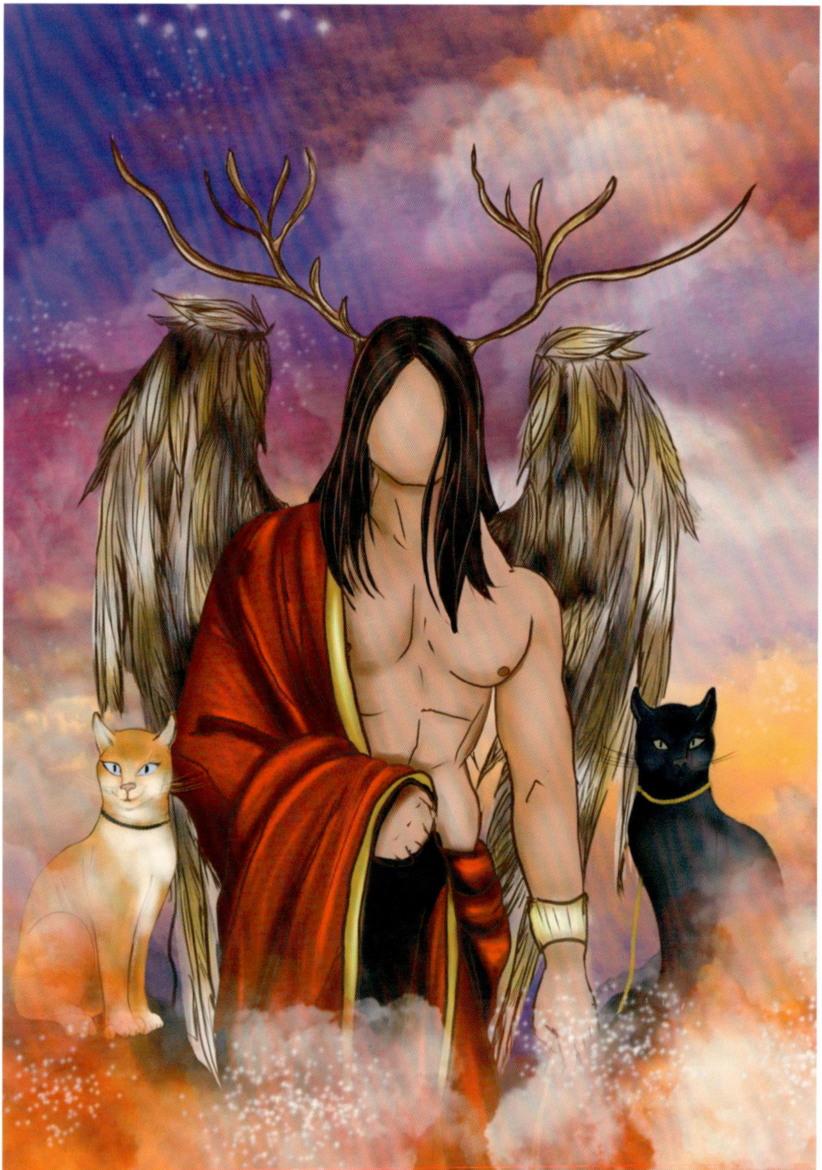

ARCANUM 15. THE DEVIL

> Eat and drink, brave Warrior,
> On this evening dedicated to you
> The pride of the tribes of the Sioux,
> The son of the nations of Manitoba.
> May your name be glorified!
> May our warrior brave and daring
> Enjoy the caresses of women
> Satisfying his thirst for passion.
>
> Can you hear how the elders sing
> Praises in your honor?
> So that from the most distant stars
> Our ancestors may hear our joy.
> And the wails and tears of
> The mothers of Athabasca's sons
> Slain by your merciless hand
> May be drowned out.

TEMPTATION — CHARISMA — PASSION

In the Tarot deck, the Fifteenth Arcanum is represented by a card depicting the Devil. This is the energy of contradiction and trials, of seduction and temptation. The devil gives a lot and sometimes does not require anything in return, but sooner or later the time will come when his lesson will have to be learned. The eternal struggle between good and evil, the goading of all that is essentially human in an individual to choose the right answer to the eternal questions: whose side are you really on? Is that really the path you are going to follow?

The energy of the Devil is the brightest and most influential of all the twenty-two Energies in the Destiny Code. The Fifteenth Arcanum can never be in the Character Zone and, therefore, end up being an individual's personal energy. There can be only one Devil, and only by observing from the sidelines does he, at his own discretion, take part in the lives of the people of this World.

Fifteens are extremely charismatic and charming, they easily make connections and other people easily fall in love with them. As a rule, people of this sort are either greatly admired or intensely hated. Whatever the case, an individual endowed with the Fifteenth Arcanum never leaves anyone indifferent. Devil people know how to make an offer that can't be refused, they can see right through everyone, see their essence and look into their Souls. It is impossible to stand up to the energy of a person with the Fifteenth Arcanum, all resistance is futile.

People with the Fifteenth Arcanum trust their intuition totally because they are utterly confident in their ability to see through others' masks, and accurately determine where the true sparkling diamond of the human soul lies and where there is nothing but emptiness. Subtly sensing the Energies of others, people with the Arcanum of the Devil, by their very presence, can lay bare other people's human essence, tempting and provoking them to take actions that are unnatural for that soul.

The Energy of the Fifteenth Arcanum connects its owner with all the dark aspects of life. Sex, perversion, alcohol, drugs, crime, violence, humiliation — Fifteens sometimes need to sink to the very bottom in order to start rising up and move towards the Light. But one must always be aware that the Fifteenth Arcanum burns with brightness not because it "burns" but because it chooses the Light. Every morning, Fifteens have to get up and choose the Light. But not every day is the same.

A combination of the Fifteenth and Fifth Arcana endows a person with the ability to gain knowledge from both sides of reality and the opportunity to accept both Light and Darkness. To take the greatest truths in the world and create a unique scheme of life for themselves and, perhaps, many other potential followers. The wider public is drawn to people with this combination of Energies like moths to a flame. The Fifteenth Arcanum is incapable of overcoming its craving to rule and the Fifth Arcanum is insanely driven to teach and this is how communities, organizations and sects are born.

The Devil has a very special Energy. The karmic task of the Fifteenth Arcanum stipulates that the individual endowed with it will have to pass through the most difficult physical and moral tests known to man. The Devil loves to torment people, dragging them to the bottom, testing their tenacity and distorting their consciousness. But there can be no remaining in these "dark waters". The individual must come through the darkness to see the Light. Quite often, people who have gone through serious tests in life and found themselves on the very edge can help others cope with similar situations through their unique experiences. By passing tests of extreme physical violence, serious alcohol or drug addiction, by "selling" their Soul to the dark side of life, Fifteens come through this experience of "falling" in order to attain the Light and share their experiences with others.

WATCHWORDS

The Arcanum of the Devil endows its owner with superpowers to see, feel and understand. These skills instil a high degree of self-confidence and a sense of superiority over others. On each occasion that these skills are confirmed, the Ego grows. The higher the status of a person with the Fifteenth Energy, the more powerful his or her abilities. When Fifteens finally perceive these abilities they no longer have the power to curtail them and they use them to manipulate, provoke and tempt others.

- Nothing that you feel is what you think it is.
- If you see a wolf, become a wolf. If you see a sheep, remain a wolf.
- Any person can be persuaded to agree with you, you just need to know what you need to offer them.

FINANCES

The devil reveals the dark side and provides hidden opportunities that cannot be seen with the naked eye. The Energy of the Fifteenth Arcanum provokes those endowed with it to go big, place a king's ransom on a single horse and has little time for common sense and doing the right thing, which it considers small-minded and petty. It has no qualms about preying on human vices and weaknesses.

Good connections, power, manipulation, the use of the human factor, the realization of the needs of the dark side of life — these are, perhaps, the main interests of a person with the Energy of the Devil.

When the Fifteenth Arcanum is in the Finance zone, it whispers in the ear of the people endowed with it that they will be more successful in informal employment than by working in good faith under a contract; that by receiving their pay in cash in an envelope, their earnings will be higher; that by taking risks and getting involved in shady deals and dodgy business, they will have good prospects for successful self-realization.

Fifteens should not be afraid to take risks, in their case risks are justified and manifestly successful.

Professions based on communication with other people are well suited to Fifteens and guarantee productivity. Fifteens make brilliant realtors, brokers, HR people, advertisers and marketers, political consultants, PR specialists and, of course, representatives of power at all possible levels.

Fifteens love money, status and power. They strive hard to achieve what they want and see no obstacles in their path. There are no mitigating vindications that can stop the Devil once he is set on achieving his ends, there is nothing and no one that can stop this wild energy.

Statistically, the majority of the most legendary swindlers and fraudsters had a combination of the Fifteenth and Fifth Arcana in their matrix. This explosive mixture of energies opens up unlimited opportunities to take everything that their possessors can wish for from life. However, it is worth remembering the special karmic program inherent in the Fifteenth Arcanum and the fact that everything will always have to be paid for in the end.

HEALTH

A tendency to addiction tends to wear the body out very quickly. They need to, at least occasionally, undertake recovery programs and cleanse their bodies of toxins and other harmful components. However, their spiritual wounds and psychological traumas are naturally not so easy to heal, but still, it is worth letting in a little Light and allowing Fifteens to alleviate the condition of their bodies and souls.

Fifteens often follow a special diet of "intermittent fasting" which comprises coffee and cigarettes until midday and then eating whatever they want as long as it is followed by large amounts of whiskey after six in the evening. And little else beyond that.

RELATIONSHIPS

It is difficult to build what is considered to be a normal relationship in the classic sense with a Fifteen. They are too charismatic, too free-willed and passionate to limit themselves to a relationship with just one partner. Their insatiable appetites, wild passion, sexuality and ambition make them great lovers but unbearably difficult partners.

However, the Energy of the Fifteenth Arcanum can also have the opposite effect on the character. Like the wild side of the Devil, the craving for the Light can also be extremely difficult for a partner to put up with. Their tendency to play at being "holier than thou" will also exasperate their partner, failing to satisfy the needs of either party in the relationship.

When in a relationship with a Fifteen, the best approach is to relax, learn to enjoy their best sides and try not to limit, judge or make too many demands of them.

If the Fifteenth Energy is in the Relationship zone, this indicates that the partners in this person's life will leave a heavy mark in his or her memory, and perhaps physically as well. In these situations, there is a chance that these Fifteens, having passed through a testing relationship with the Dark Side, will have the opportunity to find the Light — after their liaison with a demon, they might end up finding themselves in the arms of an angel.

INDICATIONS THAT THIS ENERGY IS IN A −

- Hypocritical piety.
- Anger and aggression towards other people.
- Dissatisfaction with their desires.
- The condemnation and defilement of other people's lives.
- An obsession with their faith in the Light and a constant struggle with their essence.

INDICATIONS THAT THIS ENERGY IS IN A +

- The possession of power over the souls and minds of men.
- A vivid, bright personality and captivating charisma.
- A predilection for that which is forbidden and sinful.
- Treating life as a game.

KARMIC TASKS:

- to take everything they want from life;
- to accept the shadow side of themselves;
- to be aware of the presence of both good and evil in all things;
- to pass the trials and tests facing them;
- to control their criticism of others — everyone has the right to be who they are;

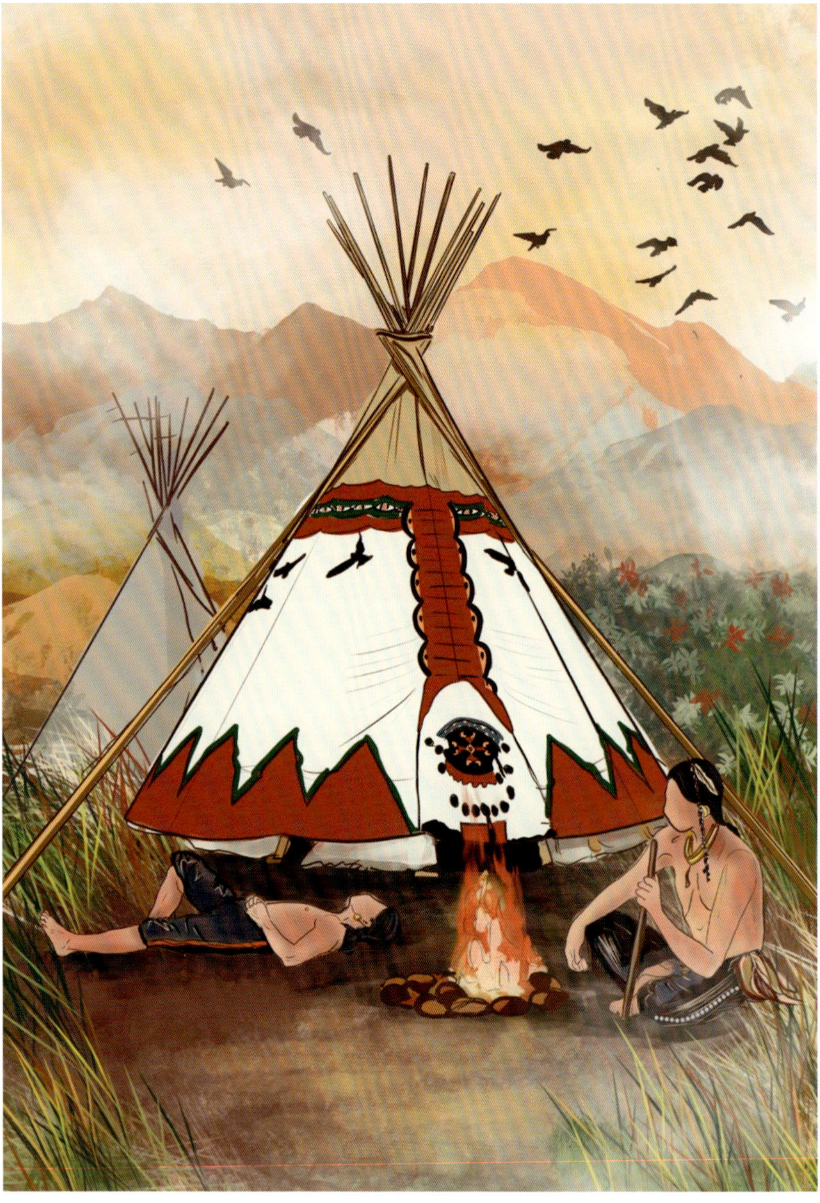

ARCANUM 16. THE TOWER

> On a harsh, cold, winter day, a hunter came in from the forest,
> Having spent the previous moon in the cold, he dreamed of the warmth of the wigwam,
> Where hot food carefully prepared by his hostess awaited him,
> And the hearth of this cherished house was guarded by the great spirit of the fire.
> Brave Wengu saw neither wigwam nor hostess,
> But only the ashes of the Fire scattered by the cold wind.
> Do not be sad, poor Wengu! Keep the memory in your heart
> To keep you warm on the way to new lands.

RECONSTRUCTION — GROWTH — DEVELOPMENT

The life of a person endowed with the Sixteenth energy in their Destiny Code Matrix is represented by a path travelling through thorns to reach the stars. It is a testing fate that resembles the plot of a blockbuster. It is extremely rare for a person to have the energy of the Sixteenth Arcana located in the Character Zone, and an individual endowed with such a unique karmic program is likely to be involved in some significant global event in the life of his or her contemporaries.

People with the Energy of the Tower are destined to live bright, eventful lives. Regular house moves, fires, natural disasters, accidents, wars, high-profile incidents, coups, revolutions, riots, and changes of power, as well as various other global and historical events. Sixteens do not have to be direct participants in these events, and having this power does not mean that they are somehow able to influence destiny, but these incidents nevertheless have a huge impact on their personal lives, perhaps accidentally making them somehow tangentially involved in what has happened. The energy of the Tower is primarily about destruction, and with a high degree of probability, the events in the life of a person with a Sixteen in their matrix will be destructive. It's possible that something will destroy their plans, deprive them of what they have achieved and break and destroy what they have or what they have long aspired to.

In the Tarot deck, the Sixteenth Arcanum is represented by the Tower. It is the energy of destruction and final completion. The Sixteenth card depicts a high tower, it has been doggedly raised by people over a long period of time, and they have made every effort to ensure that it has been built to a high standard and to be long lasting. But when it is almost completed and these people find themselves on top of it, they feel the earth tremble beneath them and everything shudder. Destiny has decreed that today of all days an earthquake should occur. The foundations have started to crack and the people that had only just now stood proudly atop their Tower now fall head first from its heights — their bodies lie strewn among its ruins. Only ashes and dust hang in the air — nothing remains: neither the Tower nor the people who built it.

The energy of the Sixteenth Arcanum teaches people that they need to go through life's trials with dignity, it is important to learn the lessons that each crisis teaches them and become stronger, taller, smarter and more cunning without becoming spiteful, respectfully accepting every test in order to survive.

The Sixteenth Energy has the fragile nature of a soap bubble or a dormant volcano. One way or another, spinning like a whirlwind, the eventfulness of life will change its pace and rhythm and sooner or later lead to a point of no return ending in an explosion, a fracture, a collapse. But, on the other hand, this energy motivates people to change. People build their towers higher in order to extend the boundaries of their vision, to increase their opportunities and prospects. By investing itself in quality, durability and reliability, the Sixteenth Arcanum gives itself completely to the cause — it builds honestly, conscientiously, without deceit or cutting corners.

When the Sixteenth Arcanum stands in the Zone of the Higher Essence, this indicates that the person endowed with this energy has a talent to be a revolutionary, an activist, a person who can smash foundations and break the rules, destroy stereotypes, overthrow power and topple everything in its path.

However, when the Sixteenth energy destroys, it does so in the name of liberation, to remove shackles and burdens. People with the energy of the Tower bear the mission of liberating everyone from imaginary beliefs, blind faith, lies and deceit. By bracing themselves against the walls of injustice and the inadequacies of the world around them, they inevitably face risks. The karmic task of these people is to remove all obstacles using the Sixteenth energy, they tear down the walls that hide the true reality lying behind them and, creating a solid foundation, they build the Tower of Truth.

People with the Sixteenth Energy spend their whole lives building something. They build businesses, careers or just plans. It is important for them to approach each issue using basic principles from the foundation up, they need to plan processes step by step and know exactly what it is and how much they will need for their "building". People with a Major Sixteenth Arcanum in their Destiny Code Matrix are the architects of life, the engineers of events — conscientious and scrupulous implementers and doers.

Stability and balance are qualities that are more important to Sixteens than others. When there is a plan and an estimate for what is needed, Sixteens sense that the process is under way and that they are doing things right. But any deviation from the plan, any unpredictable change in conditions, strikes them a serious blow, depriving them of a vitally important quality — their confidence. When these situations arise in an everyday context, it all might look rather ridiculous to people endowed with other energies. For example, a Sixteen might be doing their shopping and find that the brand of milk they needed on their shopping list is not available — suddenly they experience outright horror and their world collapses around them, all their plans instantly go up in smoke because the thing they expected to be in its rightful place isn't there. Any Three, Four, Five or Thirteen witnessing this would simply shake their head and think these people had a screw loose. But they would have no clue what a catastrophe has just befallen the Sixteen they are observing.

When the Energy of the Sixteenth Arcanum has been in a minus state for a long time, there is a high likelihood that this individual is in danger of losing their property, loved ones, faith, hope and love in their lives. Statistically, Sixteens are at a high risk of spending the rest of their lives in nursing homes, hospitals, hospices, prisons or war zones.

Likewise, Sixteens are more likely than others to witness unusual events of a global significance. Sixteens have a miraculous ability to escape catastrophes, survive terrible natural disasters and extricate themselves from the most extraordinary and difficult situations.

WATCHWORDS

Perhaps the most important thing in the lives of people with the Sixteenth Energy is to be prepared in a timely manner (and preferably in advance) for the unavoidable fact that it is impossible to avoid that which can't be changed. The expression that each individual can decide and

manage everything in his life rings absolutely false for Sixteens. The greatest tests of hardship and stamina are prepared especially for them, it is precisely from underneath their feet that the rug will be pulled, it is their plans that will collapse, and it is their lot to be subjected to the unexpected "surprises" that the Universe has in store for us.
- The moment you tell others about them, your plans are as good as dust.
- The higher you go, the harder you fall.
- While you are building, something constructive is going on.

FINANCES

Sixteens make excellent soldiers, athletes, climbers, stuntmen and racing drivers. Sixteens are the sort of people who find their calling in professions that can entail life-threatening risks. In addition, among other professions, they make for highly professional builders, architects, engineers, developers, businessmen and entrepreneurs — all occupations that require the painstaking construction of long-term projects from the foundations up.

The professions for which the Sixteenth Energy can be used are, of course, not just limited to the above range of professions and Sixteens can find themselves in absolutely any business — the main thing is that these activities make it possible for Sixteens to build their own business and actualize themselves independently of anyone else, using only their own blueprints, solutions and plans.

Like it or not, the destructive tendencies inherent to the Sixteenth Arcanum, one way or another leave their imprint on the sphere of work and self-realization of the individual endowed with it. Sixteens are constantly changing their employment as a result of dismissals, work disputes and the influence of other circumstances in their lives. When the Sixteenth Arcanum is in the Finance zone, there is a high likelihood that these individuals have the ability to make plans for long-term projects but lose everything in an instant because their business has collapsed, they have been dismissed for some inexplicable reason, they couldn't get on with the team they are in or they were laid off.

A Sixteen with the Sixteenth Energy in the Material Karma Zone should be very wary when engaging in business as their energy will interfere with its development at every stage of its "construction". People with the Energy of the Tower in this zone are advised not to put their money into stocks, banks, savings accounts, and other electronic assets. There is a very high risk of them losing their savings and everything else overnight.

Individuals with the Sixteenth Arcanum in the Higher Essence Zone should not announce their professional plans and projects before they are implemented — on many occasions it has been proven that they will inevitably go wrong and collapse as soon as these ideas are aired.

People with the energy of the Tower like to strive for comfort and prosperity because, after all, their road is hard and strewn with many trials. Sixteens have to work very hard to attain wealth and prosperity and every cent earned is highly valued (a person with the Sixteenth Energy understands this better than anyone else). This would appear to be a good place for me to give a valuable piece of advice to every person with a Major Sixteenth Energy in their matrix. It has long been noted that there is a certain pattern at play when a person is building something. During the planning stage when the final goal is still not in sight — everything goes well in measured and timely stages while the project is still not exposed to the risks that emanate from the Universe. But as soon as you feel you get close to the final stage, already thinking that your goal has been achieved — then an unexpected mishap occurs and everything starts to go completely differently from how you expected. It is very important to raise the bar with each brick laid and to add new items to your plan with each new step you take. As long as the process continues to carry on — it will not stop.

HEALTH

People with the Sixteenth Energy in the Destiny Code Matrix (regardless of its position on it) are more familiar with the force of gravity than other people. Sixteens are prone to falls and trips and often end up with fractures, dislocations, bruises and abrasions. They are extremely accident-prone. These are the sort of people who are constantly walking into walls and doors.

Just as Sixteens are prone to accidents that harm their bodies so, on the spiritual level, their psyches are also prone to trauma. People with the Energy of the Tower are prone to depression as a result of the total collapse of their convictions following the destruction of their well-laid life plans. Here, the important thing is to catch these individuals at a moment before they are beyond the point of no return, and help them realize that their life is not a total disaster zone (with no possibility of raising anything from out of the ashes), but only a building site (where the process is in full swing regardless of the cycle and where every human being's participation is extremely important and valuable).

RELATIONSHIPS

Perhaps the main feature of a person with the Energy of the Tower is the desire to create plans and to build a common cause together with others. And these aspirations are reflected when it comes to their relationships. It is very important for Sixteens that their partners are a part of the process they are involved in, so that they are united by a common cause. Perhaps the most ideal way to see their way through the Sixteenth Energy's karmic program would be to work on the construction or repair of a home together —in every sense of the expression.

When the Sixteenth Energy is in the Relationship Zone, the indications are that individuals of this sort will need a partner who will help them structure their lives, someone who will make plans with them and inspire joint activities. In these relationships, mutual support will be an important factor, each of the partners will need to be "on standby": when one passes a brick, the other will need to be on hand to catch it. The common project, the joint construction of a life together will strengthen and develop the union.

In addition, the Sixteenth Arcanum provides a good indication of a potential partner's sexual temperament, their impulsiveness and inflexibility in relationships. The Sixteenth Arcanum endows a person with an unflinching steadfastness and adamantine outer shell. Therefore, a Sixteen who appears to be decorous and unemotional on the surface will actually be ardent and passionate inside. And also, extremely susceptible and yielding to the charms of the opposite sex. All you need to remember is that balance and stability are extremely important to Sixteens — so all you have to do to have your way with them is take them by surprise, and not give them the chance to build a behavior strategy — and soon enough you will have pulled the rug from under their feet.

When the Sixteenth energy is in a minus state, there is a high likelihood of frequent divorces, separations from their partners and the revelation of adultery and betrayal after being many years in a relationship. The Sixteenth Arcanum can indicate the possible loss of a partner and widowhood. It can also possibly portend circumstances which make maintaining and continuing a relationship impossible. In addition, having the Sixteenth Energy in the Relationship Zone indicates being dependent on one's partner in terms of finances and status.

INDICATIONS THAT THIS ENERGY IS IN A –

- Creating plans that are not implemented.
- Evident fear of taking action in order not to lose what they already have.
- Superficiality and dishonesty.
- Spontaneity and failure to think out their ideas and actions.
- Small goals and limited desires.

INDICATIONS THAT THIS ENERGY IS IN A +

- Willingness to follow the plan and constantly work at it.
- The desire to raise the bar and see new heights up ahead.
- Faith that all will be for the best.
- The ability to get up off their knees, dust themselves down and move on.
- The desire to always be captivated by the idea and process of "building castles in the air".
- The conscientious and total immersion into the implementation of their plans.
- Taking their journey step by step from start to finish.
- The courage to knock down low-quality buildings and build newer better ones.
- The ability to open other people's eyes by removing their masks and crushing their false and naive beliefs.
- The ability to make and complete revolutions.

KARMIC TASKS:

- to learn to build;
- to never fear the summit — to build higher and stronger;
- to learn from their mistakes;
- to walk their path from the beginning to the very end;
- to value the process rather than the result;
- to believe in their strengths and capabilities.
- to always look ahead.

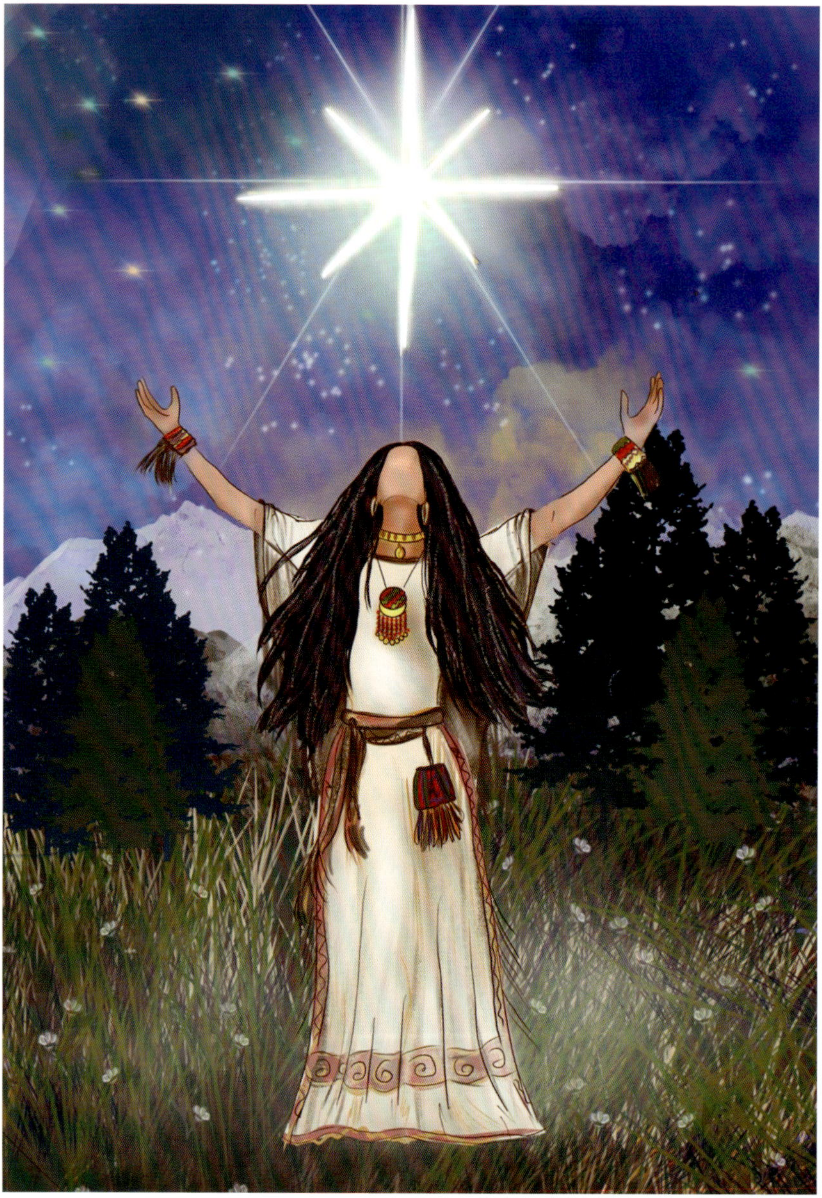

ARCANUM 17. THE STAR

Shining like a slither of white crescent moon, dissolving into the dark night,
Fair Nokomis went to dance with the prairie winds.
With the frail beauty of the fallow deer, with the silent step of the bobcat.
She will light up the land like the brightest star.
And all the sons of the great tribes will bow down to her like slaves
Offering her endless praises for her delight.

PURITY — RADIANCE — TALENT

The Energy of the Star is all about the exceptional and unique, the summit of professionalism, talent, fame and popularity. People become professionals in their chosen field because they strive to make the world a better place, give the best of themselves and realize their potential to the maximum for the benefit of society, as well as to leave a little bit of their starlight to shine on after them in history.

People endowed with the Seventeenth Arcanum in their Destiny Code Matrix strive to actualize themselves through their popularity, acknowledgement and approval in society. Sometimes, their popularity comes to them before their professionalism, and in these instances, the "shelf life" of the star will depend on their aspirations, their professional skills and their desire to "shine".

The Seventeenth Arcanum cannot stand in the Character Zone. A star cannot be hidden on the inside — it has to be visible, otherwise there would be no point in it shining. The major positions where it will have the greatest impact are the Portrait, Karmic Tail and Higher Essence Zones.

Seventeens seek recognition and popularity in everything they do, sometimes, perhaps, even hiding their desires in the process, but inevitably doing things that demand and receive the attention of those around them. Their behavior is remarkable to everyone who encounters them. In any case, one way or another, their creativity and sometimes theatricality will attract attention.

People with the Energy of the Star are kind-hearted, selfless and willing to do good deeds and work for noble causes. Their rich imaginations make them daydreamers who are remote from reality and completely impractical when it comes to everyday and worldly life. For Seventeens, the beauty of the view outside their window trumps any consideration of the chaos and disorder in their homes, people with the Energy of the Star get distracted by their creativity and can lose track of time, forgetting to eat, sleep and carry out their everyday chores, surrendering themselves to the creative process and flying far, far away towards Sirius and the other stars.

It goes without saying, that people with the Seventeenth Arcanum in their Destiny Code Matrix have been born under a lucky star, they are among the Universe's most favoured children, and the Universe has a very special mission prepared for them.

When they find themselves in sad and difficult moments it is important for Seventeens to never forget their dreams, their lofty goals and the fact that they are able to change the world. The success and the ability of a Star to realize its potential depends largely on the scale of its radiance — the brighter the Star shines, the more it illuminates everything around itself.

It is absolutely impossible for a person endowed with the energy of the Star to live a mousey life of gray mediocrity. Their lives need to be bright, rich, active and very unlike those of the people around them. It does not matter how this brightness and eventfulness is manifested — the main thing is that it comes into existence. Some Seventeens color their lives with their passion for going to various concerts, exhibitions and performances by becoming film critics or literary experts, while others perform the concerts, paint the pictures, stage the performances and create the masterpieces themselves. In either case, their energy will thus be realized.

The main task set by the Seventeenth Energy for the person endowed with it is to develop, manifest and realize their talents. It is important to remember that everything that a person gives will return to him or her a hundredfold. And everything that a person hides — will perish without a trace. Unique talent must be seen, discovered and shared. The words of a song that millions of people have heard will only captivate the hearts of several thousand of them.

WATCHWORDS

The Energy of the Star encourages the person endowed with it to shine and reach out and radiate it towards others. When light comes into being, it becomes a source of energy, giving everything and everyone around it something that they are not capable of creating on their own. The world needs Stars because beyond them there is no alternative source of beautiful radiance, and Stars need the world as the stage on which they can realize their talents.

- A Star must shine — without its radiance, a Star would not be visible on its own.
- Talent should be realized, otherwise, how would it become possible to understand that it is a great talent, and not just simply a skill.

FINANCES

Talent equals professional excellence. A person with the Seventeenth Energy in their Destiny Code Matrix is naturally endowed with special skills and is predisposed to develop these skills. Each skill is honed gradually step by step, professionalism comes with experience and dedication to one's aspirations and by believing in your dreams.

For Seventeens, everything starts with a dream. If their work and activities in life coincide with their dreams, then success is guaranteed. The stars favor dreamers, and circumstances miraculously help such people to realize themselves and their dreams and take their place in the firmament.

Regardless of which profession they take up, a Seventeen will be the star of whatever occupation they are involved in: a star in the field of dentistry or surgery, a star in the world of politics or education, a TV star or even just a celebrity. Everyone with the energy of the Star will stand out from the crowd in one way or another, shine and enrich those around them with their talents.

A career is built on fame, the more people know about a person with the Seventeenth Energy, the more successful they will be in their chosen activity. Seventeens need to strive to constantly improve and expand their skills, it is important to strengthen their talent and never rest on their laurels. They are constantly looking to improve their education and find new platforms on which they can perform in order to shine ever more brightly.

Fame and money come quickly to people with the Seventeenth Energy — the moment they open their arms to the world for it to receive them. They have the most brilliant prospects in store in all areas of life. The value of their talents and professionalism is increased when they are awarded prizes, acknowledgement, recognition, cups, stars on their epaulettes and huge numbers of subscribers and followers. But initially, it is extremely important for them not to be afraid to discover their talents and to be sure to take the first step.

Fifteen-minute wonders are people who, having made it to the top are satisfied that they have made it and now relax. The Energy of the Seventeenth Arcanum needs to be constantly shining, it allows for no let up for a peaceful and measured life. As soon as the light is allowed to go out, there will be no trace of the Star.

When the Seventeenth energy is located in the Karmic Tail, it suggests that this individual is endowed with a special talent that must be realized at all costs as a matter of vital importance to this incarnation of their Soul. In a past life, this person concealed his or her abilities and failed to realize what he or she needed to do. And for that reason, he or she has a debt they owe to the Universe. The answer for these people should be sought in their hobbies and interests because it is precisely here that their true destinies will lie, for which they came into the world to shine. And the same is true of these people's dreams — they should never renounce their dreams, because the true embodiment of their essence, and therefore, their potential lies in their dreams.

HEALTH

People with the Energy of the Star radiate light, energy, inspiration and life. The key to their physical and mental health is their inspiration, their elated ideas and their desire to move mountains. But this state is so unstable and fragile that it can very easily be turned on its head with a single careless word, a foolish incident or an absurd accident of circumstances.

Nature has endowed Seventeens with appearances that seem to defy the process of age with good skin, youthfulness, radiance and freshness. Seventeens love to laugh and smile and on a psychological level, they are able to inspire anyone with their positivity. But when their inner glow no longer shines as a result of illness, a crisis, psychological trauma, or just a bad mood — their appearance instantly changes, turning them into timid gray mice (their skin color deteriorates, their voices crack and their energy dries up).

When the Energy of the Seventeenth Arcanum is in a negative state the already fairly high risk that the individual will become depleted of vital energy is only increased. As a result, these individuals are unable to get out of bed, have no strength to eat or drink, are constantly falling asleep and unable to restore the source of their energy without outside help. When Seventeens are in this state, they are unable to see the world around them and depending on the degree of the problem, they risk developing problems with their vision, which can result in them losing their sight completely.

In addition, Stars are very sensitive to pollution levels in their immediate environment. Factors such as air pollution, sudden changes in climate and bad food and water have a more negative affect on Seventeens than others. Seventeens are hypersensitive both emotionally and physically. Therefore, what may appear normal for the majority of people is not all acceptable for them.

People with the Seventeenth Energy have a higher risk of drowning and ending up in life-threatening situations near water.

RELATIONSHIPS

When a person is endowed with the Seventeenth Energy in the Relationship Zone, this indicates that a sensitive, faithful, caring and attentive partner will make their ideal soul mate. These unions are based primarily on spiritual mutual love, where a unity of souls is more important to the partners than the unity of bodies. They are special, airy affairs, based on the subtle stuff of their partners' dreams and inspiration. As long as there is a mutual feeling of admiration, their love will burn and burn.

Seventeens are good psychologists and can accurately guess their partner's moods and desires. In their relationships, they seek to achieve complete unity with their partner and find mutual trust, satisfaction and understanding.

The Energy of the Star consists of a subtle, light sexuality, playfulness and a certain studied refinement. Like a scene from an old movie set in an old palazzo somewhere on the coast of the Mediterranean Sea lit by candlelight and a perfect sunset with crisp linen and silk sheets. Stars experience an intense need for romance and for a fire that will ignite their energy, which will envelop both partners. If a Seventeen is feeling uninspired, if he or she does not sense a slight flutter in the air, then the flame will not take hold and fail to take light.

When a Seventeen's energy is in a negative state, they can show indifference and coldness towards their partners. If this is the case, then their partners must create a spark and throw more wood on the fire to provide the light that is so vital for the Seventeenth Energy.

INDICATIONS THAT THIS ENERGY IS IN A −
- Laziness and pessimism.
- The absence of dreams and inspiration.
- A refusal to use the chances and opportunities that the Universe sends.
- Feelings of worthlessness, a refusal to find and recognize their talents.
- Unfinished business in life, an unfinished book, an unfinished speech, an unproven theorem or theory.
- A one-day wonder (a forgotten personality or talent).

INDICATIONS THAT THIS ENERGY IS IN A +
- A bright and vibrant life.
- Many fans and followers.
- Talents and dreams that are realized.
- Reaching the heights of recognition and professionalism in their field of activity.
- Actively and openly in communication with the world.
- The desire to shine and receive attention.
- Surrounded by cleanliness, comfort and beauty.
- Creativity.
- Pure in their aspirations and inspired by their dreams.
- Open to accepting new ideas and moving forward, unafraid to show their true motives.

KARMIC TASKS:
- to unleash their potential — develop their talents;
- to develop their self-esteem — to have dignity and self-confidence;
- to show their abilities to the world;

- to become a guiding star, a ray of hope;
- to accept their unique nature;
- to find sincerity in their relations with themselves;
- to shine

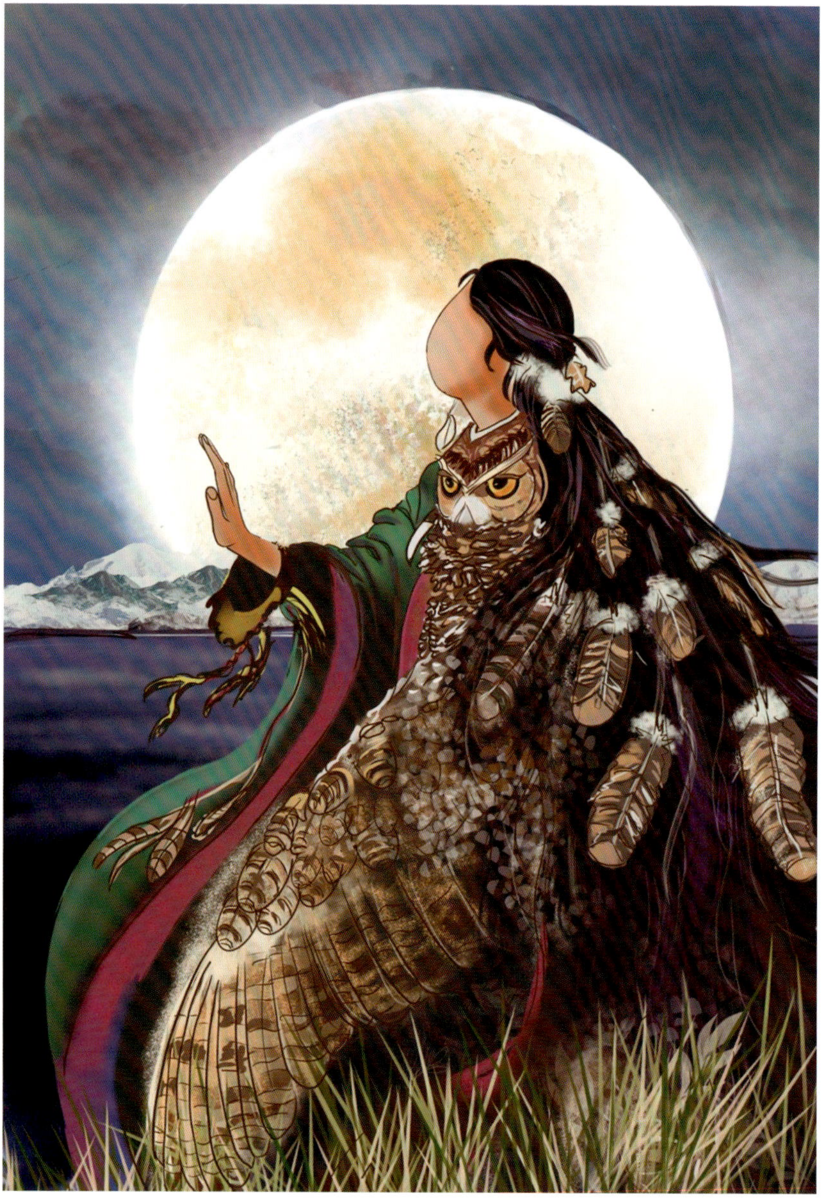

ARCANUM 18. THE MOON

> The silence of the night shuddered,
> And at the Spirits' command, the song of the Forest was silenced.
> Then the Eagle's mother went hunting
> The Stikini — dressed in their owl feathers.
> Hey you, strange birds, keep your beak to yourself!
> Her clawed talon is wrapped around your throat and
> She will mercilessly pluck out your
> Bloodied heart, still thirsting for life

GENIUS — MAGIC — INSANITY

The Energy of the Moon is the most mysterious and ambiguous of all the twenty-two Energies in the Destiny Code. The Eighteenth Arcanum gives the person endowed with it the superpower to materialize any thoughts. However, thoughts can be both good and bad. Eighteens need to learn that both their desires and fears can end up being realized, and people with the Energy of the Moon have plenty of both.

The symbol of the Thirteenth Arcana in the Tarot deck is Death. Sorcery and magic in its purest form. Under the cover of night, the Moon becomes the mistress of the world, she knows all and sees everything. Nothing can hide from her keen gaze, nothing can be kept concealed or silent — everything will come out into the open, everything will be revealed. The Arcanum of the Moon reveals all the cards, painting the situation as it really is, it lays bare people's motives and reveals their true face. At night, under the radiance of the stars, under the calm, subtle light of the moon, the most deeply hidden things come to the surface, all those things that are hidden deep inside during the daytime in the secure hope that they will not be revealed to prying eyes. The Eighteenth Arcanum reveals the individual's greatest apprehensions and fears and urges him or her to look them straight in the eye without hesitation.

When the Eighteenth Energy stands at the top of the Ancestral Square, there is a strong likelihood that these individuals are endowed with talents and skills of a magical nature. They are able to see what others cannot, to make words materialize, to influence events in their lives and those of others with their desires. This is an extremely special bonus that the Universe has generously shared with them, and it should be used for the good.

The Energy of the Moon is very strong, creative and mysterious, but also very ambiguous. At some completely uncontrolled moment, the Energy of the Moon turns all its magic, creativity, the ability to materialize ideas and all the other delights of its manifestation into a tendency to provoke those around it, a tendency to self-harm, destructive behavior, schizophrenia and subsequently to its own self-destruction. The moon is ambiguous: it is difficult to determine whether it is one's dreams or fears that are likely to appear first and what exactly causes one or the other to arise — the desire to create or the desire to destroy. It is sometimes impossible to determine at first glance who Eighteens really are, whether they are geniuses or insane.

It is good when a person with the Eighteenth Energy understands this problem for themselves, when they are capable of admitting that they are losing their sense of reality, that they are going crazy and need to put things right. Sadly, however, this is practically impossible. Eighteens are introverts, they do not trust other people and they find it difficult to open up to those around them, their inner world lives under the light of the Moon, and the familiar Sun frightens them. Eighteens have no notion of an ordinary, measured life or the need to go with the flow, that sort of life is not possible for them. It is the equivalent of throwing a bird into the sea or a fish onto dry land.

WATCHWORDS

The specific characteristics of the Eighteenth Arcanum are its mystery and supernatural nature. Whether they like it or not, magic and sorcery will accompany people endowed with the Energy of the Moon throughout their lives. Secret signs, coincidences, evident influences on events — everything in their lives is filled with the inexplicable. Perhaps one of the most important lessons that Eighteens have to learn is to voluntarily accept the powers that have been given to them by the Universe and to learn how to control them and use them for the greater good. Otherwise, the energy will look for alternative ways to realize itself and, unable to find a legitimate route to the outside world, will start causing havoc and destruction to the individual's inner world.

- Everything that can be imagined is within your grasp.
- You just have to want it — dreams really do come true.

- You should never give in to fear — otherwise, it will become a reality.

FINANCES

The Energy of the Eighteenth Arcanum and illusions are inseparable. Individuals can remain trapped in their illusions, which destroy and spoil their lives, or they can make a business out of trading in these illusions. After all, you can plunge into your hidden fantasy world and, slowly going crazy, drown in it, losing touch with reality. Or you can become a magician, a director of science fiction films, or a theater director and give vent to these fantasies and bring them to life. In order to find themselves, Eighteens need to decide what role they are ready to play in the performance that is life — the role of a spectator or creator: to be the one who drowns in the illusory world or the one who creates, controls and opens this world up to others.

People with the Energy of the moon need to choose a profession where they can be completely independent, relying solely on themselves. The Eighteenth Arcanum's life rhythms are chaotic, there is no clear seasonality in their activity or passivity, there are no clear graphs showing when they are in an excellent mood or a prolonged period of depression. If an Eighteen is to realize him or herself in any profession, the environment will need to feel natural, unconstrained, free and comfortable. Unlike the other energies (with perhaps the exception of the 12th and 13th) the Eighteenth is unable to adapt to circumstances, follow a system or change the system to its purposes and, as a result, the Energy of the Moon will go into eclipse.

A job, which allows them a free schedule, working until late or through the night is well suited to a person with the Eighteenth Arcanum in the Finance Zone. These individuals make successful creators: writers, artists, poets, musicians, psychologists, philosophers and, of course, illusionists and magicians. Whatever the activity these people take up, it should always allow them to express and transfer their internal state to the external world. The Energy of the Moon must be allowed to rise and be fully realized. The freer the individual is allowed to be with their energy flows, the more confidently he or she will be able to control and manage them and the more fruitful his or her activity and success will be.

The Energy of the Moon reveals things that the majority of people would not be able to see or understand on their own. Therefore, Eighteens act as a conduit for this magical power and this is the karmic program that they have been set: to cast aside the veil of secrecy, to reveal that which has not yet been seen, to inspire, enchant and bewitch.

Money and prosperity are perceived by Eighteens as a very useful tool to solve the most important problems in their lives — their everyday problems and issues. Money helps them not to be too distracted by worldly problems such as food, looking for money and what passes for typical work. It's vital that Eighteens are able to resolve this issue and concentrate on realizing themselves because if a person with the Eighteenth Arcanum is forced to live an ordinary life, do an average job, deal with taxes and electricity bills, they will literally go crazy.

When the energy of the moon enters into a minus state, the person endowed with it becomes overwhelmed by their fears. Overwhelmed and drowning in their prejudices they will not be able to find a job or complete or find the time to do the tasks they have been set. In their everyday lives and professional activities, Eighteens are gripped by their fears.

When they are in this state, they prefer to find part-time jobs, doing two or three at a time. Official jobs do not suit them because they are often cheated or deceived of their wages or benefits owed them. Many Eighteens live from one pay check to the next or run up large debts — living on a basic diet of bread and water is a common state of affairs for them. Thus, trapped in poverty, they often, unknown to their contemporaries, work on their magic in secret, creating great masterpieces, which are only recognized posthumously after their deaths.

HEALTH

The causes of most of the diseases and illnesses Eighteens suffer from arise from the way they have learned how to master their energy. Any violation of the balance between the spirit and the body and a failure to realize the inner essence of the Moon in the outside world will provoke the Eighteenth Energy to affect the physical and mental health of the individual endowed with it.

These imbalances are characterized by a high probability of developing mental and genetic diseases such as autism, senile dementia (earlier than usual), depression, suicidal tendencies and completely losing touch with reality. And vice versa, physical diseases such as paralysis, and genetic diseases that prevent the victim from controlling their body can develop in individuals of sound mind and memory, when they are deprived of the opportunity to manifest themselves in the world. In addition, people with Eighteen in the Character Zone very often have congenital or incurable diseases of the mind or physical body.

Eighteens are sensitive to the phases of the moon and the movement of the cosmic bodies as well as changes in the weather and they often suffer from insomnia, recurring nightmares, hallucinations and are prone to sleepwalk. They are also prone to hysteria and obsessive persecution complexes. All of the above conditions can subsequently lead to problems with their speech, stuttering, mutism, difficulty in expressing themselves and dyslexia.

It is vital for a person with the Energy of the Moon in the Destiny Code Matrix to get the support and help they need promptly. It is also important that Eighteens are told that something new and important awaits him beyond the next threshold and that they need to summon up their courage and take the first step by crossing it. It is important for them to learn how to overcome their fears; they should not allow any ghostly illusions to overshadow reality and they should try to maintain their clarity of mind.

RELATIONSHIPS

There is no denying that Eighteens are mysterious in their ordinary everyday lives and their relationships are no exception either. They share a certain similarity with Nines in that when it comes to a partner the thing they seek most of all is a unity of souls. But beyond that, they differ from Nines completely.

When they fall in love, Eighteens find themselves completely in the power of their subconscious. They become captivated by a magnetic attraction and cosmic attachment to their "chosen one". They are absolutely unique lovers who, through sex, strive to gain as deep a knowledge of their partner's soul as possible to form a complete spiritual unity with them: through flights of insanity and sensuality to the stars — an almost astral experience. Eighteens' passion and the success of a union with them are based on their fantasies and special vibrations with their partner.

However, on the other side of the coin, they can easily be blinded by their partners and an illusion of normality can be created in conditions that could end up destroying both partners. Unfortunately, turning a blind eye to betrayal and enduring violence and suffering in their relationships is considered normal for many individuals with the energy of the moon in their Destiny Code Matrix. In cases such as these, outside help is needed to bring these individuals back to a sense of reality, to dispel illusions and open their eyes to the abnormality of what is going on.

There is no need for them to howl at the moon and tear themselves to pieces out of their loneliness because the moon will always be with them for company.

INDICATIONS THAT THIS ENERGY IS IN A −

When describing some of the negative states of the Eighteenth energy, it is very important to take into account their peculiar binary nature. For example, Eighteens can simultaneously deceive themselves and be deceived by others and both of these states are manifestations of their negative energy.

- A rejection of reality.
- Oblivion.
- A tendency to allow themselves to go with the flow.
- Hints, half-truths and not completely revealing information.
- False projections of themselves and insincere mannerisms, behavior and relationships.
- Self-doubt, fearfulness, subservience and self-hatred.
- Fears and anxiety.
- Worrying about everyday domestic life.
- The unconscious gaining the upper hand over common sense.
- Wild instincts caused by dark energies.

INDICATIONS THAT THIS ENERGY IS IN A +

- Mystery and authenticity.
- Highly developed intuition and energy superpowers.
- The ability to disconnect the mind from the body.
- The ability to make internal fantasies manifest into external reality.
- Control over the mind and the subconscious.
- Control over their own thoughts and fears.
- The ability to realize their talents.
- The ability to open up to others, if not to everyone, then to those they have chosen.
- The ability to accept help from others.

- The ability to love themselves and the world around them.
- The ability to accept the truth and be honest in return.

KARMIC TASKS:
- to rid themselves of fear at all levels of their consciousness;
- to accept their ability to know and see more than others;
- to be honest — to avoid secrets and lies;
- to accept their sexuality and power of attraction;
- to learn to observe without interfering in the process;
- to read the hidden meanings in life;
- to be the architect of destinies;

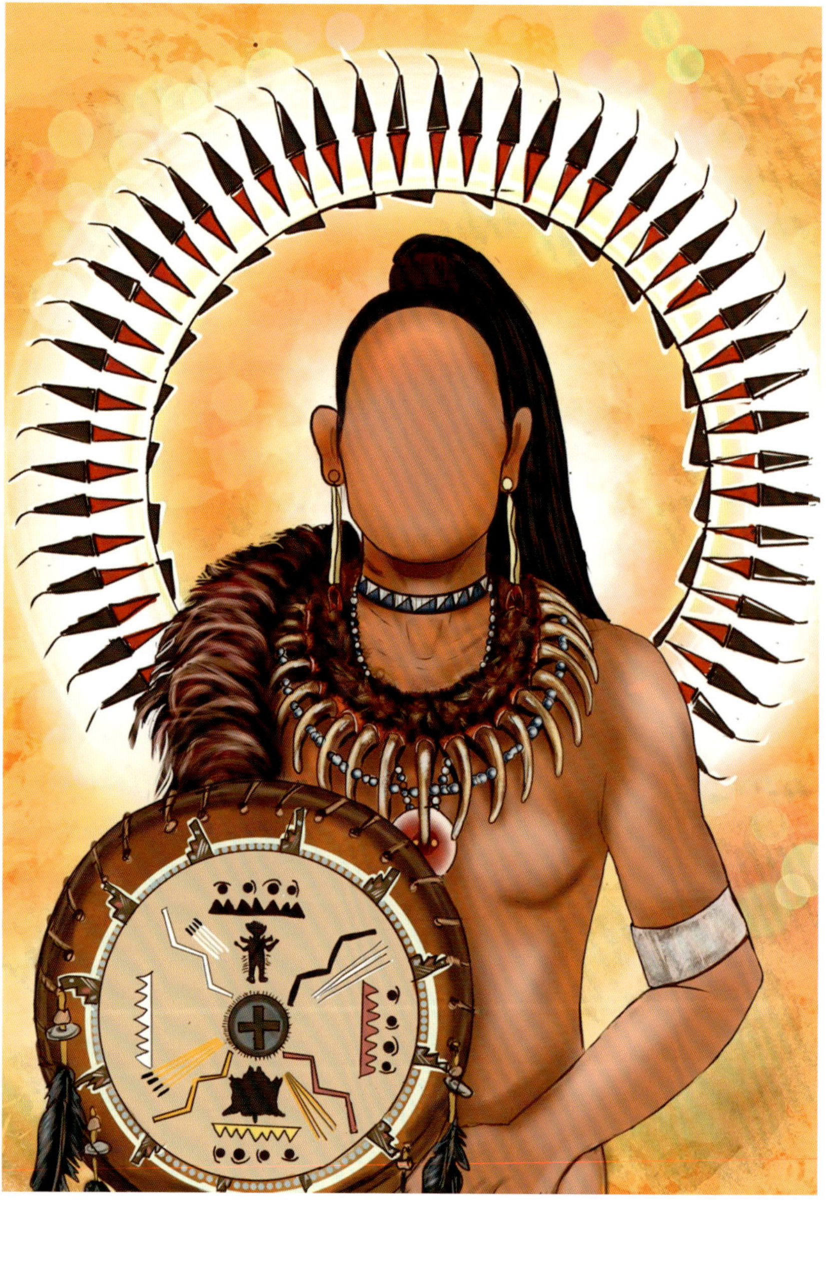

ARCANUM 19. THE SUN

> Blaze with fire, Luminary of the World.
> Fearless Warrior and Lord,
> Great Chief Bear Claw.
> Our strength will be with you.
> Keeping their Covenant
> The Sons and daughters of Nacotchtank,
> will set off with you
> For the fertile plains
> And the abundant forests.

ABUNDANCE — GENEROSITY — OPTIMISM

The Sun bears the energy of generosity, wealth and well-being. It is the energy of influence, power and high status. There is a high probability that those endowed with the Nineteenth Energy in the Destiny Code Matrix will achieve important positions in society and become the center of attention. They are sunny, open, happy people, who know how to enjoy life and teach others to do likewise.

The Energy of the Nineteenth Arcanum has an improving effect on the individual's Destiny Code Matrix as a whole, making it more positive, and, therefore makes the individual's life more open to prosperity and well-being. The life of a person with the Energy of the Sun acquires special shades of destiny's generosity — a certain cheerfulness in their perception of the world and a friendly yet bellicose character. People with the Nineteenth Arcanum in their Destiny Code Matrix are leaders and role models to those around them, their admirers follow their successes and set them up as an example to others. The Energy of the Sun enhances such qualities as honesty, frankness, clarity and openness. Nineteens need to live up to the expectations placed upon them and be the one that others look up to and aspire to, and they strive to be a role model and motivators for others to reach the levels of development they attain.

Nineteens have as much energy as the Sun. If they focus their attention on a particular problem or a certain task then their energy is like a sunbeam directed straight at its target — inevitably reducing it to ashes. The sun needs to shine on everyone, evenly and carefully distributing its energy, so that everyone is happy, and so that no one will suffer. As it is impossible to avoid the attentions of the Sun, then the only thing that one can do is to welcome it — resistance is futile. "Whoever I want to make happy is going to be happy and that's all there is to it!"

Staying positive and generous requires affluence and material resources. And in order for these resources to be available to a person with the Nineteenth Energy, they need to remain positive and generous. This may seem like a virtuous circle but Nineteens must learn to find where their point of "despondency" in this circle lies and learn to leap over it each time it comes around in order to prevent any self-doubt creeping in.

People with the Energy of the Sun in their Destiny Code Matrix must never forget to be generous in life. They need to lavish attention on themselves, those around them and especially their loved ones. They must allow themselves to relax, buy gifts, eat fine food and do whatever they want. They need to be generous in every possible life situation that they find themselves in. For example, they should leave a good tip in cafes and restaurants and they should invest generously in the development of themselves, their loved ones, those around them and the world as a whole. One particularly interesting and intriguing fact about them is that it is not a good thing for them to buy too many things at a bargain price in the sales — they are always better off buying one thing, but as expensive as possible. Practice proves that for Nineteens this motivates the Universe to be more generous to them, if they exhibit tight-fisted pettiness then the flow of prosperity and well-being soon dries up.

When the Nineteenth Arcanum is located in the Highest Essence Zone, it is an indication that this is an individual who consumes and requires a large amount of energy in the form of the attention paid to his person and is inspired to be a standard bearer and a role model to others. From early childhood, these sorts of people either tend to be straight-A students and natural leaders gathering their peers around them, or vice versa, they try to attract attention by becoming hooligans, getting into alternative subcultures or organizing riots and protests.

One way or another, a person endowed with the Energy of the Sun in their Destiny Code Matrix will become the center of the firmament in their own environment. Nineteens manifest their Sunshine in accordance with the zone that this Arcanum is located in, bestowing its special light on everything around. When they are in a positive state, they will inspire and motivate everyone around them. When the energy of the Sun is in a negative state, it will burn itself out because its energy is too powerful to be directed back in on itself.

WATCHWORDS

The Energy of the Nineteenth Arcanum gives its owner a special charm, an unusual outlook on life, a pronounced desire to live life well, and the desire to achieve a high level of prosperity and to do things on a global scale. All life on planet Earth depends on the Sun: if it is absent for too long people suffer depression, the crops fail to ripen and sometimes droughts result from its powerful rays. One way or another, everything depends on the energy provided by the main star in our firmament. And so it is with people's destinies: the energy of the Sun inevitably affects how their lives will develop.

- Shine like the Sun and light the path that leads others to happiness.
- Positivity and self-confidence are key to inner strength.
- No one will believe in you until you learn to believe in yourself.

FINANCES

People with the Energy of the Sun are endowed with access to the goodwill of the Universe. They are the Universe's chosen ones. Every possibility for self-realization is opened up to them. And every generally accepted human notion of wealth, social status, power and influence are genuinely available, accessible and achievable for them. They only have to learn how to distribute their energy, to take a broader view of the world and its issues, to avoid setting limits for themselves and to expand the opportunities available to them — to truly allow themselves to become a shining luminary.

Individuals with the Nineteenth Arcanum in the Finance Zone are very successful when it comes to money and finances. They have a special grasp and an exceptional sense of strategic thinking and they are able to apply it brilliantly to various fields of activity. First and foremost, these are business people, the sort of people who primarily and subconsciously see business as being about money and an exchange of resources. The sort of people who build up their own business to create a special product and share it with the world, the sort of people who build businesses that improve other people's living conditions, the sort of people who educate and develop themselves in order to become as famous as possible and leave their mark and name on history, the sort of people who are happy to be useful to society but people endowed with the Energy of the Sun primarily see money as their goal.

Provided that their energy is in a well-balanced state, Nineteens always stand out in their team or the company they keep. They are bright and charismatic and they attract and concentrate everyone's attention on themselves. These people strive to get to the top, they are happy to climb Olympus and even further and higher. They are career people, engines of industry, in a word, they are the people who motivate everyone around them with their light and energy. There is a certain similarity with the Seventh Energy, although the main difference is that the Energy of Movement motivates its owner to rush onward without ever looking back. Whereas Sun people, while leading from the front, turn to face their team, with their backs facing towards their goals because for them it is the attention of others on them that is of paramount importance and not the goal at their back.

An individual with the Energy of the Nineteenth Arcanum in the Finance Zone is highly likely to make "serious money" in their lives. When the Energy of the Sun lies at the junction of relationships, this indicates a high likelihood of coming into an inheritance or financial capital from a partner or family member and likewise a fast ascent in social status possibly through a successful marriage.

Any areas of activity which involve working directly with money such as banking, finance, investments and stock market trading are the most likely to activate the Nineteen's ability to really get the cash flowing. Accountancy, payroll and fundraising are also activities that stimulate the Energy of the Sun.

Activities that literally involve working with the Sun are also successful places of work for Nineteens. These might involve the creation and installation of solar panels, work with power and electricity, the development of alternative sources of electricity, astronomy and space development.

Obtaining universal recognition, awards, titles and connections with the government and state — are all things that actively help the energy of the Sun to develop and grow. Every Nineteen needs to determine in which specific zone of their Destiny Code matrix their energy lies and then use it in a sphere of life that corresponds to this zone. This is a unique bonus that is not given to everyone and Nineteens should never doubt the power of this gift and fail to use it in their lives. The Energy of the Sun opens up endless possibilities for those endowed with it to achieve a high level of wealth, power, money and influence.

HEALTH

People with the Nineteenth Arcanum in the Destiny Code Matrix are endowed with excellent health. The Sun blesses its children with longevity, large families and great stamina, energy and a love of life. These people draw their strength from physical activity and positive thinking. The more active and eventful their lives are, the more strength they have.

Ironically, people with the Nineteenth Energy in their matrix are often very sensitive to sunlight. It is not uncommon for them to have skin diseases caused by exposure to sunlight, allergies and burns. They are more likely to experience heat stroke and are worse affected by magnetic storms and solar flares than others.

RELATIONSHIPS

When the Nineteenth energy is in the Relationship zone, this indicates that these individuals are destined to meet a prosperous educated and ambitious partner with excellent prospects. Nineteens have very high requirements of their partners, they cannot afford to allow themselves to be content with little and settle for less, they won't waste their energy on boring and mundane relationships, they prefer to wait until someone who truly meets their desires and expectations comes along. The partner they are looking for will have to meet their ideals and special selection criteria and be life-defining. The energy of the Sun always radiates out the best of things, and this is a chance that should not be missed.

People endowed with the energy of the Sun are very bright and vivid individuals, they light up everything around them, they can create a festive holiday atmosphere anywhere, concentrate everyone's attention on themselves and inspire those around them. They are smiling, cheerful people who love life and have a good sense of humor — everyone looks at and admires them, sometimes even with a certain touch of envy.

The reverse side of the coin with the Nineteenth Energy is its relentless, merciless ruthlessness. With its irresistibly powerful rays, the sun can raze anything in its path to ashes, leaving deep scars. The Nineteenth Energy always leaves a trace in the memory of others — both happy and sad. People of the Sun are special, unique people and their appearance in anyone's life, even for a short period, remains with them forever.

INDICATIONS THAT THIS ENERGY IS IN A –
- Narcissism.
- Greed and pettiness.
- Poverty (a lack of funds).
- Lies and flattery.
- Self-deception and farce.
- Officiousness.
- A lack of attention towards others.
- Monotony — a lack of bright and vivid events in their lives.
- Being overweight and failing to look after their appearance.
- Living a low-maintenance lifestyle with few and modest requirements and needs.
- Purchases bought in the sales at a discount.
- Cutting down on expenses and saving money.
- Prejudice, bias and preconceptions.
- Complaints about and dissatisfaction with themselves, their life and their circumstances.

INDICATIONS THAT THIS ENERGY IS IN A +
- Generosity, prosperity and wealth.
- Cheerfulness and positive thinking.
- Openness and sociability.
- Being a person of the Sun.
- An exemplary personality.
- Honesty, frankness and nobility.
- Success, recognition (awards and titles).
- An active life.
- A taste and lust for life.
- A secure and serene pleasure in things.
- An internal and external beauty.
- Luxury, money, quality and comfort.

KARMIC TASKS:

- to learn to think positively and accept life as it is;
- to find meaning;
- to accept joy and happiness in themselves;
- to let go of prejudice;
- to rid themselves of guilt;
- to eradicate feelings of fastidiousness and disgust;
- to become the best version of themselves.

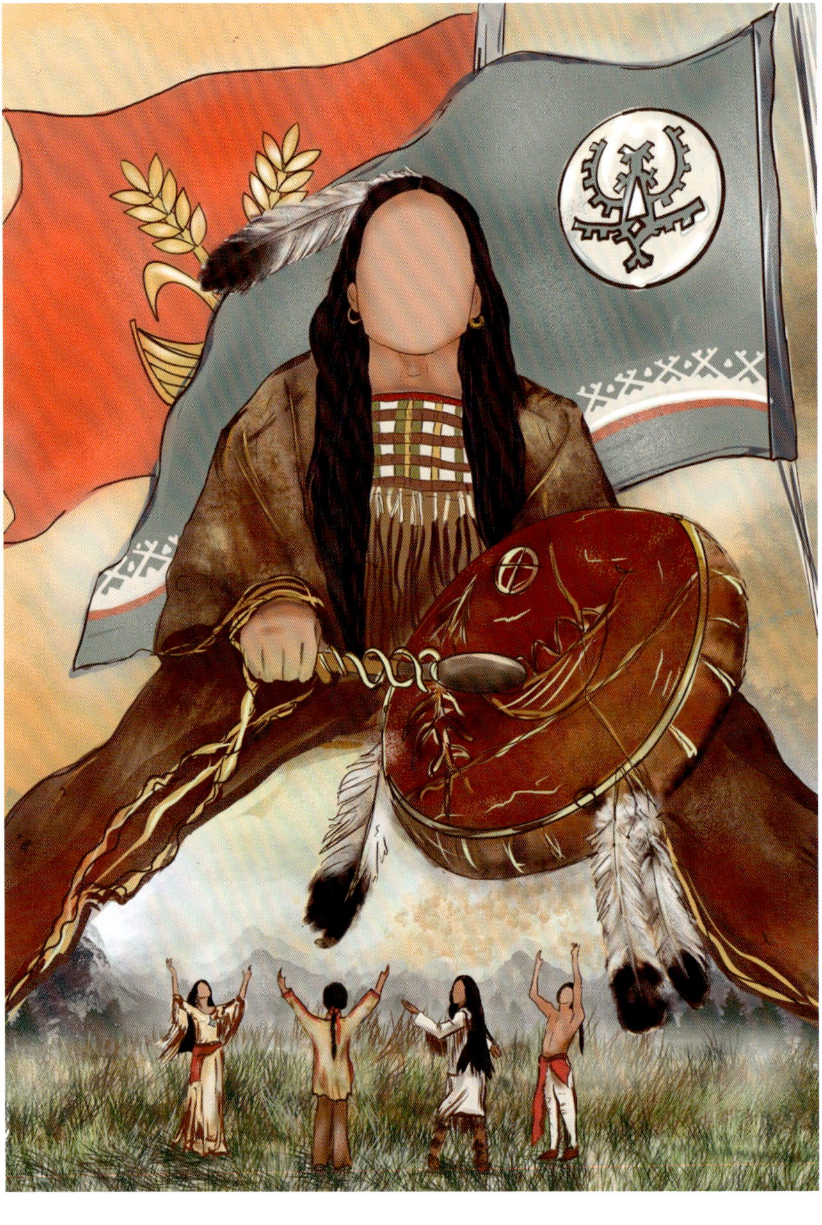

ARCANUM 20. JUDGEMENT

> Take a handful of your native soil in your fist,
> And looking far beyond the cliffs and canyons
> Tell me Warrior, who are you?
> And what you will now become?
> We are the children of Mother Earth
> Our Father is the Spirit of the Elements.
> You are the Elder brother from the great Mountains,
> And I am the son of the plains.
> So, let us stand at this hour
> On our different shores
> I will stretch out my hand to you
> My only blood brother.

FAMILY — PATRIOTISM — VOCATION

In the Tarot deck, the Twentieth Arcanum is Judgement, the Energy of honor, dignity, courage and duty. It symbolizes the struggle for one's principles, foundations and duty. The struggle against the ghosts of the past with erroneous attitudes and mindsets, the fight for one's family, homeland and truth. The Twentieth Arcanum calls for purification, renewal, upholding freedoms and rights, for an awareness of and appeal to the origins of things, to their beginning and birth.

The Twentieth Energy's karmic program is primarily about sorting out the karma of the Family Line. The task facing Twenties is to bring their Family Line up to the next level, to solve the problems of their family line, to restore communications within the family clan, to return relatives back to the bosom of the family, and restore ancestral family lines. Many routes can be taken to work out this program and the tasks set can vary completely — however, the essential thing is that a person with the Twentieth Arcanum has come into this world in this incarnation to resolve family issues, to put right the past faults of the wider family and family line.

The Energy of the Twentieth Arcanum calls on the individuals endowed with it to solve any problem, old or new, encouraging them to preserve their poise and to guard and defend honor and dignity. People with the Energy of Judgement find themselves having to wait, but no one can tell them how long that wait might be. However, one way or another, the time will come when the clarion call will summon them to battle. And this is the vital moment when a person has to decide whose side they are on, under whose flag they are ready to go and defend honor. It is at these moments that these people find their true way, their true task is revealed to them and they find and occupy their place in life.

Under no circumstances should Twenties ever speak badly about their family, their clan, the land in which they were born and live or about the authorities "whose yoke" they have agreed to live under. They must never dishonor the Family, Tribe and Motherland.

People with the Twentieth Arcanum in their matrix are above all patriots and people of honor and dignity. They will never preach false ideas and defend the interests of the enemy. They are devoted to their principles to the marrow of their bones, they have an inner core and backbone that cannot be broken. They are a truly heroic personality type.

People with the Twentieth Energy are truly unique. Even when they move to another city or emigrate abroad, their hearts and minds remain in their native birthplace. Gratitude, love, praise and fond memories of their Homeland (family and clan) strengthen their energy and give them vitality. Recalling pleasant childhood memories, communicating with relatives, maintaining family and cultural traditions and preserving ancestral artifacts are all things that inspire, nourish and guide Twenties towards the realization of their tasks. The Spirit of the Family opens up incredible opportunities for them and provides them with benefits and recognition both in moral and material terms. But when these memories are defiled, when negative or offensive comments are made about their country or homeland, their clan and family members or their parents and children, the Energy of the Twentieth Arcana is sucked out of their lives and this will block their path and opportunities in life. By speaking badly about their Homeland and Family they create a cage of circumstances for themselves that makes them a hostage and prisoner to their own false beliefs, which sooner or later they will renounce, leading them to a trial of these beliefs in the face of their personal truths, a frank debate with their consciences and eventual repentance and an acceptance that they were wrong. And incidentally, the trials that Twenties have to go through are very harsh and painful ones. It is very important for Twenties to maintain their honest devotion and gratitude to the land they have come from, as well as those who will follow them and those to whom they owe their lives.

As a rule, the majority of the people who one is surrounded by share the same nationality or citizenship as oneself. People who speak badly about their own country and, in particular, their people, are ultimately criticising and belittling themselves. Their people and country are an inalienable part of what they talk about and where they have lived, currently live and will live. By speaking negatively about something, people accumulate negative energy within themselves, darkening the chakras and absorbing this negativity inside until one day they find themselves filled to the brim with it. When this happens, their internal flows of pure energy are directed at processing the negative and their resources only suffice for this internal battle. Therefore, these individuals lack the strength to manifest their energy in life and they have no strength left to live.

By speaking badly about their relatives, parents or children, these individuals transfer this negativity onto themselves personally. The universe considers each and every one of us to be a particle of a certain common "kind", kin or family. Each person is like a twig that has grown out of a branch, that in turn has grown from the common tree of life. It turns out that by speaking badly about their family, an individual is actually speaking badly about him or herself. And anyway, who wants to be a part of something negative, to be involved in something bad?

In order to begin to work on adjusting their Twentieth Energy, those endowed with it need to initially turn their train of thought in the opposite direction. They should not speak badly about their relatives, they should search for their plus points and deliberately seek to voice them. If the family has caused them pain, it is important to find the reasons for this and defend the honor of the family and to strengthen it by restoring the truth. It is important to find the good and the light, and deliberately express it out loud. It is important to restore and strengthen the family each and every day. If an individual is endowed with the Twentieth Energy in their matrix, it is vital that they implement their karmic program and act as a warrior for and guardian of their Family and Homeland. They must fulfil their karmic duty.

WATCHWORDS

Family, Kin and Motherland, honor, courage and dignity, patriotism, fidelity and duty — these are the values, on which the Energy of the Twentieth Arcanum are built. It is important to be useful and actualize

yourself while promoting the common good. It is important to make oneself of use to one's family, kin and homeland and to serve them faithfully. Everything should be as precise and clear as it is in the army or national service.
- Duty calls! Your country needs you!
- Family values are the highest value of all. They are our everything — our ideas, joys, goals, love and our world.

FINANCES

A professional activity that praises the fundamental core values of the Twentieth Energy will always be an excellent option for a Twenty in their search and striving for self-realization. Propaganda, espionage, work for the government, military services, government departments — any area where it is important to serve for the good of one's homeland and country. This might involve working abroad in a foreign state but for the benefit of one's native country in order to promote its national interests.

People with the Twentieth Energy in the Finance Zone are endowed with the wonderful gift of public speaking. They have the ability to develop this skill very quickly and effectively so that they can implant the right thoughts and ideas into other people's heads. And everything they do is exclusively for the good of their homeland. The Twentieth Arcanum prompts those endowed with it to patronize the arts, sciences and celebrities who are popular with the wider public. Work involving the search for sponsors, supporters and lobbying interests are all areas of activity that Twenties excel at.

Twenties make excellent PR people, head hunters, scouts, agitators, speakers and spin doctors. They are also loyal, reliable and outstanding military personnel, reaching a very high rank in their long service. But, when their energy is in a negative state, they can be traitors to their national interests, spies, war criminals, defectors and terrorists.

As a rule, the material side of any issue is of secondary importance to them. For Twenties, prosperity and rewards come in the form of honors and recognition for their service. However, earning big money can be extremely important to them if it is done in the service of their family, clan and homeland.

HEALTH

The Energy of the Twentieth Arcanum, the Energy of the Family endows individuals with the remarkable gift of being able to rise again from the ashes like the Phoenix. A person with a Twenty in their Destiny Code matrix can get into shape, heal, rejuvenate and recover very quickly after any kind of illness or injury. Their ability to heal their wounds, reset their bones and return to good health is one of their seeming superpowers.

Treatments involving the purification and cleansing of the body seem to suit Twenties best. These might involve detox programs, strict diets and any other procedures that cleanse their bodies of excess.

People endowed with the Twentieth Arcanum are very sensitive to pain. The greater their fear and the more acute the physical sensation of their pain, the more difficult things become with the state of their energy. Pain is an important indicator of how well-tuned a Twenty's energy flow is: if the pain is felt strongly, then this indicates that this individual is not open to their calling to fulfil their ancestral (karmic) duty, when they experience no fear of pain and are able to endure physical discomfort (within reason, of course) this is an indicator that they have their energy under control and that it is flowing at the right pace and in the correct direction.

Very often, when Twenties' energy is in a negative state, they are at a greater risk of injury in the workplace, in the service or in the struggle to defend the interests and honor of their homeland, family and clan.

They are also susceptible to asymptomatic, complex and sometimes incurable diseases and injuries such as cerebral palsy and Down's Syndrome, as well as asthma, migraines, complex neurological diseases, brain clots and the nervous system.

RELATIONSHIPS

For Twenties, everything revolves and exists around the nuclear and wider family. Twenties are looking to meet a partner with similar interests, for whom the family is also sacred. Perhaps the best example of this would be the archetypal "Italian family", consisting of large numbers of close relatives who are constantly quarrelling, sorting out their relationships, criticizing each other, and eventually making up, but who ultimately unquestioningly love and appreciate one another. The Twentieth Energy envelops individuals with values that go beyond their platonic or physical experiences, their familial relationships are their duty, they are their work and central to their lives. When the opposite is true, when a Twenty deliberately pushes their family away, then this is a distinct sign that their energy is in a negative state. As a rule, in these situations, it is worth taking a look at and working on their chakra systems because they are evidently suffering from some pathology or other.

For Twenties, relationships should be strong, reliable and for life, this is all about two people uniting two different branches of their family and Kin together. This is about the sudden acquisition and building of a new "family". This is the forgiveness of the past and acceptance of love and kinship regardless of the obstacles involved.

Even if their relationships are not as vivid and emotional as they would like, the Twentieth Energy is, first and foremost, about loyalty, respect and duty, which are sometimes much more important than cheap thrills and empty words.

INDICATIONS THAT THIS ENERGY IS IN A −
- Leaving the family (clan).
- Betrayal.
- Condemnation of others.
- Slander, flattery, and lies, leading to injury and harm.
- Living on welfare or at someone else's expense (at the expense of the family or the state).
- Wandering aimlessly from one place to another.
- Being uncertain of their opinions and judgements.
- Refusing to perform their duty (wherever it might arise and whatever form it might take).

INDICATIONS THAT THIS ENERGY IS IN A +
- Strong bonds with their family and country.
- Renewal from and redemption of their past sins.
- Restoration of justice and the revelation of the primary source of truth.
- Resolution and settlement of family matters.
- The re-establishment and restoration of relations between the wider family and the return (reunification) of distant relatives.
- Serving one's homeland for the benefit of the greater good.
- Patriotism and faith in one's family and homeland.
- Preserving and maintaining traditions.

KARMIC TASKS:
- to heal the soul and body;
- to forgive their family and loved ones
- to pay off the debts owed by the wider family;
- to accept their inherent sense of duty;
- to learn to put their interests in the background;
- to accept and forgive betrayal;
- to be true to themselves, their family and their cause.

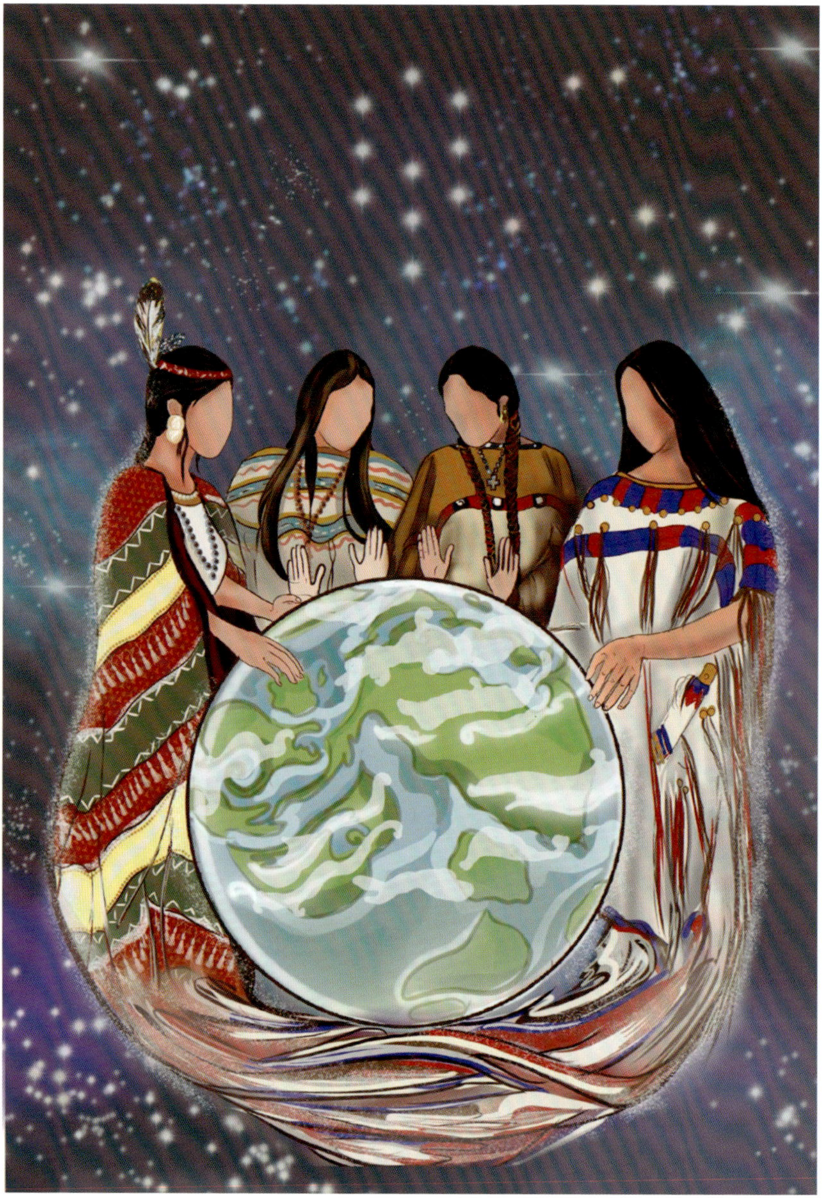

ARCANUM 21. THE WORLD

At the evening hour, in the dark of the night after the Corn Dance has been completed
The children of the Sun will gather around the sacred Fire.
So that the bravest warrior from the banks of the Missouri
Might pass the test of the Okipa through the strength of his will
In the dance of the Black Buffalo — the great beast and totemic strength of the Sioux.
So that everyone will now see that the Soul of the nation is strong
And that there is no limit to its power, only fear knows it.
That having released the Beasts into battle, one should not be afraid of the Will.
The Power of the Spirit is boundless — seek for it beyond the limits.

BEYOND THE LIMITS OF THE POSSIBLE

The Energy of the Twenty-First Arcanum bears the boundlessness of our possibilities and the limiting nature of our beliefs. The world, globality, total permission. However, the Energy of the World softens the matrix and thus gives the other energies the chance to manifest themselves in it although not too radically. The Twenty-First Arcanum expands the boundaries of perception and during each moment of life calls on the individual to look at things from a greater height, to assess the situation globally, and see other possible routes that might lead to more productive results. The Energy of the Twenty-First Arcanum gives individuals endowed with it the ability to overcome any restrictions or boundaries and move onto a more global level not only in terms of their ideas but also their goals and deeds.

The Arcanum of the World is linked with everything "foreign", everything abroad that lies "beyond the border". These might be foreign countries, foreign languages or foreigners themselves, or travel or emigration abroad. Likewise, the Twenty-First Energy entails overcoming "boundaries" and "limitations" both in the way individuals think, believe and perceive, as well as physical limitations such as debilitating diseases and other conditions that might physically limit them.

Having the Twenty-First Energy in your Destiny Code Matrix is a huge bonus, a wonderful and highly valuable gift from the Universe. Twenty-Ones are given a "magic key" that can open any door, overcome any obstacles and help them traverse any boundary. However, it is always worth remembering that nothing happens by accident and that any gift received from the Universe, as a rule, will entail corresponding difficulties for that individual in his or her journey through life and indicate what those possible difficulties that he or she is destined to face will be. Depending on where the energy is located in the Destiny Code Matrix, you can see where a person's strengths lie and therefore precisely where things will be most difficult for this individual in his or her life. After evaluating the bonuses and gifts that an individual has been given, it becomes easier to determine the vital karmic lessons and tasks that this person, in all likelihood, will have to go through in this incarnation.

Throughout their lives, Twenty-Ones are destined to face the most amazing events that cannot be explained from a commonsense point of view. There is always a successful way out of even the most hopeless of situations. Very generally speaking, Twenty-Ones never get lost in the forest — the Universe will always show them the way and direct them along the right path. Twenty-Ones can overcome any frontier post or talk their way past any border guard because they have a "passport of the world" that has been issued to them from above. There are no boundaries that can contain people with the Twenty-First Energy — however, they may have internal barriers and limitations that need to be broken and overcome.

Beliefs, convictions, behavior patterns and boundaries that limit what is permitted are some of the elements in life that force individuals to pigeonhole themselves into a small box from which it is very difficult for them to spread their wings and escape. The Energy of the World pushes those endowed with it to climb higher, to take a broader view and to go further at every stage of their lives. When a Twenty-One is content with their "box", it is a sure sign that their energy is in a deeply negative state and that they urgently need to destroy and escape the barriers and boundaries that the shelter of this box represents.

Regardless of where their energy is located on their matrix, Twenty-Ones all share the same fear of "departure". In the majority of cases, Twenty-Ones are initially afraid of going beyond the limits, to permit themselves to do something supernatural, something beyond what is considered reasonable or acceptable. Therefore, they are often indecisive at first. When, a Twenty-One is overly decisive, without any sense of where they are in space, where the brake pedal is and where the bounds of decency lie, this is an indication that he or she is suffering from a pathology of the chakra, on which their Twenty-First Energy is located. This state of chakra hyperactivity when combined with the Sixth, Twelfth, Fifteenth, Eighteenth, Twentieth, Twenty-First and Twenty-Second Energies can be extremely negative not only for the individual himself but sometimes a source of danger for those around them.

The Energy of the World in an individual's Destiny Zone indicates that one of the options for this person getting through their karmic program might be to emigrate. In order to change the course of their life and resolve any issue they might be facing, these individuals simply need to change their country of residence. In addition, the Twenty-First Energy generally speaks of a close connection with all things foreign. A person with the Twenty-First Arcanum may be subconsciously drawn to study the cultures, languages, cuisine, music and people of other countries. Likewise, the Twenty-First Arcanum is about everything that is "beyond" that which is permitted, accessible or possible. The Energy of the World pushes those endowed with it to always go further afield, to think more globally, to want more. Any thought or idea originating from the Twenty-First Arcanum will be on a huge scale encompassing everything around it.

In addition to all of the above, the Twenty-First Arcanum is about overcoming. It just so happens that the Twenty-First Arcanum's karmic program is all about the deliberate passage through beliefs, convictions or physical boundaries that limit the individual. Therefore, this can include serious physical ailments, disabilities and unusual physical features. The individual that can overcome these types of limitations will find themselves on an equal footing with other people who have not been burdened with them and will be perceived by them to be a perfectly ordinary and healthy individual. Sometimes even many of those in a Twenty-One's circle are unaware of how difficult their path has been: these are the people whose path to "normality" has always been hard. As a result, those around fail to even notice the impediments they might have been born with and only see the noble qualities they now possess.

WATCHWORDS

"And why not?" The spirit of experimentation and the desire to learn something beyond the generally accepted pushes Twenty-Ones to expand their interests in all directions and try and conduct different experiments.

- ◉ Everything new is interesting. Everything old is past and gone.
- ◉ Horizons beckon and call.
- ◉ The sun is always brighter and the sky clearer in those places where we have never been.
- ◉ Everything needs to be tried and everything has to be experienced
- ◉ For the sake of experiment, you can have a go at anything. And, indeed, why not?

FINANCES

The irrepressible need for freedom and self-expression and the desire to find one's place in life on a global scale are the main incentives spurring the development of individuals endowed with the Twenty-First Energy. Twenty-Ones' ideas and plans are global by nature and intended to be so in terms of the scale for their implementation. They are quite incapable of thinking narrowly and one-sidedly. Even when carrying out ordinary routine work, they are thinking about how this work might change the life of an entire city, country or the world as a whole. They are globalists, the sort of people who are able to see processes as a whole, to perceive actions with all the possible outcomes of their consequences.

Even when they start right at the bottom, people with the Twenty-First Arcanum in their Finance and Destiny Zone who are engaged in creative work and promoting global ideas are able to achieve fame and glory on a truly global scale.

It is important for people with the Twenty-First Arcanum in the Finance Zone to bear in mind that their energy encourages working closely with all things that are considered "foreign". Consequently, they should seriously consider working for or collaborating with foreign companies using foreign languages and overseas innovative technologies. Areas of work involving global change to accepted norms and practices are professional areas and environments that are also particularly productive for their individual and professional realization. Cash flow really begins to open up for them in the event of emigration, partnerships with foreign companies and activities carried out on the Internet using the world wide web to spread information about their projects.

Absolutely all roads are open to Twenty-Ones in terms of both their personal and professional self-realization. These people are ambitious, with rich imaginations, broad ideas and global goals. Twenty-Ones are at their most productive in large teams, on international projects and doing activities that require high levels of implementation with a global scale of influence.

The Energy of the World is about recognizing the universal value and benefit of what has been done. Therefore, Twenty-Ones often really are capable of changing the course of global processes through one very small action. It is always important for Twenty-Ones to go and see things for themselves. Even if they are living in a small provincial town doing a very routine job, there is a high likelihood that one fine day they will make a discovery or change those around them in a way that will have a profound influence on the world.

Twenty-Ones have the ability to establish connections and ties on all sides of the barricades. They are able to engage with others in a highly productive manner, regardless of their age, nationality or social status. Their ability to fully integrate into any process and rise above the situation, evaluating everything from a great height, gives them superior chances of resolving issues and ensures the most productive outcome. This is all down to the undeniable advantages they possess.

When the Twenty-First energy is in the Portrait Zone, this often indicates individuals who can change their life suddenly and dramatically, radically dismantling all the preconceptions that those in their circle have about them and take steps that no one would have expected of them. Sometimes when the Twenty-First Arcanum is in the Portrait Zone, these individuals do not immediately find their place in life, and if they are dissatisfied with their lot, they simply need to be persuaded to take the fateful step and cross over the border that will change everything and expand their circle of perception. Emigration, working for another country's government, foreign languages and partnerships – these are the sorts of decisions that immediately put Twenty-Ones at their ease and make them productive and better able to realize themselves.

For a person endowed with the Twenty-First Arcanum, emigration abroad promises an increase in income, collaboration with foreign partners guarantees taking their business to a higher level and doing business online opens up broader prospects for development. At each step of their journey, Twenty-Ones need to assess the situation globally, to consider what benefits their business will bring to the global community and how it will affect the world as a whole.

When the Twenty-First Energy gives its owner the power to expand the boundaries of their desires, this also expands the possibilities of what they can achieve materially. When Twenty-Ones know precisely what they desire and how to get it. All that remains for them to do is resolve the question of realizing themselves and liberating themselves from those factors that limit and restrict them.

Twenty-Ones should never be content with what they have. They need to take everything they can from life and attain everything that they dream of. Even if at some point they believe that the best moments of their lives have already passed, they should not stop there. They must be always looking beyond the horizon, seeing their new goals and realizing them. Everything that a person does is right, regardless of the value judgements of others. Each person has the right to everything that he or she possesses and wants to possess.

When the Energy of the World is in a minus state it can restrict and limit their convictions towards people and groups that are different to theirs and provoke them to even manifest expressions of hatred towards them. The manifestations of this hostility might be concealed or open, or based on the grounds of social, national, religious or other considerations.

HEALTH

The moral and physical restrictions in a person with the Twenty-First Energy in their Destiny Code Matrix are a specific and idiosyncratic feature of this Arcanum that leaves a trail in all areas of their lives and their health is no exception.

People endowed with the Energy of the World are able to overcome all sorts of ailments and diseases and make remarkable and even miraculous recoveries just by the power of their minds and attitude. The will to overcome and the desire to cross all borders are of particular help to them in situations where, sometimes, medicine might be powerless.

As mentioned above, Twenty-Ones are sometimes hostages to their own self-inflicted restrictions and limitations. Sometimes these restrictions are caused by a fear of thinking more broadly and out of the box, and sometimes by physical limitations (in the literal sense) as a result of severe illness and disability. But as is often the case, they have been given a special tool to lighten the burdens imposed on them. Thanks to their willpower, striving and desire, they are capable of overcoming any restrictions and putting themselves on a level footing and even surpassing those who enjoy perfect health and are endowed with more opportunities to succeed.

There is a certain pattern of behavior that puts Twenty-Ones at a greater risk of contracting rare and exotic diseases. They also have certain distinctive external features that make them stand out from other people around them.

RELATIONSHIPS

The Energy of the World provides the individuals endowed with it with the gift of perceiving others "as a whole", to love them not so much for something specific, but for everything at once, building relationships with partners that simultaneously accept their good and bad qualities at once. Of all the energies, the Energy of the World drives relationships to a higher level than any of the others. The Energy of the World reveals to the individual endowed with it the infinitesimal unlimited boundlessness of the human essence and motivates them to study their partner closely and help them reveal all their facets. Understanding, acceptance, tolerance and loyalty to the common cause, the desire to give the person they have chosen "the entire world" and to perceive the partner as the center of the Universe — this is what relationships with a person influenced by the Twenty-First Energy are built on.

People with the Twenty-First Arcanum in their Destiny Code Matrix do not take fundamental positions, or set specific boundaries when socializing and communicating with other people. They easily open themselves and others up to communication from the very first second they meet someone, easily becoming familiar with their interlocutors and can share personal stories from their lives with strangers easily and without any confusion or misunderstanding. For a person with the Twenty-First Energy, any form of communication is considered perfectly normal and natural: for example, they won't have any qualms about having little or no physical contact with a partner in a romantic relationship for a long time (sometimes even months or years), but on the other hand, they would be quite happy to enter into an intimate relationship with someone on the very first day of their acquaintance. On the whole, it is worth noting that Twenty-Ones perceive any event in their lives as an experiment, and, accordingly, their relationships are built along the same principles.

The energy of the Twenty-First Arcanum expands and stretches the boundaries of what is permissible. Therefore, if it is located in the Portrait, Material Karma, Higher Essence or the Overall Destiny Zones, this indicates that these individuals are open to homosexual and bisexual experiences. Their approach in this instance is slightly different to those of the Third or Fifteenth energies — Twenty-Ones perceive these sorts of relationships as an experience, as an experiment and as a challenge: "And why not?" The Twenty-First Arcanum knows no boundaries, no restricting convictions or beliefs, therefore, those endowed with it are interested in all the opportunities that can be gained by looking beyond what is permitted and permissible.

When the Twenty-First Energy is in the Relationship Zone, this indicates a strong and reliable alliance with their partner who is likely to be from a different country, or who they might have met abroad. It also indicates the possibility of both partners emigrating abroad and taking on the status and challenges of being an outsider together.

An interesting statistical pattern has been observed that many women with the Twenty-First Arcanum in the Portrait or the Higher Essence Zones, end up getting married several times, significantly increasing their standing and standard of living after each divorce (or separation).

When a Twenty-One's Energy is in a minus state, they can be seized by prejudices, false convictions and self-imposed limitations. Individuals in this state tend to create difficulties in their relationships by forcing their partners to share these convictions and comply with these restrictions. In these instances, the Twenty-First Arcanum can push an individual to take restrictive and repressive actions against their partners: forbidding them to do certain things, communicate with certain people, and thus limit their personal freedoms.

INDICATIONS THAT THIS ENERGY IS IN A –
- The inability to "bend" circumstances to their will.
- Placing restrictions on their thinking, physical location and everyday existence.
- A fear of crossing the line (borders).
- Restricting their lives to one place (at one point).

- Choosing personal comfort over their personal development.
- Inactivity and stagnation.
- Rejection of the freedoms, morals and customs of others.
- Criticism and condemnation of others.
- Prejudices and restricted and restrictive beliefs and convictions.

INDICATIONS THAT THIS ENERGY IS IN A +

- Openness and tolerance.
- Constantly striving to gain new 'experiences' and try out new experiments.
- Satisfying their need to express themselves.
- Taking a broad view of everything.
- Enthusiasm and adventurism.
- Emigration and a sympathy for and connection with all things foreign.
- Taking their ideas and actions to a global level.
- Freedom of thought, choice and action.

KARMIC TASKS:

- to expand the scope of their perceptions — to broaden their horizons, to want more, to go further;
- to accept all facets of the possible;
- to never stand still — to be constantly changing location;
- to accept the fact that there is no such thing as good or bad — there are merely different versions of the same thing;
- to fulfil their mission as a peacemaker — in every sense and on every scale;
- to abandon stereotypes and prejudices.

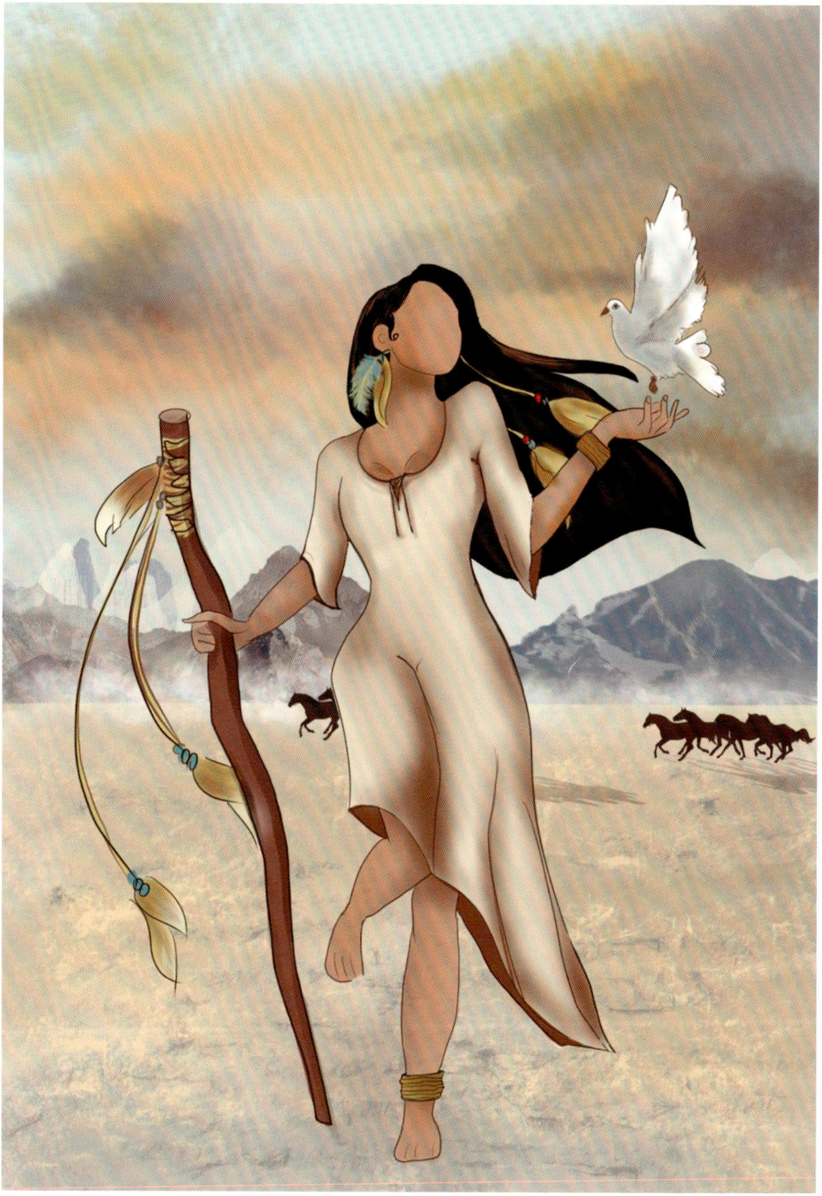

ARCANUM 22. THE FOOL

How gloriously the sun shines in the sky, how beautiful the forests that cover the earth.
The stream gurgles, the dew glistens. Everything is verdant and flourishes.
The soul stands on the threshold of new journeys and distant adventures.
However, there is no desire to rush towards these goals, to listen to advice or to wait for happiness.
It is as if a wild Niagara of passions rages deep inside the river!
Hearts are on fire, waiting for the adventure of youth.
It doesn't matter if the sun rises tomorrow, it doesn't matter if there is food on the table...
Winged youth flies, from the precipice of the cliffs — but it does not soar on an upwards trajectory.

FREEDOM — THE HERE AND THE NOW

The Energy of the Twenty-Second Arcanum is all about kindness, openness, spiritual purity, sincerity and, at the same time, the complete inability to adapt to the practicalities of life.

In the Tarot deck, the Twenty-Second Arcanum is represented by the "Fool" (or "Jester"). Wanton, bumptious and overconfident — he fools around, has fun, sincerely rejoices in life and knows how to please others. It is not with his mind nor his eyes that he considers everything but with his heart. And he suffers greatly for this over and over again. The Twenty-Second Arcanum is the energy of the child, jollity, recklessness, wisdom in all its simplicity and purity of soul and levity in its dealings with life.

The Universe has thus decreed that the Twenty-Second Energy endows its owner with a pure childish approach to life. Viewed from the sidelines by those around them, Twenty-Twos are often considered as "not being of this world", sometimes they appear strange, lacking in reason and reckless. The levity of their attitude to life more often than not irritates others rather than delighting them. But very few of these critics bother to examine the truth of the Fool's message that there is little point in complicating your life when you can just enjoy it and accept it for what it is.

The Twenty-Second Energy has certain common qualities with the Twenty-First in that it also strives to remove restrictions, limitations and boundaries and will not let them get in their way. Both of these energies are united by a craving for freedom, but in the case of the Twenty-Second Energy, they differ in that Twenty-Twos require freedom for the sake of freedom rather than to go out and conquer the world.

People with the Twenty-Second Energy in their Character Zone are extremely rare. And just as they are an extremely rare and unique phenomenon in the Destiny Code Matrix, so they are pretty unique and rare in the wider world. They are unlike anyone else in terms of their appearance, mindset or the rhythm of their lives. They simply love to live and enjoy life in "the here and now", without any "maybes", "what ifs" or "buts".

A person with the Twenty-Second Arcanum in their Destiny Code Matrix is an uncomplicated and simple soul but endowed with a complex destiny and an extraordinary life story. Their off-beat nature, refusal to fit in and otherness often irritates wider society and leads to them not being accepted. Those around them often push them away or at the very least prefer not to notice them. Of course, there are some Twenty-twos whose idiosyncrasies and unusual character traits fit the needs of their environment and their destiny is actualized by following the rules and norms of society. But for the most part, in practice, their stories and destinies unfold otherwise and, unfortunately, they are often not the most joyful or successful ones.

A strange peculiarity of the Twenty-Second Arcanum is its gullibility. It turns out that it is the Fool who is unlucky in life. There is a certain pattern regularly backed by statistics that suggests that Twenty-Twos are more likely than most to get entangled with crime, alcoholism, drugs and tragic and unhappy life situations. Twenty-Twos become overly engaged in what they are doing. Like children, they get too involved with the games they play and are sometimes unable to distinguish between the rules of the game and the rules of life. Being strongly drawn to fun, levity and simple emotions makes them easy victims of terrible addictions and cruel circumstances.

"Fools" are completely unable to judge other people's characters, take their words at face value and are unable to distinguish between truth and falsehood. They often get into bad company and easily become swayed by bad influences. Twenty-Twos are malleable and easily manipulated —

they only have to be given something of value, and they will unthinkingly do whatever they are asked to. Even if they have been lucky with their fate, and enjoy a prosperous and happy life, there is a very high chance of them losing everything as the result of a stupid and absurd combination of circumstances.

Often when an individual has the Twenty-Second Energy in the Character Zone and it is in a minus state, even their outward appearance takes on that of a Fool. Their disorderly behavior and appearance repel other people from them and the craziness of their thinking not only irritates but also truly frightens those around them. It is almost impossible to redirect the energy of the Fool once it is in a minus state, which makes the destiny of a person in this state unenviably sad.

But when the energy of the Twenty-Second Arcanum is positive, when an individual is open to the world, appreciates every day of their life and is not tempted by its easily accessible temptations, when these people manage to find the harmony and balance between what they want, what they can do and what needs to be done — their life will be a happy, productive and beautiful one that is often the envy of others.

Being childishly carefree and light is a wonderful gift and it is precisely this levity and lightness that many of the other energies, perhaps, lack. But Twenty-Twos need to avoid getting carried away and becoming a reckless lunatic, they should also avoid convincing themselves that they are the sharpest tool in the box. If a Twenty-Two tries to deceive the Universe, getting carried away with their jokes and light-heartedness and abusing their innate freedom, then the Universe will inevitably show them that they will have to answer for such behavior.

WATCHWORDS

Levity and recklessness give a person with the Twenty-Second Energy courage and fearlessness. Just as children have no fear of heights and other dangers and do not think about the obvious consequences, so the Fool looks at all risks with the sneer of the insanely brave.

- The new day will provide!
- We need to think about today — today, and tomorrow — tomorrow.
- Live every day as if it were your last.
- I'll do as I please!

FINANCES

Individuals with the Energy of the Twenty-Second Arcanum in the Finance or Material Karma Zone have a very good chance of realizing their abilities thanks to two specific qualities of the Energy of the Fool — fearlessness and an open nature. Everything "Fools" do is done sincerely and from the bottom of their hearts, if they are passionate about a job, they will see no difficulties in getting it done and will not be tempted into laziness. They are the sort of people who can be successful in several different areas of activity at the same time, but only on the condition that they are given complete freedom of action. They are passionate people with great potential, whose thinking, imagination and plans know no limits. But depending on the circumstances, these "creative flights of fancy" can very easily be disrupted and come crashing down when they are restricted to strict frameworks and schedules. Sooner or later, a bird flying freely down a narrow gorge will surely hit a cliff or an outcrop of rocks and rapidly spiral out of control.

People with the energy of the Fool are spendthrifts by nature, they do not understand the value of money and treat it irresponsibly and with a deliberate degree of skepticism. "Birds don't need money", the Twenty-Second Arcanum argues and pushes the Twenty-Two to value the process itself over the results and material rewards. For Twenty-Twos, more than anyone else, the most important thing in life is to savor the delight and enjoyment of what is happening in the here and now. Even when they find themselves in the gutter, they can see the heavens and stars reflected in the puddles rather than the filth and the dirt.

Individuals with the Twenty-Second Energy in the Finance zone will be happiest and most likely to find success in professions associated with children, and with joy, delight, and creativity. Twenty-Twos need to be completely captivated and carried away by the process, therefore, first and foremost, their profession needs to be a joyful one. This might involve the organization of festivals and events, exhibitions, concerts, shows, painting, art and writing (especially for children) along with any job that involves working with children and families whatever the format.

Twenty-Twos find it very difficult to make plans, analyze situations and get to grips with objectivity in general. Having to think about tomorrow or make plans and strategies in advance creates additional restrictions in their minds that can literally drive them crazy.

Occupations that involve working as a freelancer with a free schedule on projects that are not restricted by time and resources are the ideal activities for Fools. The ability to live only for today may appear unreliable and irresponsible to others, and perhaps it is so, but taking this view of the world does have one huge advantage: it means they do not see or accept any restrictions or difficulties as an obstacle in their path. Everything in the world is possible to them, but not everything in it delights or interests them.

The Twenty-Two's love of freedom often ends up playing a cruel joke on them. On the one hand, they love their freedom too much to work for someone else within the framework of their instructions. However, at the same time, their love of being free at any moment of the day makes it almost impossible to set up their own business and work effectively for themselves. Freedom requires absolute liberty.

When an individual is endowed with the Tenth, Seventeenth, Nineteenth, or Twenty-First Energy in addition to a Major Twenty-Second Energy in their Destiny Code Matrix, there is a high probability that they will have a brilliant (crazy) idea, which will bring them unprecedented prosperity and fame.

Having the Arcanum of the Fool in one of the Major positions of the matrix is also considered a sign and marker of "homelessness". Twenty-Twos can live for decades without a livelihood, a home, resources and opportunities, but will nevertheless end up outliving many people who enjoy these benefits.

HEALTH

As a rule, Twenty-Twos tend to enjoy good physical health. They are hardy, strong and have a good immune system. But their psychological health is unstable and fragile. People with the Energy of the Fool in their psyche are very similar to children. They are emotionally unstable and prone to sudden mood swings. The spectrum of their emotional state ranges from total despair to unconditional delight and joy.

Twenty-Twos often suffer from memory lapses, bipolar disorder, dementia, chronic alcoholism, violent insanity, impaired brain function, relapses into childish hysterics and moral degradation. They are also prone to falling into depraved and immoral behavior and losing control over their instincts and any sense of social propriety.

A person with the Twenty-Second Energy in the Destiny Code Matrix needs to understand that while "being a child" is no bad thing, life is arranged in such a way that everyone has to be responsible and answer for their actions, and that sometimes even children have to first do their "household chores" before going on to do whatever they want. It is important to learn not only to enjoy doing what you want but also to find the beauty inherent in doing what is required.

RELATIONSHIPS

For Twenty-Twos, the most valuable thing in life is freedom — in their actions, emotions, feelings and choices. As a rule, the Fool is here today and gone tomorrow, and there is no thing or no one that can keep him in one place. Fools are the sort of people who choose independent relationships free of obligations and oaths of allegiance. It stands to reason, therefore, that they are not destined to live happy and harmonious family lives. Their amorousness and enthusiasm can intoxicate and drive others out of their minds. And their constant procession of new emotions and moods can spread to their partner, igniting and inspiring reciprocal passions. However, the flames of these passions can go out as quickly as they are ignited. The image of the Fool is that of a loner and vagabond throughout their lives. They are loving, kind and open to everyone but they belong to no one but themselves and their interests and needs will always take precedence over those of others.

When the Twenty-Second Energy is in the Relationship zone, there is a high probability that there will be a large age difference between this individual and their potential partner. They often enter into marriages of convenience where the partners only meet from time to time without any obligations, or perhaps an open relationship where they are free to see other people. There is also a likelihood that the Twenty-Two's love of freedom and probable sexual activity outside the relationship will cause problems in their relationships triggering breakups and crises between them and their partners.

If a Fool is in love, then he will love with all his heart and with every fiber of his body. Their flirting is sincere and carefree, it is the result of their freedom of action and their need to satisfy their every whim by throwing themselves headfirst into the powerful tides of eroticism and desire. The most important factor in their relationships is an element of levity and lightness, it is vital for Twenty-Twos that they are able to fool around, treat difficult situations with a bit of humor, and sometimes turn acute moments of conflict into a joke.

The weaknesses of the Twenty-Second Energy in the context of relationships are the unreliability and frivolity that is inherent in the nature of the Fool. Nothing will hold him back if he decides to leave — neither money, nor promises, nor children, no one and nothing can stop him. The Fool is one of life's wanderers, the wise course of action is simply to thank him for the goodness he has brought into your life, as well as the lessons that he has forced you to experience. You should simply be grateful and then let him go (otherwise things will only get worse).

The Energy of the Twenty-Second Arcanum is also all about children — having lots of them and the joy that having lots of children can bring. I have no practical statistical evidence to show that children can strengthen a partnership with a Twenty-Two but in theory, it is recommended as a part of the methodology of the Destiny Code Matrix.

INDICATIONS THAT THIS ENERGY IS IN A −

- Getting overly immersed in the processes of life (alcoholism, drug addiction, gambling).
- An amenability and vulnerability to outside influence.
- Recklessness and irresponsibility.
- Open indifference.
- Disdain for other people, their obligations and the consequences of their deeds.
- Reckless and irrational behavior.
- Playing the role of a child.
- A tendency to get into trouble (provoke other people).
- Being untidy and allowing their appearance to become off-putting.
- Insanity.

INDICATIONS THAT THIS ENERGY IS IN A +

- Spontaneity and adventurousness.
- Optimism and a faith in the good.
- Openness to the world and to others.
- Honesty and sincerity.
- The ability to enjoy life and the ability to please others.
- The ability to live as an entertainer.

- Living for today, but with a purpose for tomorrow.
- Accepting all the opportunities that the Universe has to offer them without prejudice.
- Knowing that wisdom lies in simplicity.

KARMIC TASKS:
- to preserve freedom of thought, action and purpose;
- to learn not to restrict others by their actions;
- to learn to set priorities
- to avoid clinging to the material (things, money, people);
- to learn to enjoy life with a childlike wonder;
- to observe and respect law and order;
- to learn to accept life's failures as an opportunity to start over.

26 PROGRAMS OF THE PAST

THE ENERGIES OF THE KARMIC TAIL

The Destiny Code is synthesized at the time of a person's birth and set down in their date of birth, which bears the personality, makeup and tasks prescribed that each individual person in the Universe is endowed with and the karmic programs they need to undergo in the upcoming incarnation of their Soul. However, up to this moment, according to the theory of reincarnation, the Soul has probably lived through many other incarnations. On each occasion, it has collected knowledge and gained unique experiences that are stored in its memory and transmitted with each rebirth of this person as its own kind of personal baggage.

As part of learning how to interpret a person's Destiny Code Matrix using their date of birth, there is a theoretical element, according to which, at a hypothetical level, the experience of a Soul's past incarnations can be analyzed using the karmic programs embedded in its Destiny Code Matrix. The arcana of the Karmic Tail in the matrix make up special groups of energies, which together form special karmic programs of the past and indicate what this personal baggage (the Soul's memory) of these past incarnations might be and which will undoubtedly have a big influence on this person's current incarnation.

Some believe that it is karmically harmful to study the previous incarnations of the Soul. They argue that by doing this, the individual might waste their energy by directing it towards an initial negative interpretation of their past karmic programs and thereby run the risk of getting stuck in these past states without the prospect of working out the programs that have been set for their current life. Others believe that there is no point delving into the Memory of the Soul and the past, as this might provoke the release of negative energies into the present — that if a person repeatedly returns to the past, he or she will be forced to repeat these experiences all over again and thus remain stuck in them.

In my opinion, having knowledge of the past and taking it into account when interpreting an individual's Destiny Code Matrix is as important as determining the causes of a particular disease they might be suffering. When a person understands the interconnection of events, when the starting point of this or that storyline is revealed, then, in theory, it is possible to return to it and use this experience to avoid repeating the mistakes of the past in the future. The personal luggage that is the Soul's

Memory is a unique source of information that provides us with a huge store of potential opportunities to correct and control the current life that a person is living. This is a very valuable additional tool, and once having learned to use it, individuals can live their lives more productively and realize their potential more effectively.

The Energies of the Karmic Tail in the Destiny Code Matrix can hypothetically reveal the possible life scenarios that the Soul might have been through in its previous incarnations. The Karmic Tail provides us with an unspecified picture, a summary of the most significant and uncompleted tasks of the past. It does not provide a specific overview of a past life from birth to death — it is a general picture of the energetic nature of the Soul's past, containing its most painful and negative characteristics, which the Soul has not been able to pass through over the span of all its possible incarnations. The Universe sets tasks in order to achieve their final resolution. One way or another, these lessons must be learned and these final examinations passed. So, time after time, from one life to another, the Soul bears its own special karmic task — its Program of the Past.

This methodology for reading and interpreting the Destiny Code contains twenty-six programs of the past, which represent certain scenarios depicting the likely development of events in previous incarnations. These experiences impose specific features on the current life a person is living and have an influence on it. A triple-up of energies in the Karmic Tail is considered to be a negative factor of influence, and initially, each of these energies is endowed to the individual in a minus state. Each of these programs indicates what difficulties the Soul might have faced in its past incarnations and what precisely it needs to work on and learn to overcome in its current life. The Karmic Tail indicates the mistakes of the past, which are useful to know when working with energies and trying to bring them into a positive state.

The following are a number of suppositions about what a person's life might have been like in a past incarnation of their Soul, taking into account the characteristics of the energies and Triple ups of their Karmic Tail, which we can metaphorically use to represent the probable story of a particular Destiny.

9—12—3. ISOLATION

In one of its past incarnations, this Soul was a woman. The female energy endowed it with beauty and attraction but something went wrong, and this person was forced to remain alone, having lost a partner and never finding happiness again. It is likely that this individual lost or voluntarily cut all ties with a loved one, having been forced to make a sacrifice in a difficult situation. This individual is now required to go against the grain and prove their importance and worth step by step. Loneliness, rejection and voluntary surrender are not an option for them. For a long time in their current life, individuals with this karmic program might find themselves alone without a partner.

3—13—10. SUICIDE

Life is a priceless gift. The life of every person is important, regardless of the circumstances they find themselves in or how they imagine them to be. However, the perception and awareness of this fact do not come immediately to everybody, and sometimes it comes too late. In one of their past incarnations, this individual did not value their life and, in an effort to acquire new sensations, lost it. Now the Universe wants to teach this Soul a lesson and is sending trials and tribulations to this person in their current incarnation to test and teach them to gain a sense of the value of life. In this life, on more than one occasion, they will have to fall down, pick themselves up again and move on. Losing everything, they will have to pull themselves together and head back into life's struggles all over again from scratch. Each time they do so, they will discover their true emotions and calling to love life more and more. This Karmic Tail bears a Feminine energy.

3—22—19. THE UNBORN CHILD

It's time to be allowed to grow up. In its past incarnations, this Soul has not had the opportunity to become an adult, repeatedly parting from its life at an early stage after its acquisition. In its current incarnation, this Soul will strive with all its might to attain "adulthood", but out of habit will continue to play childish games upon reaching it. This childishness will interfere with this person's life and lead him or her into ridiculous situations. They need to regard these situations in an adult manner, without passing it off as a joke or an act of folly. The Universe is demanding that the Soul finally grows up in this incarnation.

3—7—22. THE PRISONER

The Soul must be free whatever the circumstances or conditions. In one of its past incarnations, this person was deprived of their freedom and became a prisoner. It is not important if this was because they ended up in prison as a criminal, a prisoner of war, an unwilling concubine or lost their freedom through the bonds of marriage. The Soul maintains the memory of the restrictions placed on the free will of the body and Soul during that incarnation. In this incarnation, this individual is tasked with breaking out of the captivity of the prejudices that surround them and destroying the shackles of the circumstances that restrict them — to do everything in their power to breathe freely whatever the cost.

6—14—8. THE DICTATOR

Cold-bloodedness, power and the observance of personal codes of honor. In a previous incarnation, these Souls ended up in the body of an heir to an important inheritance. They spent their time from early childhood, honing the skills needed to become a ruler and emotions, feelings and personal needs were suppressed and eradicated. The ruthlessness of this life has deprived them of all the most beautiful moments in life, deprived them of their childhood, deprived them of carefree joy and deprived them of happiness. The Soul recalls this and continues to keep this memory alive. In their current lives, these individuals are likely to cut short any manifestation of weakness, emotion and openness to their true desires and feelings. Sometimes feelings of happiness and inspiration may frighten and repel them. They have been set this lesson to find a balance and learn that it is possible, by observing the law and performing the tasks assigned to them that they can be a happy person, regardless of the burden of responsibility and duty placed on them. They need to learn to give free rein to their feelings while observing the internal boundaries of what is permitted.

6—17—11. WASTED TALENT

In one of their past incarnations, these Souls possessed special skills and abilities, but for some reason did not have the time to realize their talents. Now in this life, these people are forced to constantly search for their true nature — they feel at a subconscious level that they are "special", but exactly what it is that makes them different to others remains a mystery to them. In this current incarnation, these people are given a chance to correct what has happened in the past and realize their talents. Their entire current life will revolve around this "self-realization". These people will need to learn to try new things out for themselves and to look for interesting ways to implement their skills. More than anything else they will be tormented by the idea that they are wasting their lives and will not have time to complete something important. However, the important thing for them is to listen to their inner calling, to determine what their special abilities are, to discover them step by step and not hide them from the world, otherwise, these talents will once again remain unrealized and perish.

6—20—14. THE VICTIM

People rarely appreciate what they have, and it's even rarer that they are grateful for what they have. In one of their past incarnations, the Universe was extremely generous to these Souls in terms of the bonuses and opportunities they were given. However, in this past life, this person only took without giving anything in return, even their gratitude. Until one day, they took so much that they were brought to trial and deprived of their life — thus becoming a victim. In this life, these people find themselves with limited opportunities and forced to make constant painful choices, where compromise and balance are the key to making the right choice. In this instance, the Universe has decided to teach these people the lesson that it is important to appreciate every moment in life and appreciate every chance and every opportunity.

6—5—17. PRIDE

People quickly become accustomed to the good life, to comfort, to wealth, to other people's favorable disposition towards them. But sooner or later everything comes to an end. In a previous incarnation, these Souls were probably showered with attention, honors and privileges, they then became full of pride about their importance, power and influence. In this past life, they had everything done for them, but now the time has come for them to do everything for themselves and serve and show goodwill towards others. But the memory of their past life makes these people too proud and they find it impossible to admit that they are no longer top of the pile in this life. In their current incarnation, these people are forced to face the discrepancy between their perceptions and how their environment accepts them. Pride and arrogance, disdain and prejudice — are the qualities that these people will need to work on in order to pass through this karmic program.

6—8—20. ESTRANGED FROM THEIR FAMILY

In one of their past incarnations, these Souls were expelled or became estranged from their Family. There is no point in trying to determine what the causes were. However, in their current incarnation, it is very important that they remain a part of the family, help the wider family and maintain the unity of the family. But, as luck would have it, in this current life, there is a high degree of probability that circumstances will make it hard for these people to keep in touch with their relatives. Possible disagreements, the loss of relatives, a tragedy in the family — there will be no excuses for inaction on their part. The Universe knows exactly who the true guardians of the Family are — those who at one time were estranged or expelled from it. One option for passing this karmic program might be the creation of their own large new family with its own strong tight-knit and affectionate relationships.

9—15—6. THE LIBERTINE

Love in all its manifestations is the most wonderful and beautiful thing and there is little point arguing against this. But the quantity of love experienced matters a lot. Too much restraint over one's feelings or, on the contrary, a lack of it are qualities that can change a situation dramatically. In a past life, these people loved "to love" so much that they ended up giving themselves to others without leaving a trace in return. And when the time came for them to choose between their true "beloved" and a "lover", they made the fatal mistake of choosing the latter, which ended up ruining their life. In their current incarnation, debauchery is never far from the surface of these people's lives, quietly biding its time to break free. It begins to manifest itself in their youth when they begin to become consumed by their love affairs. The Universe is repeating the lesson of their previous life and giving them a chance to make the right choice.

9—3—21. THE OVERSEER

Once someone has developed a taste for blood, it is impossible to ever rid them of it again. Likewise, when a person has been given ultimate power, even if it is only for a split second, it is impossible to ever forget its sweetness again. In the past, these Souls were once put in charge of other people and ended up torturing and tormenting them. Oppressing and showing aggression towards the weak in order to satisfy their own feeling of superiority once gave strength and nourished their Soul. And it is likely that this behavior turned into a way of life. It is very difficult to get rid of habits, especially those that delight and bring pleasure to the individual. In this life, these people need to learn that the habits of their past life merely satisfied their need to feel stronger. Often this manifests itself in these people's current lives in childhood when they are aggressive towards weaker children, their brothers and sisters, and animals. In adulthood, they can turn into secret tyrants, who play a weak and subservient role when in the presence of those who are stronger than them but at the first opportunity try to find a victim who they can take their pent-up aggression out on.

12—16—4. THE SOVEREIGN

It is likely that in a previous incarnation, these Souls were endowed with great power as a ruler, emperor or lord — in a word, these people were in charge, they were the Boss. Reveling in their power, they failed to learn to respect others, behaved in an arrogant fashion and did not take into account other people's right to life. In this current incarnation, they will find it difficult to attain power and strengthen their position in society and they will have to put the interests of others before their own. This karmic program bears the Masculine energy of the Fourth Arcanum — women with this Karmic Tail in their matrix need to subdue their pride and try to balance their craving to exert their superiority over men because this will cause complications and difficulties in their relationships. Men endowed with this triple-up in their Karmic Tail will have to fight much harder than others to maintain their positions — it is very important for them to win power and become the master of their lives.

12—19—7. THE WARRIOR

A warrior is brave and strong in life, but he is only considered a warrior while the battle is raging. In one of their past incarnations, these Souls did a lot of fighting. In their current incarnation, they find it very difficult to stay calm and sit still and, according to theory, are very eager for a fight. During their current incarnation, these people will provoke a lot of difficulties for themselves, creating an extremely hard path for themselves in the process. Even when peaceful ways of resolving a situation are evident and available, the Warrior will choose the path of greatest struggle and resistance.

15—20—5. THE REBEL

In a past life, these Souls have been heirs to a noble and powerful family. At one time, their relatives had high hopes and expectations of them but these did not come to fruition. In their current incarnation, these Souls often end up in families that are broken and have become estranged from each other. Because of their memories of the lack of care and attention they received in the past, the spirit of "rebellion" arises in their souls once more and once again they come up against their family's expectations. This karmic program suggests that these individuals will face difficulties in life due to their family relationships. There is a high probability that they might even encounter violence and by getting through this experience, manage to pacify the rebel inside.

15—5—8. THE HOLY INQUISITION

In a previous life, in the name of a Universal Truth, these Souls played a part in a mission of some Holy Inquisition or other. Knowing the law of karma, they have carried evil in their souls under the cover of pious intentions and thus violated it. Marching under false banners and slogans, these people have been tempted and fooled in their past lives into acting for the benefit of the Universal order, without realizing that they were actually doing dark terrible deeds and creating chaos all around them. In their current life, these people will be forced to choose which side they should be on, and regardless of their choice, will be drawn to do the opposite all their life. While creating lawlessness and excess, these people will seek the Light, striving to be pure in faith and truth but will always be on the lookout for hidden ways to satisfy their dark desires. These individuals must learn to forgive others, subdue their passions and adopt a healthy view of the multifaceted nature of life without having to go to extremes.

15—8—11. VIOLENCE

In their past incarnations, these Souls have reveled and given full rein to their worst vices and addictions. Causing suffering to others, they experienced suffering themselves. In all likelihood, these people led a wild life in one of their previous incarnations and, using their strength, imposed their wishes and desires on others using violent means. In their current life, these people are destined, through their personal experience, to experience what it is like to be an injured party. This Karmic Tail can often predict tragic events in these people's current incarnation. There is a high probability that they will become a victim of physical violence or end up in prison or a relationship where their life itself might be at risk.

18—6—6. AFFAIRS OF THE HEART

In their past incarnations, these Souls have probably suffered for love many times. Flying with their head in the clouds, they rushed into numerous romantic adventures, their Souls sinking without a trace each time. In their current life, these people crave love and attention, but they can never get enough of it. Unbridled romance, whispered sweet nothings and immersing themselves in an ocean of tender embraces is not going to work as an end in itself. Time after time, while searching for sensations instead of genuine feelings, these people inevitably make the same mistakes of the past. Also worth mentioning is that in this life, these people are ready to take any steps necessary — even going as far as to use love magic.

18—9—9. MAGICAL KNOWLEDGE

It is likely that in one of their past incarnations, these Souls acquired some kind of unique magical knowledge but did not want to share it with anyone else, keeping it carefully concealed and protected. For fear of being discovered and losing this valuable knowledge, these people abandoned the company of others, becoming a hermit and voluntarily dooming themselves to a life of loneliness. In this incarnation, these Souls, having understood the lesson of their past life, will strive with all their effort to remember and restore this valuable knowledge to others, but all in vain. In their current life, these people will be given ways to recover this information, but obstacles and difficulties will be strewn in their path preventing them from disclosing this knowledge and putting it into practice.

9—9—18 THE SECRET MAGUS

These Souls have come a long way through their reincarnations. In their past lives, these persons will have received unique abilities and successfully applied them in practice, but evidently, something went wrong and they ended up deciding not to develop and use this gift. In their current lives, these people are extremely afraid of taking on responsibility or making decisions because they are afraid of making a mistake. Despite possessing superpowers, understanding the structure of the world and its interconnections and sensing what is right and what is not, these people are tormented by the fact that they cannot decide how to manifest their true powers and apply these skills in life.

9—18—9. MAGICAL ENSLAVEMENT

In their current lives, these people deliberately avoid anything magical or secret. Their fear of falling under the influence of others or becoming a victim of outside control drives them into a corner. They are crushed by the memory of their past, because in a previous incarnation they were the victim of circumstances connected with their manipulation and pressure. In one of their previous lives, these people wanted to leave a place, taking only the gifts they had been given from above, but someone else had their own plans for their gifts and prevented them from doing so. This Karmic

Program presupposes that these Souls have been endowed with a magical gift.

18—3—12. EMPATHY

These Souls have passed through difficult paths in their past incarnations and lived the life of a person suffering from a serious illness, they might have suffered a physical accident or been born with developmental or serious physical disabilities. In their current lives, they are terrified by the recollections preserved in their Souls' memories and become afraid of getting sick or seeking treatment. These people are also often dismissive of people with physical disabilities and ailments and have a habit of criticizing minor deviations in other people from what they consider to be the standards of "normality". These people's strength of spirit will be tested by the weakness and powerlessness of the body, both their own and those of the people around them who will need their help.

18—6—15. DARK MATTERS

These Souls have experience of working with magic at a high level in their past. Their memory of this allows them to work with it in their current life. They are endowed with the ability to materialize their thoughts and words and this can simultaneously be the strong and weak point of their personalities. They need to be careful how they use this gift and work on their energies to realize its potential for their development, and not for the acquisition of material goods.

21—10—7. THE CRUSADER

Freedom is a personal choice for each individual. In one of their past incarnations, these Souls have brought their knowledge and faith to others under the banner of the liberation of these other people's destinies, while expanding the boundaries of the territories they have acquired. Ignoring others' wishes and opinions, these people have imposed their mission on others while failing to see and take into account the desire and willingness of these other people to accept their notion of freedom. Therefore, in this current incarnation, these people are constantly violating other people's boundaries and thus complicating their own way in life. As a test, the Universe teaches them a lesson and deliberately limits their opportunities, by creating conditions that these people can only overcome with the support of other people and by taking into account the interests of those around them.

21—4—10. THE OPPRESSED SOUL

The energy of the Fourth Arcanum in the Karmic Tail indicates that in a past life these Souls were probably incarnated in the body of a man. And since this Arcanum has been given to these individuals for karmic development in their current lives, this indicates that their Souls were unable to cope with their role as a man in their past life. It is therefore very important for them in this current life to find the happy medium between what their environment requires from them and what they themselves want to get out of life. If this karmic program is located in a woman's Destiny Code, this indicates the importance of them of not "wearing the breeches" in their relationships and taking on burdens that are too heavy for their shoulders. If it is located in a man's matrix, then the opposite is true: they will need to finally manifest their true masculinity and take responsibility and not restrict their lives with prejudices and erroneous attitudes.

21—7—13. THE CASTIGATOR

A member of a punitive expedition that has destroyed many lives. There is a likelihood that in the past these Souls might have been involved in mass murders and massacres or were a victim of circumstances related to them. Therefore, with the imprint of their involvement in these actions, these Souls now bear the burden of responsibility for what they have done. In their current incarnation, these people are destined to save and help other lives and pay the debt of their past.

21—10—16. THE CULT SERVANT

One way or another, experience rewards us by helping us overcome obstacles and strive to grow ever upwards. Striving upward towards one's goal under the banner of a Faith or a Cult fills the experience gained with the historical significance of the path that has been traveled. In one of their previous incarnations, these Souls did not have time to transfer their knowledge and fulfill their mission of serving their cult. In their current incarnation, these people are already endowed with a mission thanks to this karmic program — their goal is to be a mentor and guide to lost souls, to open up to them prospects of overcoming what lies beyond their horizons.

CONCLUSION

Amidst the hectic days of everyday lives,
In pursuit of happiness and prosperity,
Not everyone can allow themselves
A moment of personal weakness.
Not everyone wants to decide in an instant
What is true and what is false.
But everyone can and needs to look back

On the path they have traveled.
And then, the heart constricts inside.
Dreams and desires will be resurrected.
You will feel yourself in that sacred moment,
When you ask yourself what your next choice will be?
Will you go, rushing after the crowd again
To conquer peaks that are alien to you
Or will you allow yourself to be needed by this World?

Do you want to embrace the trees,
Or maybe look for inspiration?
Did you perhaps want to become an artist,
But found yourself confined to oblivion and silence.
Stop! Take stock. Listen to yourself.
The veil of the Soul is parted.
Decipher the Code of your Destiny, learn "Who you are"
And walk along the Path of Revelation.

In their everyday lives, people are bombarded by a tsunami of unnecessary information and an endless number of small jobs that need to be done but which nevertheless distract them from what is important and essential. They have to go to work because they need to support their families and pay for their food, clothing and housing. With all these worries, sometimes they lack the time to think about where all this is leading them. What is the meaning of it all? Are they being true to themselves in everything that they do? Is this really their destiny?

Thus, a talented artist might find herself in a gray office, where she is forced to perform work which she finds boring and monotonous. While other people might do well at what they do but it is still very much not the place they should be — like, for example, a person who ends up managing a large factory, while dreaming of conducting a symphony orchestra. As a result, all of these people suffer. And together with them, the whole of humanity suffers because it is not developing in the way that it should be. Therefore, in an attempt to make life easier for themselves, people end up complicating everything, and the Universe's initial true system of organizing things begins to come into conflict with the social and moral order that our current civilization has developed into. Many people are not where they should be because they simply do not have the opportunity to stop and comprehend their true essence — to define who they truly are.

Knowledge does not oblige us to apply it right here and now. Although it is extremely valuable! Knowledge is given so that people might simply know. How one should proceed with this knowledge is a personal matter for each and every individual. The Destiny Code is an additional tool to knowledge and should only be used in an advisory way. No one is obliged to strictly follow its instructions. However, by learning how to use it, people are able to provide themselves with the opportunity to change their life for the better and apply the knowledge they gain every day to follow the path of their true destiny — the path that leads to their true Selves.

Each person's birth date contains a unique Code. The numbers contained in it are just labels, which allow us to identify and trace the nuances of our Destinies. Of course, it is vital to look at them in slightly broader terms than simply as plain numbers.

All people are individuals. Each person is special, and each has his or her own unique Destiny, which is an inherent part of the overall system. An important part. The Major Arcana of the Tarot deck that are used in the Destiny Code, helps to reveal how this system works. Each of the Twenty-Two Arcana is an archetype. After reading them, you can clearly determine which type any given individual belongs to, and what tasks the Universe has set for him or her. This system provides important knowledge — a person might have come into this world, for example, to create beauty, to teach or heal other people, or simply to enjoy life.

The Destiny Code is unique in that, unlike anything else, it helps us to find answers to the most pressing questions that every person asks themselves at a certain moment in their life. The Destiny Code opens up a path which makes it easier for people to determine their goals, choose the right route and, most importantly, find Themselves.

If a person is rich and talented, this does not necessarily mean that he or she is a good person. Each person is significant, but not everyone is capable of attaining global accomplishments. Often, small, routine things done the right way can carry more weight for the overall good of society. People are accustomed to the notion that values are universally accepted and fundamental for each and every one of us. It is believed that if one person desperately strives for recognition, fame and wealth, then others should strive for this as well. However, the reality is that each individual should only take from life that which he or she really needs. But at the same time, in reality, the quality and quantity of the things that a person wants to take — depends solely on him or herself. The desires and needs of each individual are formed subconsciously and are based on the quantity and quality of resources that are needed for them to realize their personal Destiny, to realize and attain their True Self.

In this way, a person only receives that which he or she agrees to receive. These boundaries are dependent solely on the individual, and no "Universe" or otherworldly forces can influence this. A person takes from life only what he or she really wants to take (and not a cent more). So, why do people constantly complain about not getting what they want?

People don't get what they want for the simple reason that they don't understand what they truly need and don't have a sense and acceptance of their True Self. They want many things only because it is the done or customary thing to want them and this overshadows their true inner desires.

All knowledge that has been given to people is extremely important and precious. However, its value lies not only in the fact that it preserves the events and facts of human history. A thorough knowledge of the past is the best textbook for learning how to prepare for the present and the future, and karma, while being inevitable, is also a complex set of processes. By looking back, you can learn and understand the consequences of certain actions. By understanding the consequences of these actions in the past, it is possible to avoid them in the future.

The ancient civilizations of the world were very similar to each other. When we look at the histories of the Indigenous peoples of North and South America and compare them with those of the indigenous peoples of Greenland, Siberia and Australia, the ancient peoples of China, India and the smaller nations of Asia, we see very clear similarities in the spiritual and material organization of their lives despite being located a long way away from each other. Their geographical locations and the names of their Gods may have differed but the essential elements of their lives were strikingly close. Within the structure of these indigenous people's lives, each member of the tribe had their own precise role and meaning. People occupied a defined place in the Circle of Life. And even every animal, element, substance and phenomenon was given its place there. Warriors, hunters, gatherers, farmers and builders were all born into the tribe – and they all knew their path in life from birth. Everyone accepted their destiny.

My book is about learning to be unafraid to return to these roots, to be unafraid to use the knowledge that mankind has uncovered and preserved for each of us. The past does not just provide us with an excursion into history that provides us with knowledge about how things were previously. The past opens up perspectives into the future because time is cyclical. Everything that once was will, sooner or later, come again. The movement of energy is the Wheel of Life. And it is important for each individual to take their place in the mechanism of its organization. And, as everyone knows, the journey begins with finding this (your) place in it in accordance with the number on the ticket that you have been issued.

Mankind today stands at a crossroads in time where it needs to re-evaluate all the knowledge that it has accumulated over the past centuries. And through this analysis, each individual needs to determine where he or she stands in all of this. What place do each of us occupy in the world? What is our personal role here?

The Destiny Code is a unique technique that reveals the knowledge each individual needs to know about him or herself, about the people in their lives and about the meanings that lie behind every act and event in his or her life. Many people have different attitudes towards occultism, magic and other esoteric practices that reveal the secrets of sacred knowledge. But there is no denying their inherent weight and power. All you need to do is to simply allow yourself to look a little beyond conventional wisdom and just start using this knowledge. The Destiny Code is a robustly structured technique that is based on an important global algorithm that reveals the structure and organization of the universe. You only need to try it once to put its recommendations into practice and, step by step, the effective route that you need to take to follow the way to your true Self will become clear.